MW00676820

CONTENTS

WELCOME

TO THE *FOUNDATIONS CURRICULUM*

"I just wanted to find a way to help parents homeschool."

—LEIGH BORTINS

Dear Families,

In 1997, I hosted a group of homeschool students and parents in my home each week. At our meetings we studied Latin, completed science labs, debated current events, solved problem sets, and discussed literature, history, and philosophy. Shortly after, hundreds of families asked to share in this vibrant experience of classical, Christian education.

I worked with many of my friends (and their friends) who were interested in classical, Christian homeschooling to develop a program to disciple and mentor families with students aged twelve to eighteen. We quickly realized that our children lacked a solid grammatical foundation, so we developed the *Foundations Curriculum* and launched weekly programs for families of younger children. We wanted our younger children to engage more confidently with the dialectic and rhetoric stages of their education.

I spent the next decade practicing the Foundations memory work at home with our children while training Foundations community leaders and working closely with families. It was slow, hard work, but we all agreed with world memory champion Dominic O'Brien—we were being given new brains.

As I reflect on this fifth edition of the *Foundations Curriculum*, I have the same words of advice as I did twenty years ago when I started this program: Enjoy these precious years with your young children. Delight in their continual discoveries of new truths about God's world. Praise them for working hard to memorize and recite His truths.

All of us learn best through gentle repetition over extended periods of time. Do not approach the memory work as trivia or try to learn it by cramming for a weekly test. Information acquired in this way is soon forgotten. Instead, as classical, Christian parents, strive to impart a body of knowledge that will remain with your family for a lifetime.

Expose your children and students to a broad base of knowledge in a wide range of subjects: Scripture, math, Latin, science, English, history, and geography. Give them an education rich in content. Provide plenty of opportunities for review and recitation wherever you are—in the car, waiting at the dentist, and in line at the grocery store. Exchange impatient moments for purposeful memories. Give your children the tools needed to parent your grandchildren well. As a grandmother, I already see our growing family echoing in celebration the things my husband and I have passed on.

Proverbs 25:2 says, "It is the glory of God to conceal a thing: but the honour of kings is to search out a matter." Welcome to a life of hide-and-seek.

Love,

Leigh

Leigh A. Bortins

Classical Conversations Founder and Chief Visionary Officer

WHAT IS CLASSICAL CONVERSATIONS®?

CHRISTIAN

WE BELIEVE
the purpose of education is to know God and to make Him known.

Our mission is to know God and to make Him known. In every subject, God has hidden His truth and beauty. It is our pleasure as students and teachers to discover Him as we learn. Our studies should also prepare us to reason clearly, speak eloquently, calculate accurately, and write convincingly so that we have the ability to make God known to others.

Children are stamped with the physical image of their biological parents. This physical resemblance is one way we know our children are our responsibility. It is the parents' job to model what it means to bear God's image, and all other institutions should support parents in that effort, not supplant them.

We raise our sons and daughters to become brothers and sisters in Christ. Parents have the divinely appointed duty to love and train their children in the way they should go, embodying Christ's love in all things and in every circumstance. We commit to studying God's Word throughout our lives—we should be no less committed when it comes to studying His world.

WE BELIEVE

classical education teaches a child how to learn using the arts of grammar, dialectic, and rhetoric.

We hide God's Word in our heart, align our thoughts to God's, and share the love of Christ with our neighbor. He has perfectly equipped each one of us to obey Him. Words, thoughts, and actions are analogous to the classical arts of grammar, dialectic, and rhetoric.

"I am the way, the truth, and the life," our Lord Jesus taught of himself. Parents must pray unceasingly for the grace and mercy needed to better reflect the image of God while demonstrating how to love God with their whole body, mind, and soul.

We examine the words, thoughts, and actions of the past and present, of Christians and non-Christians, and of neighboring and distant cultures in order to stand like Paul and be all things to all people, ready with an answer for the hope within us.

We believe that each child is uniquely and wonderfully made, and the people who know and love a child best—the parents—are the ones most motivated to help that child succeed. Within the framework of a biblical worldview, Classical Conversations® equips parents to use the classical model—the tools for learning any subject.

CLASSICAL

"True education should prepare us to love learning and to see the world from God's side of the sky."

–LEIGH A. BORTINS
ECHO IN CELEBRATION

5

Through wisdom is
an house builded; and
by understanding it is
established: And by
knowledge shall the
chambers be filled
with all precious and
pleasant riches.

PROVERBS 24:3–4

The classical model consists of the seven liberal arts. The first three are:

1) The art of grammar—training the brain to retain a foundation of knowledge in important subjects, with emphasis on memory

2) The art of dialectic—growing in understanding, with emphasis on questions and discussion

3) The art of rhetoric—displaying wisdom and virtue, with emphasis on the arts of persuasion

The Bible refers to these arts in Proverbs 24:3–4 as knowledge, understanding, and wisdom.

WE BELIEVE
the support of community enhances our ability to fulfill parental duties.

The classical education community—along with our church, our neighbors, and our extended family— remains close to our family's interests and well-being. We need their example and encouragement to help us to enjoy our responsibilities as parents.

The classical education community allows us to strengthen clear thinking skills while learning to love our neighbor. For harmonious community, we must put others before ourselves, just as we practice at home with our family.

The pursuit of truth requires self-denial, courage, and perseverance. Even if you feel inadequate, your community will be there to help as you and your student wrestle with hard ideas, words, and deeds.

- Foundations: K4–6th grade—Memorize and recite!

- Essentials: 4th–6th grade—Memorize, dialogue, and write!

- Challenge: 7th–12th grade (ages 12+)—Dialogue, think, write, share, and lead!

In community, parents find the support and encouragement they need. Likewise, students develop wisdom under the tutelage of trustworthy mentors, and they develop positive peer relationships by learning together, working together on projects, and challenging each other.

7

BUILDING A FIRM
FOUNDATION

Launch *your* adventure from a firm foundation by pairing our proven curriculum with the consistency of a licensed community.

Congratulations! You are about to join an international network of 2,000+ licensed Foundations programs. For more than twenty years, Classical Conversations® has labored to uncover the "lost tools of learning" that help parents give their children a better education. As our community grows in understanding classical, Christian education, we work hard to share our new insights with you. Participating in a licensed Classical Conversations community not only honors the continuing training of our academic leadership teams but also offers you the benefits of Foundations tutor training, free Parent Practicums, and quality educational materials.

We are committed to:

❋ Consistent Community

No matter where the Lord leads your family, we strive to develop a classical, Christian community to support your homeschooling. We develop consistent Christian business training for our Foundations directors and classical academic training materials for Foundations tutors, parents, and students. No matter where you move, your family will join a community that feels like the one you left.

❋ Classical Training

Our licensed directors attend annual in-person business licensing and academic orientation each year. In addition, they have access to online mentoring from experienced academic advisors and face-to-face support from local leadership.

✸ Christian Vetting of Community Leaders

We believe the purpose of education is "to know God and to make Him known." We ask our directors to affirm a statement of faith and lead from a Christ-centered worldview that informs every aspect of learning. We seek to employ the Matthew 18 model of conflict resolution at every opportunity.

✸ Modeling Classical Education

We choose to not simply replicate a modern education at home. Instead, one homeschooling tutor guides parents and their children through all subjects, modeling the skills to be learned and demonstrating the integration and unity of all subjects within a Christ-centered worldview.

✸ Honoring Parents

You are your child's first and best teacher. In the Foundations program, a parent is required to attend community day once a week with his or her child so that the parents too can improve as classical educators. Parents remain the primary teacher in middle and high school.

✸ Complete K4–12 Curriculum

We are committed to supporting parents along their entire homeschooling journey. Students can begin with the Foundations program for K4–6th, then supplement with English and math in our Essentials program in grades 4–6. Both programs prepare students for success in the Challenge programs: grades 7–12. We also offer a wide range of supplemental services, including standardized testing, help with transcripts, college and scholarship searches, and dual-enrollment opportunities.

Thank you for joining the big, messy, beautiful story of Christians across the globe seeking to help their children know God and make Him known.

BECOMING
TRANSFORMED

To make the homeschooling years a success, parents need one another, and our children need to find good friends. Homeschooling can be lonely, and raising the standard of education in our homes is a challenge. Your local community will provide accountability, support, and encouragement; however, you may also need to replace some popular ideas about education with timeless ones.

First, pray that you will see your children as God sees them—they are "royalty worth dying for." The "royalty" part helps you hold your children to a higher standard. It also helps students understand why they may face different expectations than their non-Christian friends and why they have to work harder. They are not being raised to be average—they are being raised to lead as servant-kings! The "worth dying for" part helps parents remember that their sacrifice of time and energy is of eternal value and worth.

Do you agree? Then let's get started.

INSTEAD OF "I'm not an expert educator."

REMEMBER You are your child's first and best teacher.

Every parent naturally begins by interacting with his or her child, naming and calling attention to countless experiences with the world. From naming, parents proceed to songs, jingles, ABCs, numbers, colors, Bible verses, prayers, and good stories as the child begins to mimic what he or she sees and hears. With practice, these tendencies become useful tools for studying any subject (see "Tools for Teaching the Art of Grammar" on page 18). Outside of the Foundations memory work, all you will need to add are language arts and math programs that suit your family. Foundations students in fourth grade and up can take advantage of the Classical Conversations® Essentials program to hone the "three Rs" (reading, writing, and arithmetic) in community each week.

INSTEAD OF "I'm not a 'math person'."

REMEMBER → All subjects are integrated to glorify their Creator.

It is our prayer that, as families study using the classical model set forth in Classical Conversations programs, they will develop a love for life and learning together. We want to recapture the idea that a parent who knows how to learn can share the tools of learning with his or her children. Segregating subjects may be efficient for a teacher, and it definitely benefits our finite minds as we break down a subject to its basic grammar, but we should aim to integrate anything God reveals to us.

INSTEAD OF "I have to cover all the material."

REMEMBER → Focus on solid pegs for securing knowledge.

C. S. Lewis wrote in *Letters to Children* that schools "should teach far fewer subjects far better." In "The Lost Tools of Learning," Dorothy Sayers advocated teaching students the tools needed to learn one subject and then showing them how to use those same tools to study any subject. Both ideas are modeled in our programs.

We choose important content from history, science, math, language, and geography and master as much of it as possible. The facts we memorize are the "pegs" on which to "hang" new ideas your children will meet in other contexts. As you build this strong foundation of knowledge, you are teaching your child how to memorize anything.

You may certainly choose to re-create a modern education at home, but sitting at a desk for five hours a day is a poor substitute for making the world your classroom just because that is what "school" means!

INSTEAD OF "I have to cover the material in sequence."

REMEMBER Developing the art of memory is key.

The Foundations program is structured so a new student can enroll at any given week and begin mastering the memory work. All your children cover the same material, making it efficient for you to homeschool multiple children. Even toddlers tend to learn the Latin chants and multiplication songs (and more!) with their elder siblings. Learning how to master information is the key. Even if you enter a Foundations program mid-year, there is no reason to back up to cover previous material. It doesn't matter where you begin—just begin!

INSTEAD OF "I need to keep up with the latest technology."

REMEMBER Start with a stick in the sand.

At Classical Conversations, we believe that simple is best. Founder Leigh Bortins often says, "If Jesus could teach His disciples by writing with a stick in the sand, then surely I can teach my kids that way, too." Focus on timeless skills that will prepare your child to work hard, enjoy learning, develop good habits, and celebrate success.

Begin your classical homeschooling journey with these basics:

- Memorization to train the mind, using excellent content in a variety of subjects
- A rigorous language arts program that progresses with your child's ability (you choose)
- A complete K4–12 math program (you choose)

- Reading, writing, and talking about ideas that help us know God and make Him known

INSTEAD OF "I just want to take it one year at a time."

REMEMBER Homeschooling in the early years prepares your family for the joys of homeschooling through high school.

If you are just starting out on your homeschooling journey, high school and graduation may seem light-years away. Enjoy your children! Also use these gentler years to think about your goals for your children's education: not **what** you want to teach them at home, but **why** you want to center their education at home (see "Preparing for This Year's Journey," page 16). Once you've built a strong foundation for your home school in these early years, you'll *want* to continue homeschooling through high school, to stay for the feast of big ideas, deep conversations, and abiding friendship with your grown children. When you are ready, be encouraged to know that the Foundations program is part of a cohesive vision for classical, Christian education all the way through high school. The Essentials and Challenge programs will be there when you are ready for the next step.

MEMORIZING
WHY, WHAT, AND HOW

Our brain is a wonderful tool, able to recall an amazing number of facts (grammar), to see relationships between innumerable pieces of information (dialectic), and to make judgments and convey ideas (rhetoric) based on those facts and relationships. The art of grammar comes naturally to young children, who love to mimic, repeat, and memorize.

"After three months of memory training, I felt that I had been given a new brain."

—DOMINIC O'BRIEN, EIGHT-TIME WORLD MEMORY CHAMPION

Why do we memorize?

The Foundations program is designed to prepare students to be confident thinkers, debaters, speakers, and leaders later in life. By memorizing a standard body of information, students can progress much more easily through a new subject and move more quickly into critical thought.

More importantly, as Christians, our children should know who did what, where, when, and why for Him. They should see His creation revealed through science. His word is a lamp unto our feet—and theirs, too. That means we must acquire, nurture, and expand our ability to store information, words, and abstract ideas. It is our prayer that, as Classical Conversations families study using the classical model, they will develop a love for life and learning together.

What do we memorize?

The Foundations curriculum provides history, science, geography, Latin, English, and math facts to cultivate a rich and robust foundation for future learning. Our memory work is arranged in three cycles, each lasting a full academic year. Cycle 1 emphasizes ancient world history and related sciences. Cycle 2 emphasizes medieval to modern world history and related sciences. Cycle 3 emphasizes national history and related sciences. Every three years we repeat exactly the same material. This gives children an opportunity to work on mastering the material at least twice from K4 to sixth grade.

How do we memorize?

In the Foundations program, we teach young children according to the way God designed them to learn—through repetition. Young children are capable of storing an immense number of facts, but like any muscle, the brain needs training, using the keys of repetition, intensity, and duration.

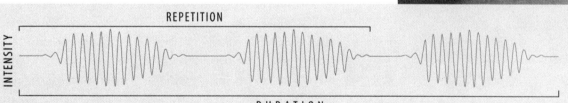

Repetition: In community one day a week and for as little as twenty minutes a day at home, tutors and parents repeat key facts.

Intensity: Songs, poems, anagrams, dances, and kinesthetic activities add intensity and make the facts memorable.

Duration: The duration of the program (up to eight years of memorizing the same material) cements the memory work.

Following this proven method, young children can store an immense number of facts, waiting to be tapped for debate, discussion, and integration during the later middle and high school years. Classical Conversations families with children of all learning styles memorize hundreds of pieces of information each semester. Your child can do it, and so can you.

"We learn through three avenues… repetition, duration, and intensity."

—LEIGH A. BORTINS

PREPARING
FOR THIS YEAR'S JOURNEY

Goals, like a road map, provide direction for the year ahead. They also provide a starting point for choosing what and how to study. *Curriculum* can be translated from Latin as the "course to be run." You will set this course at the beginning of the year; however, as you run along the course, you will encounter unforeseen events. Therefore, your course will need to be flexible and adaptable.

In his essay on marriage, Wendell Berry says, "Because the condition of marriage is worldly and its meaning communal, no one party to it can be solely in charge. What you alone think it ought to be, it is not going to be. Where you alone think you want it to go, it is not going to go. It is going where the two of you—and marriage, time, life, history, and the world—will take it. You do not know the road; you have committed your life to a way." [footnote: Berry, Wendell. "Poetry and Marriage: The Use of Old Forms (1982)." *Standing By Words*: Essays. Berkeley: Counterpoint Press, 2011.]

> "It is going where the two of you—and marriage, time, life, history, and the world—will take it. You do not know the road; you have committed your life to a way."
> —WENDELL BERRY

Remember, you alone are not setting the pace for the journey; the journey is going where you and your spouse and your children are taking it. There will be detours and obstacles, but you have committed yourself to a way.

#1 DESTINATION: START WITH THE END IN MIND

When preparing for a family vacation, first you choose the destination and then you pack; in other words, you start with the end in mind. You should prepare for your homeschool journey this year the same way you would prepare for a family vacation—start with the end in mind. Ask yourself:

- What memory work do I want to focus on and learn more this year: math, Latin, geography, timeline, science, etc.?
- How do I cultivate a child who loves God?
- How do I cultivate a child who thoughtfully listens?
- How do I cultivate a child who loves his neighbor?
- How do I cultivate a student who loves learning?

Thinking on these larger questions will help you stay oriented when your school year journey takes an unexpected turn like a health detour, a financial U-turn, or a neighbor-in-need diversion.

#2 ORIGIN: THINK ABOUT WHERE YOU ARE

Your family's circumstances are unique. Therefore, you should take time to reflect on your particular circumstances, including your strengths, needs, limits, necessities, and dreams.

- What are the ages of your children?
- What are your strengths?
- What are your child's strengths?
- What are your family's limitations this year?
- What are some commitments you have made for this year?
- How do you want this year to be remembered?

#3 GOALS: MARK OUT THE COURSE

To set your schedule, develop a weekly rhythm around your community day that fits your family. Be sure to include times for memory work review, kitchen math lessons, backyard science observations, and reading good stories together. If your student plays a more formal sport or an instrument, be sure to consider how your weekly rhythm is shaped by this pursuit.

For sample schedules that have worked for some families, please see *Classical Christian Education Made Approachable*, available from ClassicalConversationsBooks.com.

#4 ASSESS AND ADJUST: PARENT AND STUDENT

It is a good idea to assess progress at least twice a year—both your child's and yours. Refer back to the specific goals you set and then ask two powerful questions:

- What are we doing well?
- What do we need to do better?

This habit will provide time for reflection. Try to limit yourself to one or two habits that need more attention. If you have gotten busy or distracted with lesser things, these questions give you an opportunity to get back on course. However, if your circumstances have presented a crisis, you will need to rework your initial vision and plan. In this flexible accommodation, look for new kinds of lessons to be learned, often important life lessons.

For the student, it is good to assess rhythms of time and days of the week. Notice how morning and afternoon times affect your student. Notice when attentiveness and alertness seem higher or lower. Does your student have special needs? Think about how your student is engaging their memory work and lesson work. It is natural for younger students to be eager when expectations are clear and they can be successful. Memory work tends to be an arena in which younger students have clarity and can succeed with relative ease.

#5 CELEBRATE: RECOGNIZE MILESTONES ALONG THE WAY

During assessment, you will find ways to commend yourself and your child for a job well done. These moments will be a sweet reminder when you are tempted to take a costly detour on the homeschool journey.

"Knowledge of the memory work from all three cycles, especially science and Latin, has helped in all seminars during the Challenge day. It is wonderful that NOT everything is NEW each week."

–ETHAN MORROW,
CHALLENGE A STUDENT,
NATIONAL MEMORY
MASTER FINALIST

TOOLS FOR TEACHING THE ART OF GRAMMAR

Modern education has trained us to think that education starts when a child turns four or five, but as a parent, you've been teaching your baby since day one. It is worth repeating: all parents naturally begin educating by spending time with their children, naming and calling attention to countless experiences with the world. That doesn't change when your child turns four.

Understanding the way God created our littlest learners always helps us educate well. Ask yourself, "What are my children like?" "What are they good at?" "What do they enjoy?" The classical model is powerful because it is natural. We teach with the grain of a child's development, following God's design.

When you learn a new language, you start with its grammar: the basic elements and rules that govern its structure. Once you discover the system of the language, you can progress more quickly. Young children thrive on grammar because it suits their nature. Even older students and adults begin with grammar when learning something new, but we need discipline to reach beyond our inclinations and to cultivate good habits.

The *Foundations Curriculum* emphasizes the art of grammar—ways to build copious ideas and vocabulary. The classical art of grammar teaches us to think systematically about any subject by naming, attending, memorizing, expressing, and storytelling.

NAMING	**ATTENDING**	**MEMORIZING**	**EXPRESSING**	**STORYTELLING**
Name things specifically.	Look and listen closely.	Soak up facts and ideas.	Express ideas creatively.	Hear and retell stories.

18

Enjoy learning the best and most common *naming* of things and their parts, reflecting on the categories they belong to. Enjoy *attending* to things, using all five senses—including taste, smell, touch—and comparing things. Enjoy *memorizing* facts and relations of things to recall, connect, and expand new ideas to older ones from a rich storehouse and firm foundation of memory. Enjoy *expressing* what you remember through various forms such as reciting, drawing, dancing, and singing. And finally, make lots of time to enjoy *story-telling*. Read many good stories aloud together and have your student narrate back what he or she remembers; children absorb stories all around them and will one day decide which stories to imitate and live by.

By forming these *five core habits*™ *of grammar*—naming, attending, memorizing, expressing, and storytelling—we learn how to grasp the basic elements, vocabulary, and rules of any subject, allowing us to progress more quickly toward comprehension and creativity in future studies. As students continue through Classical Conversations programs, they will build on these core habits using other tools. Continuing on in the art of dialectic, students will learn the importance of good questions using the *five common topics*, and for the art of rhetoric, students will learn categories of expression using the *five canons of rhetoric* to seek truth and to express themselves creatively and persuasively.

TRIVIUM ART	CULTIVATING	THINK IN FIVE-NESS
Grammar	Five Core Habits™	**FORMING HABITS** Naming, Attending, Memorizing, Expressing, Storytelling
Dialectic	Five Common Topics	**ASKING GOOD QUESTIONS** Definition, Comparison, Relationship, Circumstance, Testimony
Rhetoric	Five Canons of Rhetoric	**EXPRESSING TRUTH** Invention, Arrangement, Elocution, Memory, Delivery

"Ye shall teach them diligently unto thy children, and shalt talk of them when thou sittest in thine house, when thou walkest by the way, and when thou liest down, and when thou risest up."

—DEUTERONOMY 6:9

The heart of the Foundations program is the memory work, which cultivates the fertile faculty of memory. You may be thinking, "But what do we DO?" Cultivating these uniquely human habits offers flexibility and creativity with and around each week's memory work. Therefore, we recommend enjoying the memory work first and then looking for its everyday manifestations as you live life.

Whether you are folding laundry or cooking a meal, whether you are on a nature walk or planting a garden, whether you are learning a sport or doing a math lesson, you have lots of opportunities to thoughtfully and naturally cultivate these core habits. Remember, you don't need to use all five core habits in every lesson, and you don't have to use them sequentially.

On the weeks when you are not sure what learning has occurred, remember this: your child's education is not so much the content you cover but what you cultivate across the years and across the subjects for the long term. On those days, reflect on the five core habits you have cultivated and you will be surprised at what has been learned. Remember that you have a community where memory work recitation happens weekly, and where science projects, art and music projects, and fun presentations are taking place. We are wired to learn; you are teaching your children all the time and you have a support community to help you along the way. Relax, practice the five core habits a little every day, enjoy your community day activities and fellowship, and enjoy these younger years to their fullest.

Oh, one more thing—remember to smile at your children. Not a scary smile. Not like the forced smile your child has in the family photo. Smile, because your children are heartily made in His image and wired to learn about His world, their neighbor, and themselves. Smile, because somehow in His economy, you are your child's first and best teacher. Your countenance is a special grace and mercy to your young ones as they travel on their journey.

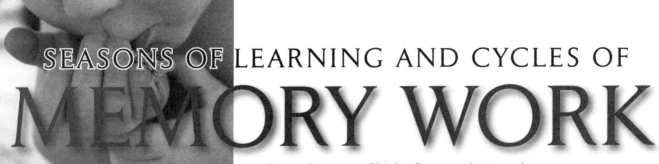

SEASONS OF LEARNING AND CYCLES OF
MEMORY WORK

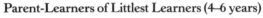

Parent-Learners of Littlest Learners (4–6 years)

In these young years, in the midst of so many physical demands, you have the distinct opportunity to take the long view of learning with your children. Enjoy playing with the memory work together as a family and capitalize on the boundless energy and curiosity of these youngest learners. Enjoy the changing seasons as you sit, walk, and lie down [Deuteronomy 6:7], by enjoying nature walks, looking closely at flowers, listening to bird songs, touching the petals of flowers, tasting new fruits, and smelling aromas that will instill a lifetime of memories.

Learning as *Formative Play* for the Littlest Learners

These little learners will have the opportunity to play with and revisit the memory work two more times. Relax and play. As you and your child revisit the memory work in later years, you will find new discoveries and connections for particular science facts, history sentences, timeline cards, math facts, Latin endings, or parts of speech as it is revisited.

Parent-Learners of Younger Learners (7–9 years)

These younger years afford you an abundant opportunity to learn with your children. Therefore, make plans to prepare a little now for the years ahead. As you learn with your child, make time to go a little further each summer in your own understanding. Are you concerned about teaching writing to your child? Do you need help with reading and math? Set aside a little time each summer to attend one of our free, three-day Parent Practicums, designed to equip you as a teacher and cultivate a love of learning in your home.

Learning as *Attentive Play* for Younger Learners

These younger learners will have the opportunity to revisit the memory work one more time (and so will you as the parent). Cultivate the faculties of attention and memory as well as the five senses by incorporating the **five core habits of grammar™** in your activities. **Name** things with greater attention to detail. Intentionally use all the senses to **attend** to the world. **Memorize** grammar, facts, and songs about things that catch their interest. **Express** facts in a variety of ways such as journaling, singing, chanting, and marching. Practice **storytelling** by having your younger learner narrate the events of the day.

Parent-Learners of Older Learners (10–12 years)

These older years continue to afford parents the opportunity to learn with their children and prepare a little more for the years ahead. In these years, you can more intentionally prepare for the dialectic arts by learning to ask good questions. Your student's awareness of ideas, assumptions, and questions often grow exponentially in these years. We can help you prepare and make the most of these fruitful years! Make time this summer to learn more about asking good questions by attending one of our free Parent Practicums.

Learning as *Purposeful Play* for Older Learners

These older learners will begin to recognize their memory work within other subjects. On community day, a science experiment, an art activity, or a music moment may also act as a catalyst, igniting a desire to learn something in greater depth. Be sure to provide time and space for exploring their interests. The exploring will be formative in cultivating the love of learning in your child's mind and heart.

In addition, stories are particularly formative as these young people become more self-aware. Your older learners are discovering the principles of self-governance. Good stories help acquaint children with timeless human struggles. Providing stories that help them develop their own virtues and confront their vices brings consolation and vision as they navigate God's unfolding story of their life.

Is this your child's second or third time through the memory work?

 TAKE TWO

If this is your child's second time through the curriculum, look for the Take Two symbol for suggestions to provide a fresh review of the memory work. The second time through a cycle brings robust gifts and hospitable familiarity.

Remember that although the memory work is familiar, your child is more mature now; also, your family is in a new season to engage with the memory work in a different way. For the student, provide time for additional discoveries regarding a chosen fact from the memory work for the weekly Foundations presentation. As the parent, look for easy ways to integrate memory work review in other forms like copy work, handwriting, and dictation practice.

Your student can become a memory master of the current cycle or compete as a National Memory Master finalist of all three cycles! Finalists come from all over the United States to compete for the National Memory Master title. Prizes include trips and scholarships. Search for "National Memory Master" on the Internet for more information on the annual Classical Conversations National Memory Master Competition.

The cycles of memory work are always applicable to your family's season of learning. Just as the sun rises and sets repeatedly, projecting a unique glow across the sky, your family will have a new experience each time you revisit the memory work.

> "Because children have abounding vitality, because they are in spirit fierce and free, therefore they want things repeated and unchanged. They always say, 'Do it again;' and the grown-up person does it again until he is nearly dead. For grown-up people are not strong enough to exult in monotony. But perhaps God is strong enough to exult in monotony."
>
> –G. K. CHESTERTON, *ORTHODOXY*

What is a memory master? A student who desires to memorize all the memory work for a cycle. Ask your local director for more details about becoming a Memory Master!

TAILORING
FOR YOUR SEASON OF LIFE

We tailor our children's work for the same reason we would tailor a garment: we want it to fit a particular person so that it is neither too big nor too small. Sometimes a child may need less work than prescribed in the curriculum in order to avoid discouragement. Sometimes a child may need work to be more challenging than the curriculum assigns in order to avoid boredom or disinterest. As the parent, you know your children best, so you are the best one to decide how to tailor your child's workload.

To learn more, we recommend the books *Classical Christian Education Made Approachable* and *The Core: Teaching Your Child the Foundations of a Classical Education.*

PLAYING WITH LEARNING

The Scribblers at-home program is a list of recommended at-home resources and activities for children ages 3 to 8. It is not a community or tuition-based program. Scribblers products give parents practical tools for fostering a love of learning in their youngest children while also providing hands-on activities to keep them engaged as parents teach their older students. Although families have the flexibility to choose programs that fit their own learning styles and interests, these recommended resources help hone fine-motor skills, develop basic literacy, reinforce Foundations memory work, and teach children about truth, goodness, and beauty.

SCRIBBLERS (Aged 3–8)	<ul><li>Read aloud—a lot!</li><li>Develop a daily habit of studying math.</li><li>Keep them with you (on your lap for the littlest) during community day.</li><li>Keep children in the room while older siblings review their memory work.</li><li>Take them along on field trips.</li><li>Have fun exploring outside.</li><li>Play with maps.</li></ul>

FIRST TIME THROUGH A CYCLE	 TAKE TWO	PREPARING FOR CHALLENGE
YOUNG CHILDREN (Aged 4–6) • Read aloud—a lot! • Review memory work for about 30 minutes daily. • Focus on rote memorization and recitation (don't worry about review games or a lot of extras). • Find connections to the memory work throughout the day. For example, at the grocery store, skip count apples; in the kitchen, practice measurements; on a road trip, review geography. • Use a finger to trace maps, slowly progressing from the colored and labeled maps to the outline maps. *Do little hands need busy work? Scribblers is for them! See the previous page.*	Suggested at-home activities for students who are going through a cycle for the second time. Intended for use only after the primary work is done very well.	Suggested at-home activities for older students focusing on preparation for the Challenge program.
OLDER CHILDREN (Aged 7–9) • Read aloud—a lot! Add books related to cycle memory work. • Review memory work for about 30 minutes daily. • Add in fun games. • Do lots of copy work. • Model the skill of asking questions about how the different memory work subjects are connected. • Trace colored labeled maps. Add abbreviated labels for locations and color in the water. • Find connections to the memory work throughout the day.	REPEAT all the activities from your first time through the cycle and ADD: • Practice Memory Master proofing.	REPEAT all the activities from your first two times through the cycle, then ADD: • Participate in the National Memory Master competition! • **Grammar**: Practice writing the Latin declensions and conjugations with macros and try out the endings on vocabulary from Henle *First Year Latin*. • **Exposition**: Read one of the Challenge literature books aloud as a family.
OLDEST CHILDREN (Aged 10–12) • Read aloud—a lot! • Assign books for independent reading. • Review memory work for 30–45 minutes daily, together and independently. • Model a doable schedule for practicing memory work independently. • Cultivate a heart for the Memory Master process. • Work on dictation of memory work. • Play lots of math fact games to help with accuracy and mastery. • Encourage questions to see how memory work subjects are connected. • Give students time to think. Don't be so quick to give an answer; let them work to formulate their thoughts. • Copy maps every day. **ESSENTIALS** • Participate in Essentials! Build on your math facts by increasing speed and accuracy through math games. • Add to your memory pegs about history by outlining and re-writing stories from history. • Solidify English grammar studies in preparation for studying Latin grammar. • Practice your keyword outlining skills by summarizing a *Classical Acts & Facts® History* or *Science* card.	REPEAT all the activities from your first time through the cycle and ADD: • Spend time engaging in conversation about what they learned and discovered. • Connect presentations to memory work.	• **Debate**: Transition from labeling and tracing maps to drawing the world freehand and then labeling it. • **Research/History**: Do a presentation on one of the science or history topics for this cycle using the five common topics. • **Rhetoric**: Use the five canons of rhetoric to write, memorize, and deliver a presentation on a great artist or composer. • **Logic**: Try more advanced math problems or discuss a more advanced math problem using the five common topics.

REMEMBERING
THE SPIRIT AND PURPOSE OF MEMORY WORK

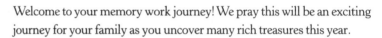

As Proverbs 25:2 tells us, "It is the glory of God to conceal a thing: but the honour of kings is to search out a matter."

Welcome to your memory work journey! We pray this will be an exciting journey for your family as you uncover many rich treasures this year.

We pray you will enjoy this game of hide and seek with the Creator this year and will search out many ideas as a family.

The *Foundations Curriculum* serves to give families a series of memory pegs on which they can hang world history, global geography, scientific discovery, mathematical relationships, and language studies. Later, your family can enjoy discussing these ideas in depth as your children grow in understanding.

We designed the **history timeline** to give students seven events from world history each week that cover important people, battles, and discoveries while introducing students to all seven continents. The **history sentences** put a little more flesh on some of these events to give our families a skeletal story of world history. Over the years, you will continue to add to this skeleton as you research, read, discuss, and discover more.

Man has been uniquely gifted with language. The **English grammar** memory work is designed to give our children an introduction to their own mother tongue in preparation for deeper studies of language through the Essentials program. The **Latin grammar** lays the groundwork for future studies of language structure and expression throughout the Challenge program.

Mathematics is a study in relationships. The **math** memory work is designed to give students a strong foundation in multiplication tables, identities, conversions, and basic geometrical relationships. Students will strengthen speed and accuracy of addition and multiplication in the Essentials program. A firm foundation in arithmetic and geometry provides children with the opportunity to experience and discover something unknown from something known.

Isn't it amazing that scientists are continually discovering more about the created world, as well as continually correcting their understanding? As a consequence, the **science** memory work may not reflect the latest consensus,

discoveries, and conversations. Therefore, we encourage you to think about the science memory work as foundational building blocks for later studies in science. Presenting scientific principles to younger children requires simplification at first, knowing the memory work will be like seed in the soil: it will grow and mature as it is fed by light and nourished by water. Especially when it comes to theories and discoveries, families will have lots of different ideas—as do scientists! The memory work gives you a solid place to start a hospitable, truth-seeking conversation in humility and love.

We call our **geography** maps keys to the geography memory work. It is important to remember that the nature of geography is that political boundaries and names of countries change over time. Therefore, families should follow their interests and do their own research about a particular area and its history. The maps in our curriculum are intended to be high-level representations to guide in memorization and to unlock family conversations about the nature of the physical and political world. They contain gridlines for students to use when tracing or drawing maps and blue shading to help younger students visually discriminate between land and water. Finally, we have included sample maps drawn by a former Challenge A student so that you can see what is possible when students are asked to draw and label the world. For more detailed maps, refer to the Classical Conversations® MultiMedia publication *Exploring the World Through Cartography* or another atlas.

The **hands-on projects** are designed to allow students to cultivate attention by looking closely and listening closely through restful fine arts projects and experiences of drawing, music theory, artists, and composers. Students also have an opportunity to express through imitation of drawing techniques and playing the tin whistle, as well as attend to sights and sounds through the great artists and composers and orchestra. The **science demonstrations** are designed to give a gentle introduction to the scientific method, allowing students to play with science and talk about their observations.

Finally, no classical education would be complete without a study of rhetoric, which we will define as "sharing the truth with our audience in the most compelling way." The Foundations **presentations** will serve as a gentle introduction to the art of rhetoric by giving students practice with public speaking twenty-four times each year.

Enjoy your journey of discovery this year! The Foundations memory work holds hidden opportunities for you and your family to seek out and discover new truths about His world and our place in His world. Uncover amazing ideas that will deepen your love for our Savior. Echo in celebration of His glorious creation and your stewardship of it!

Memory work is like a mustard seed. It starts out so small but grows larger than you can imagine given the seeming smallness of the seed. Therefore, memorize and recite a little memory work a few times a week, enjoy your hands-on projects and experiences in community, and watch the hidden, living ideas grow.

Remember to rest along the way and not to let efficiency and immediate usefulness become tyrants in your home school. He gives to his servants in their sleep (Psalm 127:2) and renews the strength of those who wait on Him (Isaiah 40:31).

NAVIGATING THE MEMORY WORK

Shows current cycle and week.

The week's memory work, including hands-on activities, with space to note tunes, motions, or helpful activities.

Jot down ideas learned each week, what your child did well, or what he or she needs to work harder on.

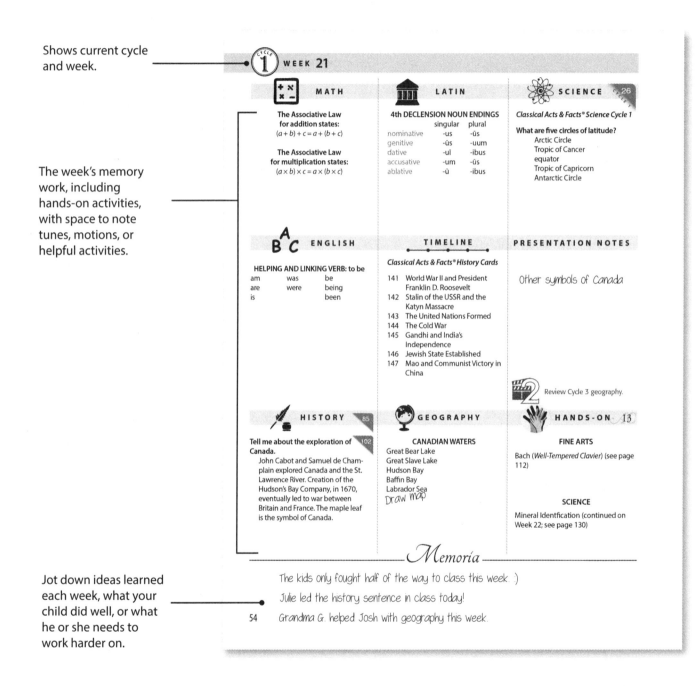

CYCLE 1 — WEEK 21

MATH

The Associative Law for addition states:
$(a + b) + c = a + (b + c)$

The Associative Law for multiplication states:
$(a \times b) \times c = a \times (b \times c)$

LATIN

4th DECLENSION NOUN ENDINGS

	singular	plural
nominative	-us	-ūs
genitive	-ūs	-uum
dative	-uī	-ibus
accusative	-um	-ūs
ablative	-ū	-ibus

SCIENCE

Classical Acts & Facts® Science Cycle 1

What are five circles of latitude?
Arctic Circle
Tropic of Cancer
equator
Tropic of Capricorn
Antarctic Circle

ENGLISH

HELPING AND LINKING VERB: to be

am	was	be
are	were	being
is		been

TIMELINE

Classical Acts & Facts® History Cards

141 World War II and President Franklin D. Roosevelt
142 Stalin of the USSR and the Katyn Massacre
143 The United Nations Formed
144 The Cold War
145 Gandhi and India's Independence
146 Jewish State Established
147 Mao and Communist Victory in China

PRESENTATION NOTES

Other symbols of Canada

Review Cycle 3 geography.

HISTORY

Tell me about the exploration of Canada.
John Cabot and Samuel de Champlain explored Canada and the St. Lawrence River. Creation of the Hudson's Bay Company, in 1670, eventually led to war between Britain and France. The maple leaf is the symbol of Canada.

GEOGRAPHY

CANADIAN WATERS
Great Bear Lake
Great Slave Lake
Hudson Bay
Baffin Bay
Labrador Sea
Draw map

HANDS-ON

FINE ARTS
Bach (*Well-Tempered Clavier*) (see page 112)

SCIENCE
Mineral Identfication (continued on Week 22; see page 130)

Memoria

The kids only fought half of the way to class this week. :)

Julie led the history sentence in class today!

Grandma G. helped Josh with geography this week.

54

Look for these handy icons to quickly identify subject content.

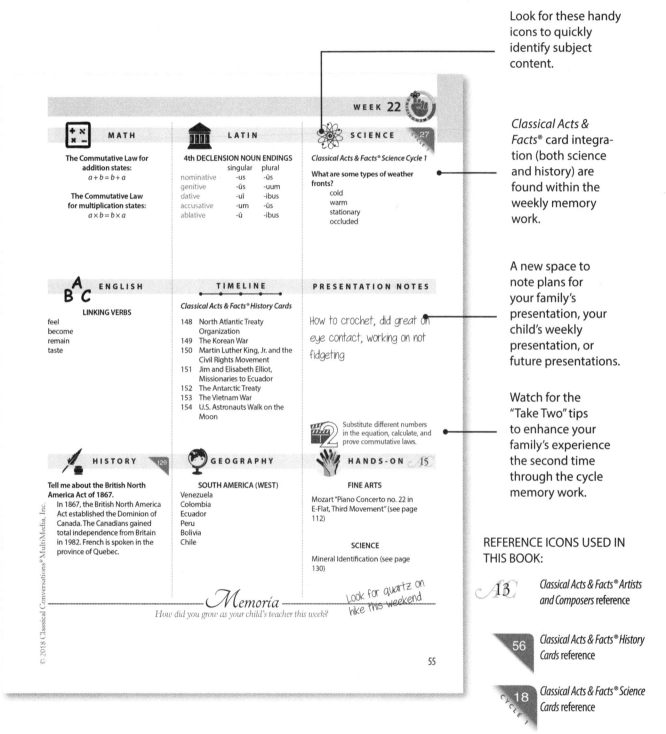

WEEK 22

MATH

The Commutative Law for addition states:
$$a + b = b + a$$

The Commutative Law for multiplication states:
$$a \times b = b \times a$$

LATIN

4th DECLENSION NOUN ENDINGS

	singular	plural
nominative	-us	-ūs
genitive	-ūs	-uum
dative	-uī	-ibus
accusative	-um	-ūs
ablative	-ū	-ibus

SCIENCE

Classical Acts & Facts® Science Cycle 1

What are some types of weather fronts?
cold
warm
stationary
occluded

Classical Acts & Facts® card integration (both science and history) are found within the weekly memory work.

ENGLISH

LINKING VERBS

feel
become
remain
taste

TIMELINE

Classical Acts & Facts® History Cards

148 North Atlantic Treaty Organization
149 The Korean War
150 Martin Luther King, Jr. and the Civil Rights Movement
151 Jim and Elisabeth Elliot, Missionaries to Ecuador
152 The Antarctic Treaty
153 The Vietnam War
154 U.S. Astronauts Walk on the Moon

PRESENTATION NOTES

How to crochet; did great on eye contact; working on not fidgeting

A new space to note plans for your family's presentation, your child's weekly presentation, or future presentations.

Substitute different numbers in the equation, calculate, and prove commutative laws.

Watch for the "Take Two" tips to enhance your family's experience the second time through the cycle memory work.

HISTORY

Tell me about the British North America Act of 1867.
In 1867, the British North America Act established the Dominion of Canada. The Canadians gained total independence from Britain in 1982. French is spoken in the province of Quebec.

GEOGRAPHY

SOUTH AMERICA (WEST)
Venezuela
Colombia
Ecuador
Peru
Bolivia
Chile

HANDS-ON

FINE ARTS

Mozart "Piano Concerto no. 22 in E-Flat, Third Movement" (see page 112)

SCIENCE

Mineral Identification (see page 130)

Memoria
How did you grow as your child's teacher this week?

Look for quartz on hike this weekend

55

REFERENCE ICONS USED IN THIS BOOK:

Classical Acts & Facts® Artists and Composers reference

Classical Acts & Facts® History Cards reference

Classical Acts & Facts® Science Cards reference

MATH	LATIN	SCIENCE	ART AND MUSIC	ENGLISH	TIMELINE, HISTORY, & GEOGRAPHY
F O U N D A T I O N S ①					
Multiplication Tables, Conversions, Geometric Formulas, Algebraic Laws	Noun Endings (Declensions)	Biology, Earth Science	Drawing, Art Masters, Music Theory, Composers	Verbs, Prepositions	Creation to Modern America; World: Historical Empires, Peoples, and Countries
F O U N D A T I O N S ②					
Same as Cycle 1	Verb Endings (Conjugations)	Ecology, Astronomy, Physics	Drawing, Impressionists, Music Theory, Composers	Pronouns, Adverbs, Conjunctions	Creation to Modern America; World: Pre-Reformation to Modern
F O U N D A T I O N S ③					
Same as Cycle 1	Translate John 1:1–7	Anatomy, Chemistry, Origins	Drawing, American Masters, Music Theory, Composers	Participles, Irregular Verb Tenses, and Clauses	Creation to Modern America; United States (or native country)
E S S E N T I A L S					
Drills and Games	Parts of Speech, Sentence Structure, Parsing	Language Arts and Composition	Language Arts and Composition	English Grammar	History-Based Writing
LOGIC	GRAMMAR	RESEARCH	REASONING	EXPOSITION	DEBATE
C H A L L E N G E Ⓐ					
Arithmetic	Latin A	Natural Science/ Biology/Science Fair	Clear Reasoning/ Apologetics	Newbery Literature	Cartography
C H A L L E N G E Ⓑ					
Pre-Algebra	Latin B	History of Astronomy	Formal & Informal Logic	Newbery Literature/ Short Stories	Current Events/ Mock Trial
C H A L L E N G E Ⓘ					
Algebra	Latin 1	Physical Science	Formal Logic/ Applied Logic	American Literature	American Government / Free Market Economics
C H A L L E N G E ⒾⒾ					
Algebra and Geometry	Latin 2	Biology	Formal Logic/ Applied Logic	British Literature	Western Cultural History
C H A L L E N G E ⒾⒾⒾ					
Pre-Calculus	Caesar and Cicero	Chemistry	Philosophy/ Applied Logic	Poetry / Shakespeare	American History
C H A L L E N G E ⒾⓋ					
Pre-Calculus/ Calculus	Language and Literature	Physics	Theology	Ancient Literature	World History

CYCLE 1

Through wisdom is an house builded; and by understanding it is established:
And by knowledge shall the chambers be filled with all precious and pleasant riches.

—PROVERBS 24:3–4

A CYCLE 1 MEMORY MASTER KNOWS...

ANCIENT KINGDOMS

161 EVENTS AND PEOPLE
in a chronological timeline

24 HISTORY SENTENCES
span SIX ancient kingdoms and add depth to the timeline

120 GEOGRAPHIC FEATURES
and political locations throughout history, all around the world

24 SCIENCE FACTS
including classifications of living things and each continent's highest mountain

45 U.S. PRESIDENTS

53 PREPOSITIONS
along with grammar facts, including 23 helping verbs and 12 linking verbs

5 LATIN NOUN ENDINGS
and their singular and plural cases

15s MULTIPLICATION TABLES
as well as common squares and cubes, basic geometry formulas, and unit conversions

not to mention drawing techniques, music theory and tin whistle, 6 great artists and related projects, introduction to orchestra and 3 classical composers, 12 science experiments, 12 science projects, and 24 oral presentations!

For practice on the go, download our mobile app!

THAT'S OVER **400** pieces of information **in one year!**

WEEK	MATH	LATIN	SCIENCE	ENGLISH	TIMELINE	HISTORY	GEOGRAPHY	PROJECTS	FINE ARTS
1	1s and 2s	nom-sub; gen-poss; dat-IO; acc-DO; abl-OP	classification	preposition	1–7	Commandments 1–5	Fertile Crescent	45 Baby Bean	5 elements of shape
2	3s and 4s		kingdoms	about–against	8–14	Commandments 6–10	Assyrian Empire	54 Telegraph Lines 56 Belly Up	mirror images
3	5s and 6s	noun endings (1st declension)	animal cell	along–atop	15–21	Greek and Roman gods	Hebrew Empire	57 Blending 58 Ground Temperature	upside-down
4	7s and 8s		plant cell	before–beside	22–28	7 Wonders	Hittite Empire	62 Pollution	abstract art
5	9s and 10s	noun endings (2nd declension)	invertebrates	between–concerning	29–35	Romans	Egyptian Empire	60 Oily Feathers 61 Tangled	perspective
6	11s and 12s		vertebrates	down–from	36–42	Ancient Greeks	Ancient Greece	65 Fooling Your Tongue 66 Trickery	final project
7	13s	noun endings (3rd declension)	reproduce	in–near	43–49	Hinduism	Roman Empire	nature walk: animals	tin whistle
8	14s		seed plants	of–out	50–56	Imperialism	Indus River Valley	nature walk: plants	dynamics
9	15s	noun endings (4th declension)	parts of plant	outside–since	57–63	Lao-Tzu	China	crayfish	note values and staff
10	squares		leaf shapes	through–toward	64–70	Heian period	Japan	owl pellets	rhythm
11	cubes	noun endings (5th declension)	parts of a flower	under–upon	71–77	Byzantine Empire	Byzantine Empire	parts of a flower	note names and scales
12	tsp. and tbsp.		plant systems	with–without	78–84	Muslim Empire	Muslim Empire	classification	review and celebration
13	liquid equivalents	nom-sub; gen-poss; dat-IO; acc-DO; abl-OP	parts of geosphere	compound preps	85–91	Kush	Western Africa	121 Tilt 127 Sinkers	Giotto
14	linear equivalents		kinds of rock	helping verb	92–98	Trade in Africa	Ancient Africa	125 Spoon Pen 126 Sampler	Ghiberti
15	metric measurements	noun endings (1st declension)	highest mountain	do, does, did	99–105	Prince Henry	Middle East	128 Prints	Angelico
16	area rectangle		kinds of volcanoes	has, have, had	106–112	Mesoamerica	African waters	130 Stretch 132 Spurt	Dürer
17	area square	noun endings (2nd declension)	parts of a volcano	may–might	113–119	Aztecs	African countries	138 Rock Bridge	Michelangelo
18	area triangle		types of ocean floor	should–would	120–126	Mound Builders	Mesoamerica regions	140 Push Up 142 Up Draft	El Greco
19	area circle	noun endings (3rd declension)	ocean zones	shall, will, can	127–133	Anasazi	Mesoamerica	crystals	Baroque and Classical
20	circumference		parts of the atmosphere	linking verb	134–140	Mexican Revolution	Dominion of Canada	layers of geosphere	Handel
21	Associative Law	noun endings (4th declension)	circles of latitude	to be	141–147	Canada	Canadian waters	mineral ID	Bach
22	Commutative Law		kinds of weather fronts	feel–taste	148–154	British North America Act	S. America (west)	more mineral ID	Mozart
23	Distributive Law	noun endings (5th declension)	types of clouds	seem–sound	155–161	South America	S. America (east)	rock structure ID	orchestra
24	Identity Law		globe	stay–grow	U. S. Presidents	Portuguese Empire	North Atlantic	compass walk	review

 MATH

MULTIPLICATION TABLES
1s and 2s

1 × 1 = 1	2 × 1 = 2
1 × 2 = 2	2 × 2 = 4
1 × 3 = 3	2 × 3 = 6
1 × 4 = 4	2 × 4 = 8
1 × 5 = 5	2 × 5 = 10
1 × 6 = 6	2 × 6 = 12
1 × 7 = 7	2 × 7 = 14
1 × 8 = 8	2 × 8 = 16
1 × 9 = 9	2 × 9 = 18
1 × 10 = 10	2 × 10 = 20
1 × 11 = 11	2 × 11 = 22
1 × 12 = 12	2 × 12 = 24
1 × 13 = 13	2 × 13 = 26
1 × 14 = 14	2 × 14 = 28
1 × 15 = 15	2 × 15 = 30

 ENGLISH

A PREPOSITION

A **preposition** relates a noun or pronoun to another word.

 LATIN

NOUN CASES

nominative—subject

genitive—possessive

dative—indirect object

accusative—direct object

ablative—object of the preposition

TIMELINE

Classical Acts & Facts® History Cards

1	**AGE OF ANCIENT EMPIRES**
2	Creation and the Fall
3	The Flood and the Tower of Babel
4	Mesopotamia and Sumer
5	Egyptians
6	Indus River Valley Civilization
7	Minoans and Mycenaeans

 SCIENCE

Classical Acts & Facts® Science Cycle 1

What are the classifications of living things?

domain
kingdom
phylum
class
order
family
genus
species

PRESENTATION NOTES

 Recite math memory work in speed rounds.

 HISTORY 18

Tell me about commandments 1–5.
Thou shalt…

1 have no other gods before me.
2 not make unto thee any graven image.
3 not take the name of the LORD thy God in vain.
4 remember the sabbath day, to keep it holy.
5 honor thy father and thy mother: that thy days may be long upon the land which the LORD thy God giveth thee.

 **GEOGRAPHY**

FERTILE CRESCENT

Mediterranean Sea
Mesopotamia
Euphrates River
Tigris River
Sumer

 HANDS-ON

FINE ARTS

Drawing Introduction (see page 80)
Five Elements of Shape (see page 81)

SCIENCE

Baby Bean (#45)

 *Memoria*

MATH

MULTIPLICATION TABLES
3s and 4s

3 × 1 = 3	4 × 1 = 4
3 × 2 = 6	4 × 2 = 8
3 × 3 = 9	4 × 3 = 12
3 × 4 = 12	4 × 4 = 16
3 × 5 = 15	4 × 5 = 20
3 × 6 = 18	4 × 6 = 24
3 × 7 = 21	4 × 7 = 28
3 × 8 = 24	4 × 8 = 32
3 × 9 = 27	4 × 9 = 36
3 × 10 = 30	4 × 10 = 40
3 × 11 = 33	4 × 11 = 44
3 × 12 = 36	4 × 12 = 48
3 × 13 = 39	4 × 13 = 52
3 × 14 = 42	4 × 14 = 56
3 × 15 = 45	4 × 15 = 60

 ENGLISH

PREPOSITIONS

about
above
across
after
against

 LATIN

NOUN CASES

nominative—subject
genitive—possessive
dative—indirect object
accusative—direct object
ablative—object of the preposition

TIMELINE

Classical Acts & Facts® History Cards

8	Seven Wonders of the Ancient World
9	Patriarchs of Israel
10	Hittites and Canaanites
11	Kush
12	Assyrians
13	Babylonians
14	China's Shang Dynasty

 SCIENCE

Classical Acts & Facts® Science Cycle 1

What are the kingdoms of living things?

animalia
plantae
fungi
protista
archaea
bacteria

PRESENTATION NOTES

 Set a goal of drawing one map a day.

 HISTORY 18

Tell me about commandments 6–10.
Thou shalt…
6 not murder.
7 not commit adultery.
8 not steal.
9 not bear false witness against thy neighbor.
10 not covet.

 **GEOGRAPHY**

ASSYRIAN EMPIRE
Red Sea
Persian Gulf
Caspian Sea
Black Sea
Babylon

HANDS-ON

FINE ARTS
Mirror Images (see page 82)

SCIENCE
Telegraph Lines (#54)
Belly Up (#56)

Memoria
What are some outside activities you enjoy at night?

 MATH

MULTIPLICATION TABLES
5s and 6s

5 × 1 = 5	6 × 1 = 6
5 × 2 = 10	6 × 2 = 12
5 × 3 = 15	6 × 3 = 18
5 × 4 = 20	6 × 4 = 24
5 × 5 = 25	6 × 5 = 30
5 × 6 = 30	6 × 6 = 36
5 × 7 = 35	6 × 7 = 42
5 × 8 = 40	6 × 8 = 48
5 × 9 = 45	6 × 9 = 54
5 × 10 = 50	6 × 10 = 60
5 × 11 = 55	6 × 11 = 66
5 × 12 = 60	6 × 12 = 72
5 × 13 = 65	6 × 13 = 78
5 × 14 = 70	6 × 14 = 84
5 × 15 = 75	6 × 15 = 90

 ENGLISH

PREPOSITIONS
along
amid
among
around
at
atop

 HISTORY 20

Tell me about the Greek and Roman gods.

GREEK	ROMAN
Zeus	Jupiter
Hera	Juno
Ares	Mars
Aphrodite	Venus
Hermes	Mercury
Athena	Minerva
Poseidon	Neptune

 LATIN

1st DECLENSION NOUN ENDINGS

	singular	plural
nominative	-a	-ae
genitive	-ae	-ārum
dative	-ae	-īs
accusative	-am	-ās
ablative	-ā	-īs

TIMELINE

Classical Acts & Facts® History Cards

15   Hinduism in India
16   Phoenicians and the Alphabet
17   Olmecs of Mesoamerica
18   Israelite Exodus and Desert Wandering
19   Israelite Conquest and Judges
20   Greek Dark Ages
21   Israel's United Kingdom

 GEOGRAPHY

HEBREW EMPIRE
Judah
Israel
Jordan River
Dead Sea
Phoenicia
Sea of Galilee

 SCIENCE 6

Classical Acts & Facts® Science Cycle 1

What are some parts of an animal cell?

nucleus
cytoplasm
vacuole
mitochondria
cell membrane
Golgi bodies

PRESENTATION NOTES

 Review Cycle 2 history.

 HANDS-ON

FINE ARTS
Upside-Down Image (see page 83)

SCIENCE

Blending (#57)
Ground Temperature (#58)

 *Memoria*

 MATH

MULTIPLICATION TABLES
7s and 8s

7 × 1 = 7	8 × 1 = 8
7 × 2 = 14	8 × 2 = 16
7 × 3 = 21	8 × 3 = 24
7 × 4 = 28	8 × 4 = 32
7 × 5 = 35	8 × 5 = 40
7 × 6 = 42	8 × 6 = 48
7 × 7 = 49	8 × 7 = 56
7 × 8 = 56	8 × 8 = 64
7 × 9 = 63	8 × 9 = 72
7 × 10 = 70	8 × 10 = 80
7 × 11 = 77	8 × 11 = 88
7 × 12 = 84	8 × 12 = 96
7 × 13 = 91	8 × 13 = 104
7 × 14 = 98	8 × 14 = 112
7 × 15 = 105	8 × 15 = 120

 ENGLISH

PREPOSITIONS
before
behind
below
beneath
beside

 HISTORY 8

Tell me about the Seven Wonders of the Ancient World.
The Seven Wonders of the Ancient World are:
Pyramids of Giza
Hanging Gardens of Babylon
Temple of Artemis at Ephesus
Statue of Zeus at Olympia
Mausoleum at Helicarnassus
Pharos Lighthouse at
  Alexandria
Colossus of Rhodes

 LATIN

1st DECLENSION NOUN ENDINGS

	singular	plural
nominative	-a	-ae
genitive	-ae	-ārum
dative	-ae	-īs
accusative	-am	-ās
ablative	-ā	-īs

 **TIMELINE**

Classical Acts & Facts® History Cards

22	Early Native Americans
23	Israel Divides into Two Kingdoms
24	Homer and Hesiod
25	Rome Founded by Romulus and Remus
26	Israel Falls to Assyria
27	Assyria Falls to Babylon
28	Lao-Tzu, Confucius, Buddha

 Review Cycle 2 English.

 **GEOGRAPHY**

HITTITE EMPIRE
Hattusa
Asia Minor
Arabian Desert
Cyprus

 SCIENCE 7

Classical Acts & Facts® Science Cycle 1

What are some parts of a plant cell?
nucleus
cytoplasm
vacuole
mitochondria
cell membrane
cell wall
chloroplasts
Golgi bodies

PRESENTATION NOTES

 **HANDS-ON**

FINE ARTS
Abstract Art (see page 84)

SCIENCE
Pollution (#62)

Memoria
What are you praying for?

MATH

MULTIPLICATION TABLES
9s and 10s

9 × 1 = 9	10 × 1 = 10
9 × 2 = 18	10 × 2 = 20
9 × 3 = 27	10 × 3 = 30
9 × 4 = 36	10 × 4 = 40
9 × 5 = 45	10 × 5 = 50
9 × 6 = 54	10 × 6 = 60
9 × 7 = 63	10 × 7 = 70
9 × 8 = 72	10 × 8 = 80
9 × 9 = 81	10 × 9 = 90
9 × 10 = 90	10 × 10 = 100
9 × 11 = 99	10 × 11 = 110
9 × 12 = 108	10 × 12 = 120
9 × 13 = 117	10 × 13 = 130
9 × 14 = 126	10 × 14 = 140
9 × 15 = 135	10 × 15 = 150

ENGLISH

PREPOSITIONS
between
beyond
but
by
concerning

LATIN

2nd DECLENSION NOUN ENDINGS

	singular	plural
nominative	-us	-ī
genitive	-ī	-ōrum
dative	-ō	-īs
accusative	-um	-ōs
ablative	-ō	-īs

TIMELINE

Classical Acts & Facts® History Cards

29	Judah falls to Babylon, Temple Destroyed
30	Babylon Falls to Persia
31	Jews Return and Rebuild the Temple
32	Roman Republic
33	Golden Age of Greece
34	Peloponnesian Wars
35	Persia Falls to Alexander the Great

SCIENCE

Classical Acts & Facts® Science Cycle 1

What are the major groups of invertebrates?
   sponges
   stinging-cell animals
   flatworms
   roundworms
   segmented worms
   mollusks
   sea stars
   arthropods

PRESENTATION NOTES

 Recite Cycle 1 Latin declensions in speed rounds.

HISTORY

Tell me about the Romans.
   The Roman Republic became the Roman Empire when Augustus was crowned emperor in 27 BC. This was followed by the *Pax Romana*. In AD 286, the empire divided into the western and eastern empires until Germanic barbarians defeated the western empire in AD 476.

GEOGRAPHY

EGYPTIAN EMPIRE
Egypt
Nile River
Upper/Lower Egypt
Nile River Delta

HANDS-ON

FINE ARTS
Perspective (see page 85)

SCIENCE
Oily Feathers (#60)
Tangled (#61)

 Memoria

MATH

MULTIPLICATION TABLES
11s and 12s

11 × 1 = 11	12 × 1 = 12
11 × 2 = 22	12 × 2 = 24
11 × 3 = 33	12 × 3 = 36
11 × 4 = 44	12 × 4 = 48
11 × 5 = 55	12 × 5 = 60
11 × 6 = 66	12 × 6 = 72
11 × 7 = 77	12 × 7 = 84
11 × 8 = 88	12 × 8 = 96
11 × 9 = 99	12 × 9 = 108
11 × 10 = 110	12 × 10 = 120
11 × 11 = 121	12 × 11 = 132
11 × 12 = 132	12 × 12 = 144
11 × 13 = 143	12 × 13 = 156
11 × 14 = 154	12 × 14 = 168
11 × 15 = 165	12 × 15 = 180

ENGLISH

PREPOSITIONS

down
during
except
for
from

LATIN

2nd DECLENSION NOUN ENDINGS

	singular	plural
nominative	-us	-ī
genitive	-ī	-ōrum
dative	-ō	-īs
accusative	-um	-ōs
ablative	-ō	-īs

TIMELINE

Classical Acts & Facts® History Cards

36	India's Mauryan Empire
37	Mayans of Mesoamerica
38	Punic Wars
39	Rome Conquers Greece
40	Roman Dictator Julius Caesar
41	Caesar Augustus and the *Pax Romana*
42	John the Baptist

SCIENCE

CYCLE 1   9

Classical Acts & Facts® Science Cycle 1

What are the major groups of vertebrates?
fish
amphibians
reptiles
mammals
birds

PRESENTATION NOTES

HISTORY   24

Tell me about some ancient Greeks.   33

Homer, a famous poet; Pythagoras, a famous mathematician; Socrates, a famous philosopher; and Archimedes, a famous inventor, shaped Western ideas. Ancient Greek city-states were among the first democracies.

GEOGRAPHY

ANCIENT GREECE
Greece
Aegean Sea
Macedonia
Crete
Rhodes

HANDS-ON

FINE ARTS
Drawing Review and Final Project
(see page 86)

SCIENCE
Fooling Your Tongue (#65)
Trickery (#66)

Memoria
What do you want to do differently next week?

 MATH

MULTIPLICATION TABLES

13s

13 × 1 = 13
13 × 2 = 26
13 × 3 = 39
13 × 4 = 52
13 × 5 = 65
13 × 6 = 78
13 × 7 = 91
13 × 8 = 104
13 × 9 = 117
13 × 10 = 130
13 × 11 = 143
13 × 12 = 156
13 × 13 = 169
13 × 14 = 182
13 × 15 = 195

 ENGLISH

PREPOSITIONS

in
inside
into
like
near

 HISTORY 15

Tell me about Hinduism and Buddhism in India. 28

Hinduism developed around 1500 BC and is known for karma, reincarnation, and the caste system.

Founded in the sixth century BC, Buddhism teaches self-denial as the path to enlightenment.

 LATIN

3rd DECLENSION NOUN ENDINGS

	singular	plural
nominative	various	-ēs
genitive	-is	-um
dative	-ī	-ibus
accusative	-em	-ēs
ablative	-e	-ibus

 **TIMELINE**

Classical Acts & Facts® History Cards

43 Jesus the Messiah
44 Pentecost and the Early Church
45 Persecution Spreads the Gospel
46 Herod's Temple Destroyed by Titus
47 Diocletian Divides the Roman Empire
48 Constantine Legalizes Christianity
49 India's Gupta Dynasty

 GEOGRAPHY

ROMAN EMPIRE

Hispania
Gaul
Germania
Alexandria
Carthage

 SCIENCE 10

Classical Acts & Facts® Science Cycle 1

What are some ways animals reproduce?

live birth
eggs
fragmentation
budding

PRESENTATION NOTES

Randomly choose a *Classical Acts & Facts® History Card* and recite cards that come after.

HANDS-ON

FINE ARTS

Music Theory and Practice Introduction (see page 87)
Parts of the Tin Whistle (see pages 88, 90–91)

SCIENCE

Animal Nature Walk (see page 118)

 *Memoria*

MATH

MULTIPLICATION TABLES
14s
$14 \times 1 = 14$
$14 \times 2 = 28$
$14 \times 3 = 42$
$14 \times 4 = 56$
$14 \times 5 = 70$
$14 \times 6 = 84$
$14 \times 7 = 98$
$14 \times 8 = 112$
$14 \times 9 = 126$
$14 \times 10 = 140$
$14 \times 11 = 154$
$14 \times 12 = 168$
$14 \times 13 = 182$
$14 \times 14 = 196$
$14 \times 15 = 210$

ENGLISH

PREPOSITIONS
of
off
on
onto
out

LATIN

3rd DECLENSION NOUN ENDINGS

	singular	plural
nominative	various	-ēs
genitive	-is	-um
dative	-ī	-ibus
accusative	-em	-ēs
ablative	-e	-ibus

TIMELINE

Classical Acts & Facts® History Cards

50	Council of Nicea
51	Augustine of Hippo
52	Jerome Completes the Vulgate
53	Visigoths Sack Rome
54	**THE MIDDLE AGES**
55	Council of Chalcedon
56	Western Roman Empire Falls to Barbarians

SCIENCE

Classical Acts & Facts® Science Cycle 1

What are some types of seed plants?
monocot
dicot
conifer

PRESENTATION NOTES

 Use *Trivium Tables®: Rhetoric* to enhance your presentation this week.

HISTORY

Tell me about the Age of Imperialism.

During the Age of Imperialism, the British established rule over India in 1858, and Queen Victoria was declared the Empress of India in 1877.

Before his assassination in 1948, Mohandas Gandhi led the passive resistance movement, which helped win India's independence.

GEOGRAPHY

INDUS RIVER VALLEY
Ganges River
Himalayas
Arabian Sea
Bay of Bengal
Great Indian Desert

HANDS-ON

FINE ARTS
Dynamics (see pages 92–93)

SCIENCE
Plant Nature Walk (see page 119)

Memoria

What new discovery about God's world brought you joy?

 MATH

MULTIPLICATION TABLES
15s
$15 \times 1 = 15$
$15 \times 2 = 30$
$15 \times 3 = 45$
$15 \times 4 = 60$
$15 \times 5 = 75$
$15 \times 6 = 90$
$15 \times 7 = 105$
$15 \times 8 = 120$
$15 \times 9 = 135$
$15 \times 10 = 150$
$15 \times 11 = 165$
$15 \times 12 = 180$
$15 \times 13 = 195$
$15 \times 14 = 210$
$15 \times 15 = 225$

 ENGLISH

PREPOSITIONS
outside
over
past
regarding
since

 LATIN

4th DECLENSION NOUN ENDINGS

	singular	plural
nominative	-us	-ūs
genitive	-ūs	-uum
dative	-uī	-ibus
accusative	-um	-ūs
ablative	-ū	-ibus

 **TIMELINE**

Classical Acts & Facts® History Cards

57	Byzantine Emperor Justinian
58	Benedict and Monasticism
59	Muhammad Founds Islam
60	Zanj and Early Ghana in Africa
61	Franks Defeat Muslims at the Battle of Tours
62	Golden Age of Islam
63	Vikings Raid and Trade

 SCIENCE

Classical Acts & Facts® Science Cycle 1

What are some parts of a plant?
leaves
stems
roots

PRESENTATION NOTES

 Review Cycle 2 science.

 HISTORY 28

Tell me about Lao-Tzu and Confucius in China.
Around the sixth century BC, Lao-Tzu founded Taoism, which emphasizes harmony with nature, and Confucius taught compassion and obedience.

 GEOGRAPHY

CHINA
Mongolia
Yellow Sea
Yellow River
Yangtze River
Beijing

 **HANDS-ON**

FINE ARTS
Note Values and Staff (see pages 94–95)

SCIENCE
Crayfish Identification (see page 120)

Memoria

 MATH

 LATIN

 SCIENCE

SQUARES

$1 \times 1 = 1$
$2 \times 2 = 4$
$3 \times 3 = 9$
$4 \times 4 = 16$
$5 \times 5 = 25$
$6 \times 6 = 36$
$7 \times 7 = 49$
$8 \times 8 = 64$
$9 \times 9 = 81$
$10 \times 10 = 100$
$11 \times 11 = 121$
$12 \times 12 = 144$
$13 \times 13 = 169$
$14 \times 14 = 196$
$15 \times 15 = 225$

4th DECLENSION NOUN ENDINGS

	singular	plural
nominative	-us	-ūs
genitive	-ūs	-uum
dative	-uī	-ibus
accusative	-um	-ūs
ablative	-ū	-ibus

Classical Acts & Facts® Science Cycle 1

What are some leaf shapes?
linear
oval
lobed
cleft
scalelike
needlelike

 ENGLISH

 **TIMELINE**

PRESENTATION NOTES

PREPOSITIONS

through
throughout
to
toward

Classical Acts & Facts® History Cards

64   Japan's Heian Period
65   Charlemagne Crowned
      Emperor of Europe
66   Alfred the Great of England
67   Erik the Red and Leif Eriksson,
      Norse Explorers
68   Vladimir I of Kiev
69   Byzantine Emperor Basil II
70   East-West Schism of the
      Church

 Review Cycle 2 geography.

 HISTORY 64

 **GEOGRAPHY**

HANDS-ON

Tell me about Japan's Heian period. 76

Around 794, Japan's emperors moved to Heian, present-day Kyoto. The Heian period ended in the twelfth century when civil war gave control to military commanders called shoguns in a feudal system where knights called samurai protected wealthy landowners.

JAPAN

Kyoto
Tokyo
Mt. Fuji
Pacific Ocean
Sea of Japan

FINE ARTS
Rhythm (see pages 96–97)

SCIENCE
Owl Pellet Dissection (see page 121)

Memoria
Share some details from a field trip.

MATH

CUBES

$1 \times 1 \times 1 = 1$
$2 \times 2 \times 2 = 8$
$3 \times 3 \times 3 = 27$
$4 \times 4 \times 4 = 64$
$5 \times 5 \times 5 = 125$
$6 \times 6 \times 6 = 216$
$7 \times 7 \times 7 = 343$
$8 \times 8 \times 8 = 512$
$9 \times 9 \times 9 = 729$
$10 \times 10 \times 10 = 1{,}000$
$11 \times 11 \times 11 = 1{,}331$
$12 \times 12 \times 12 = 1{,}728$
$13 \times 13 \times 13 = 2{,}197$
$14 \times 14 \times 14 = 2{,}744$
$15 \times 15 \times 15 = 3{,}375$

ENGLISH

PREPOSITIONS

under
underneath
until
up
upon

LATIN

5th DECLENSION NOUN ENDINGS

	singular	plural
nominative	-ēs	-ēs
genitive	-ēī	-ērum
dative	-ēī	-ēbus
accusative	-em	-ēs
ablative	-ē	-ēbus

TIMELINE

Classical Acts & Facts® History Cards

71 Norman Conquest and Feudalism in Europe
72 The Crusades
73 Zimbabwe and Early Mali in Africa
74 Aztecs of Mesoamerica
75 Francis of Assisi and Thomas Aquinas
76 Japan's Shoguns
77 Incas of South America

 Recite timeline backwards *and* forwards.

SCIENCE

15 · CYCLE 1

Classical Acts & Facts® Science Cycle 1

What are some parts of a flower?
petal
stamen
anther
pistil
sepal

PRESENTATION NOTES

HISTORY

 48

Tell me about Emperor Constantine and the Byzantine Empire. 57

Emperor Constantine stopped the persecution of Christians in the Eastern Roman Empire. In AD 330, he moved the capital to Byzantium and renamed it Constantinople. Emperor Justinian's Code became a model for legal systems. The Byzantine Empire lasted until Ottoman Turks captured Constantinople in 1453. 69 80

GEOGRAPHY

BYZANTINE EMPIRE
Constantinople
Rome
Athens
Ephesus
Antioch

HANDS-ON

FINE ARTS
Note Names and Scales (see pages 98–101)

SCIENCE
Parts of a Flower (see page 122)

 *Memoria*

MATH

TEASPOONS AND TABLESPOONS

3 teaspoons (tsp.) =
1 tablespoon (tbsp.)

2 tablespoons (tbsp.) =
1 fluid ounce (fl. oz.)

LATIN

5th DECLENSION NOUN ENDINGS

	singular	plural
nominative	-ēs	-ēs
genitive	-ēī	-ērum
dative	-ēī	-ēbus
accusative	-em	-ēs
ablative	-ē	-ēbus

SCIENCE

Classical Acts & Facts® Science Cycle 1

What are some plant systems?
photosynthesis
respiration
transpiration

16

CYCLE 1

ENGLISH

PREPOSITIONS

with
within
without

TIMELINE

Classical Acts & Facts® History Cards

78 Genghis Khan Rules the Mongols
79 England's Magna Carta
80 Ottoman Empire
81 Marco Polo's Journey to China
82 The Hundred Years' War and Black Death
83 The Renaissance
84 China's Ming Dynasty

PRESENTATION NOTES

Choose a series of history sentences and create a history story.

HISTORY

59

Tell me about the Muslim Empire. 80
In 622, Islam was founded in the Arabian Peninsula by Muhammad, who worshiped Allah. Mecca is the holy city of Islam. During the 1400s, the Ottoman Turks expanded the Muslim Empire.

GEOGRAPHY

MUSLIM EMPIRE
Mecca
Medina
Baghdad
Damascus
Tours
Syria

HANDS-ON

FINE ARTS
Review and Celebration (see page 102)

SCIENCE
Plants and Animals Classification (see page 123)

Memoria
Who are some mentors you value?

 MATH

LIQUID EQUIVALENTS

8 fluid ounces (fl. oz.) = 1 cup (c.)

2 cups (c.) = 1 pint (pt.)

2 pints (pt.) = 1 quart (qt.)

4 quarts (qt.) = 1 gallon (gal.)

 LATIN

NOUN CASES

nominative—subject

genitive—possessive

dative—indirect object

accusative—direct object

ablative—object of the preposition

 SCIENCE 17

Classical Acts & Facts® Science Cycle 1

What are some parts of the geosphere?
core
mantle
crust
hydrosphere
biosphere
atmosphere

 ENGLISH

COMPOUND PREPOSITIONS

according to
in addition to
except for
in front of
out of
instead of

 TIMELINE

Classical Acts & Facts® History Cards

85 **AGE OF EXPLORATION**
86 Prince Henry Founds School of Navigation
87 Slave Trade in Africa
88 Gutenberg's Printing Press
89 Songhai in Africa
90 Czar Ivan the Great of Russia
91 The Spanish Inquisition

PRESENTATION NOTES

 Recite all of the prepositions forwards and backwards.

 HISTORY 11

Tell me about the Kush.
The Kush mined gold along the Nile River from 2000 BC to AD 350. The Berbers traded gold, iron, and salt in the desert.

 GEOGRAPHY

WESTERN AFRICA

Atlantic Ocean
Senegal River
Niger River
Sahara Desert
Ivory Coast

 HANDS-ON

FINE ARTS

Great Artists Introduction (see pages 104–105)
Giotto (see page 106)

SCIENCE

Tilt (#121)
Sinkers (#127)

MATH

LINEAR EQUIVALENTS

2.54 centimeters (cm) = 1 inch (in.)

12 inches (in.) = 1 foot (ft.)

5,280 feet (ft.) = 1 mile (mi.)

1 kilometer (km) = ⅝ mile (mi.)

 LATIN

NOUN CASES

nominative—subject

genitive—possessive

dative—indirect object

accusative—direct object

ablative—object of the preposition

 SCIENCE CYCLE 1 18

Classical Acts & Facts® Science Cycle 1

What are three kinds of rock?
sedimentary
metamorphic
igneous

 ENGLISH

A HELPING VERB

A **helping verb** helps another verb assert action, being, or existence.

TIMELINE

Classical Acts & Facts® History Cards

92 Columbus Sails to the Caribbean

93 AGE OF ABSOLUTE MONARCHS

94 Protestant Reformation

95 Spanish Conquistadors in the Americas

96 Calvin's *Institutes of the Christian Religion*

97 Council of Trent

98 Baroque Period of the Arts

PRESENTATION NOTES

 HISTORY 60

Tell me about trade in Africa. 73

In 700, Ghana was known as "the land of gold." The Mali nation took control of the gold trade in 1240 and established Timbuktu as a center of trade, culture, and learning. By the mid-1400s, the wealthy and powerful Songhai Empire controlled trade in western Africa. 89

 GEOGRAPHY

ANCIENT AFRICA

Ancient Ghana
Ancient Mali
Western Sahara
Fez
Tangier

 HANDS-ON

FINE ARTS

Ghiberti (see page 106)

SCIENCE

Spoon Pen (#125)
Sampler (#126)

Describe God's goodness to your family.

 MATH

METRIC MEASUREMENTS

10 millimeters (mm) =
1 centimeter (cm)

100 centimeters (cm) = 1 meter (m)

1,000 meters (m) = 1 kilometer (km)

 LATIN

1st DECLENSION NOUN ENDINGS

	singular	plural
nominative	-a	-ae
genitive	-ae	-ārum
dative	-ae	-īs
accusative	-am	-ās
ablative	-ā	-īs

 SCIENCE 19

Classical Acts & Facts® Science Cycle 1

What is each continent's highest mountain?

Everest in Asia
Aconcagua in S. America
Denali in N. America
Kilimanjaro in Africa
Elbrus in Europe
Kosciuszko in Australia
Vinson Massif in Antarctica

 ENGLISH

HELPING VERBS

do
does
did

TIMELINE

Classical Acts & Facts® History Cards

99 Japan's Isolation
100 Jamestown and Plymouth Colony Founded
101 AGE OF ENLIGHTENMENT
102 Hudson's Bay Company
103 First Great Awakening
104 Classical Period of the Arts
105 The Seven Years' War

PRESENTATION NOTES

 Find a biography on Angelico.

 HISTORY 86

Tell me about Prince Henry of Portugal.

In the 1400s, Prince Henry of Portugal founded a school of navigation. His work advanced European exploration and trade, including the slave trade.

 GEOGRAPHY

MIDDLE EAST

Israel
Sinai Peninsula
Suez Canal
Cairo
Gaza Strip

 HANDS-ON

FINE ARTS

Angelico (see page 106)

SCIENCE

Prints (#124)

Memoria

 MATH

AREA OF A RECTANGLE

The area of a rectangle equals length times width.

 LATIN

1st DECLENSION NOUN ENDINGS

	singular	plural
nominative	-a	-ae
genitive	-ae	-ārum
dative	-ae	-īs
accusative	-am	-ās
ablative	-ā	-īs

 SCIENCE 20

Classical Acts & Facts® Science Cycle 1

What are four kinds of volcanoes?
active
intermittent
dormant
extinct

 ENGLISH

HELPING VERBS

has
have
had

TIMELINE

Classical Acts & Facts® History Cards

106 AGE OF INDUSTRY
107 James Cook Sails to Australia and Antarctica
108 American Revolution and Gen. George Washington
109 Madison's Constitution and the Bill of Rights
110 French Revolution
111 Second Great Awakening
112 Louisiana Purchase and Lewis and Clark Expedition

PRESENTATION NOTES

 Categorize timeline cards by continent.

 HISTORY 17

Tell me about the civilizations of Mesoamerica. 37

Three of the advanced civilizations of Mesoamerica from 1200 BC to AD 1500 were the Olmecs, the Mayans, and the Aztecs. 74

 GEOGRAPHY

AFRICAN WATERS
Congo River
Lake Victoria
Zambezi River
Orange River

  HANDS-ON 10

FINE ARTS
Dürer (see page 107)

SCIENCE
Stretch (#130)
Spurt (#132)

What are you learning about yourself?

 MATH

AREA OF A SQUARE
The area of a square equals length of its side squared.

 LATIN

2nd DECLENSION NOUN ENDINGS
	singular	plural
nominative	-us	-ī
genitive	-ī	-ōrum
dative	-ō	-īs
accusative	-um	-ōs
ablative	-ō	-īs

 SCIENCE 21

Classical Acts & Facts® Science Cycle 1

What are some parts of a volcano?
magma
vents
lava
crater
gases

 ENGLISH

HELPING VERBS
may
must
might

TIMELINE

Classical Acts & Facts® History Cards

113 Napoleon Crowned Emperor of France
114 Liberation of South America
115 The War of 1812
116 The Missouri Compromise
117 Immigrants Flock to America
118 The Monroe Doctrine
119 Romantic Period of the Arts

PRESENTATION NOTES

 In ten minutes, draw as much of the world map as you can remember, with locations and features.

 HISTORY 74

Tell me about the Aztecs.
The Aztecs used pyramids in rituals of human sacrifice. Their civilization began to fall when Hernán Cortés of Spain defeated Montezuma II in 1519.

 GEOGRAPHY

AFRICAN COUNTRIES
Ethiopia
Mozambique
Zimbabwe
South Africa
Madagascar

 HANDS-ON

FINE ARTS
Michelangelo (see page 107)

SCIENCE
Rock Bridge (#138)

Memoria

MATH

 LATIN

 SCIENCE CYCLE 1 23

AREA OF A TRIANGLE
The area of a triangle equals one-half base times height.

2nd DECLENSION NOUN ENDINGS

	singular	plural
nominative	-us	-ī
genitive	-ī	-ōrum
dative	-ō	-īs
accusative	-um	-ōs
ablative	-ō	-īs

Classical Acts & Facts® Science Cycle 1

What are four types of ocean floor?
continental shelf
abyssal plain
mid-ocean ridge
trench

 ENGLISH

 **TIMELINE**

PRESENTATION NOTES

HELPING VERBS

should
could
would

Classical Acts & Facts® History Cards

120	Cherokee Trail of Tears
121	U.S. Westward Expansion
122	Marx Publishes *The Communist Manifesto*
123	The Compromise of 1850 and the *Dred Scott* Decision
124	U.S. Restores Trade with Japan
125	British Queen Victoria's Rule Over India
126	Darwin Publishes *The Origin of Species*

 Recite Latin endings by recalling with cases (e.g., dative second declension singular and plural).

 **HISTORY** 22

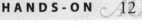 **GEOGRAPHY**

HANDS-ON *12*

Tell me about the Mound Builders.
Circa 1000 BC to AD 1450, three North American mound-building civilizations were the Adena, the Hopewell, and the Mississippians.

MESOAMERICA REGIONS
Gulf of Mexico
Yucatan Peninsula
Olmec Civilization
Maya Civilization
Aztec Civilization

FINE ARTS
El Greco (see page 107)

SCIENCE
Push Up (#140)
Up Draft (#142)

— *Memoria* —
How did your parents contribute to your success?

 MATH

AREA OF A CIRCLE
The area of a circle equals pi (3.14) times the radius squared.

 LATIN

3rd DECLENSION NOUN ENDINGS

	singular	plural
nominative	various	-ēs
genitive	-is	-um
dative	-ī	-ibus
accusative	-em	-ēs
ablative	-e	-ibus

 SCIENCE 24

Classical Acts & Facts® Science Cycle 1

What are some ocean zones?
epipelagic
mesopelagic
bathypelagic
abyssalpelagic

 ENGLISH

HELPING VERBS
shall
will
can

TIMELINE

Classical Acts & Facts® History Cards

127	Lincoln's War Between the States
128	Reconstruction of the Southern States
129	Dominion of Canada
130	Otto von Bismarck Unifies Germany
131	Boer Wars in Africa
132	The Spanish-American War
133	The Progressive Era

PRESENTATION NOTES

 Review Cycle 3 science.

 HISTORY 22

Tell me about the Anasazi.
The Anasazi of the southwestern United States built adobe villages in caves and on the sides of cliffs from 500 BC to AD 1200.

 GEOGRAPHY

MESOAMERICA
Mexico City
Chichen Itza
Lake Texcoco
Mayapan
Oaxaca

 HANDS-ON 98

FINE ARTS 104
Composers and Orchestra Introduction (see pages 108–109)
Baroque and Classical periods (see page 110)

SCIENCE

Crystals (see page 124)

MATH

CIRCUMFERENCE OF A CIRCLE
The circumference of a circle equals two times pi (3.14) times the radius.

LATIN

3rd DECLENSION NOUN ENDINGS

	singular	plural
nominative	various	-ēs
genitive	-is	-um
dative	-ī	-ibus
accusative	-em	-ēs
ablative	-e	-ibus

SCIENCE   25

Classical Acts & Facts® Science Cycle 1

What are some parts of the atmosphere?
troposphere
stratosphere
mesosphere
thermosphere
exosphere

ENGLISH

A LINKING VERB
A **linking verb** makes an assertion by joining two words.

TIMELINE

Classical Acts & Facts® History Cards

134 Australia Becomes a Commonwealth
135 Mexican Revolution
136 World War I and President Wilson
137 Lenin and the Bolshevik Revolution in Russia
138 U.S. Evangelist Billy Graham
139 Modern Period of the Arts
140 The Great Depression and the New Deal

PRESENTATION NOTES

 Review Cycle 3 English.

HISTORY   135

Tell me about the Mexican Revolution.
Circa 1910, during the Mexican Revolution, Pancho Villa and Emiliano Zapata fought the federales for "Land and Liberty."

GEOGRAPHY

DOMINION OF CANADA
Ontario
Quebec
New Brunswick
Nova Scotia

HANDS-ON   14

FINE ARTS
Handel "Water Music Suite" (see page 110)

SCIENCE
Layers of the Geosphere (see page 125)

Memoria
What did you struggle with this week?

 MATH

The Associative Law
for addition states:
$(a + b) + c = a + (b + c)$

The Associative Law
for multiplication states:
$(a \times b) \times c = a \times (b \times c)$

 LATIN

4th DECLENSION NOUN ENDINGS

	singular	plural
nominative	-us	-ūs
genitive	-ūs	-uum
dative	-uī	-ibus
accusative	-um	-ūs
ablative	-ū	-ibus

 SCIENCE 26

Classical Acts & Facts® Science Cycle 1

What are five circles of latitude?
Arctic Circle
Tropic of Cancer
equator
Tropic of Capricorn
Antarctic Circle

 ENGLISH

HELPING AND LINKING VERB: to be

am	was	be
are	were	being
is		been

TIMELINE

Classical Acts & Facts® History Cards

141 World War II and President
Franklin D. Roosevelt
142 Stalin of the USSR and the
Katyn Massacre
143 The United Nations Formed
144 The Cold War
145 Gandhi and India's
Independence
146 Jewish State Established
147 Mao and Communist Victory in
China

PRESENTATION NOTES

  Review Cycle 3 geography.

 HISTORY 85

Tell me about the exploration of 102
Canada.
John Cabot and Samuel de Champlain explored Canada and the St. Lawrence River. Creation of the Hudson's Bay Company, in 1670, eventually led to war between Britain and France. The maple leaf is the symbol of Canada.

GEOGRAPHY

CANADIAN WATERS
Great Bear Lake
Great Slave Lake
Hudson Bay
Baffin Bay
Labrador Sea

HANDS-ON 13

FINE ARTS

Bach *Well-Tempered Clavier* (see page 110)

SCIENCE

Mineral Identfication (continued on Week 22; see page 126)

 MATH

The Commutative Law
for addition states:
$a + b = b + a$

The Commutative Law
for multiplication states:
$a \times b = b \times a$

 LATIN

4th DECLENSION NOUN ENDINGS

	singular	plural
nominative	-us	-ūs
genitive	-ūs	-uum
dative	-uī	-ibus
accusative	-um	-ūs
ablative	-ū	-ibus

 SCIENCE

Classical Acts & Facts® Science Cycle 1

What are some kinds of weather fronts?
cold
warm
stationary
occluded

 ENGLISH

LINKING VERBS

feel
become
remain
taste

TIMELINE

Classical Acts & Facts® History Cards

148 North Atlantic Treaty Organization
149 The Korean War
150 Martin Luther King, Jr. and the Civil Rights Movement
151 Jim and Elisabeth Elliot, Missionaries to Ecuador
152 The Antarctic Treaty
153 The Vietnam War
154 U.S. Astronauts Walk on the Moon

PRESENTATION NOTES

 Substitute different numbers in the equation, calculate, and prove commutative laws.

 HISTORY 129

Tell me about the British North America Act of 1867.
In 1867, the British North America Act established the Dominion of Canada. The Canadians gained total independence from Britain in 1982. French is spoken in the province of Quebec.

 **GEOGRAPHY**

SOUTH AMERICA (WEST)
Venezuela
Colombia
Ecuador
Peru
Bolivia
Chile

 HANDS-ON

FINE ARTS

Mozart "Piano Concerto no. 22 in E-Flat, Third Movement" (see page 110)

SCIENCE

Mineral Identification (see page 126)

Memoria
How did your family grow this year?

 MATH

The Distributive Law states:
$a(b + c) = ab + ac$

 LATIN

5th DECLENSION NOUN ENDINGS

	singular	plural
nominative	-ēs	-ēs
genitive	-ēī	-ērum
dative	-ēī	-ēbus
accusative	-em	-ēs
ablative	-ē	-ēbus

 SCIENCE 30

Classical Acts & Facts® Science Cycle 1

What are some types of clouds?
cumulonimbus
cirrus
stratus
cumulus
stratocumulus

ENGLISH

LINKING VERBS

seem
appear
look
sound

TIMELINE

Classical Acts & Facts® History Cards

155 AGE OF INFORMATION AND GLOBALIZATION
156 Watergate, President Nixon Resigns
157 Fall of Communism in Eastern Europe
158 European Union Formed
159 Apartheid Abolished in South Africa
160 September 11, 2001
161 Rising Tide of Freedom

PRESENTATION NOTES

 Review Cycle 3 Latin.

 HISTORY 114

Tell me about the liberation of South America.
In the early 1800s, San Martín of Argentina, O'Higgins of Chile, and Bolívar of Venezuela fought to liberate South America from Spain.

GEOGRAPHY

SOUTH AMERICA (EAST)
Argentina
Uruguay
Paraguay
Brazil
French Guiana
Suriname
Guyana

 HANDS-ON

FINE ARTS
Orchestra Overview (see page 111)

SCIENCE
Rock Structure Identification (see page 126)

 *Memoria*

 MATH

The Identity Law
for addition states:
$a + 0 = a$

The Identity Law
for multiplication states:
$a \times 1 = a$

 LATIN

5th DECLENSION NOUN ENDINGS

	singular	plural
nominative	-ēs	-ēs
genitive	-ēī	-ērum
dative	-ēī	-ēbus
accusative	-em	-ēs
ablative	-ē	-ēbus

 SCIENCE 31

Classical Acts & Facts® Science Cycle 1

What are some markings on the globe?
latitude
longitude
Prime Meridian
degrees
Northern Hemisphere
Southern Hemisphere

 ENGLISH

LINKING VERBS

stay
smell
grow

 **TIMELINE**

Classical Acts & Facts® History Cards

U.S. Presidents:
Washington, Adams, Jefferson,
Madison, Monroe, Adams, Jackson,
Van Buren, Harrison, Tyler, Polk,
Taylor, Fillmore, Pierce, Buchanan,
Lincoln, Johnson, Grant, Hayes,
Garfield, Arthur, Cleveland, Harrison,
Cleveland, McKinley, Roosevelt, Taft,
Wilson, Harding, Coolidge, Hoover,
Roosevelt, Truman, Eisenhower,
Kennedy, Johnson, Nixon, Ford,
Carter, Reagan, Bush, Clinton, Bush,
Obama, Trump

PRESENTATION NOTES

 Recite the presidents' first *and* last names. List political parties of each president. List the state in which each president was born.

 HISTORY 113

Tell me about the Portuguese Empire.
When Napoleon threatened the Portuguese Empire, King John VI fled to Brazil. His son, Dom Pedro I, declared Brazil independent in 1822.

 GEOGRAPHY

NORTH ATLANTIC
Greenland
Iceland
Denmark Strait
Davis Strait

 HANDS-ON

FINE ARTS
Review and Celebration (see page 111)

SCIENCE
Compass Walk (see page 127)

 *Memoria*
Celebrate!

1 1s and 2s

- [ ] $1 \times 1 = 1$
- [ ] $1 \times 2 = 2$
- [ ] $1 \times 3 = 3$
- [ ] $1 \times 4 = 4$
- [ ] $1 \times 5 = 5$
- [ ] $1 \times 6 = 6$
- [ ] $1 \times 7 = 7$
- [ ] $1 \times 8 = 8$
- [ ] $1 \times 9 = 9$
- [ ] $1 \times 10 = 10$
- [ ] $1 \times 11 = 11$
- [ ] $1 \times 12 = 12$
- [ ] $1 \times 13 = 13$
- [ ] $1 \times 14 = 14$
- [ ] $1 \times 15 = 15$
- [ ] $2 \times 1 = 2$
- [ ] $2 \times 2 = 4$
- [ ] $2 \times 3 = 6$
- [ ] $2 \times 4 = 8$
- [ ] $2 \times 5 = 10$
- [ ] $2 \times 6 = 12$
- [ ] $2 \times 7 = 14$
- [ ] $2 \times 8 = 16$
- [ ] $2 \times 9 = 18$
- [ ] $2 \times 10 = 20$
- [ ] $2 \times 11 = 22$
- [ ] $2 \times 12 = 24$
- [ ] $2 \times 13 = 26$
- [ ] $2 \times 14 = 28$
- [ ] $2 \times 15 = 30$

2 3s and 4s

- [ ] $3 \times 1 = 3$
- [ ] $3 \times 2 = 6$
- [ ] $3 \times 3 = 9$
- [ ] $3 \times 4 = 12$
- [ ] $3 \times 5 = 15$

- [ ] $3 \times 6 = 18$
- [ ] $3 \times 7 = 21$
- [ ] $3 \times 8 = 24$
- [ ] $3 \times 9 = 27$
- [ ] $3 \times 10 = 30$
- [ ] $3 \times 11 = 33$
- [ ] $3 \times 12 = 36$
- [ ] $3 \times 13 = 39$
- [ ] $3 \times 14 = 42$
- [ ] $3 \times 15 = 45$
- [ ] $4 \times 1 = 4$
- [ ] $4 \times 2 = 8$
- [ ] $4 \times 3 = 12$
- [ ] $4 \times 4 = 16$
- [ ] $4 \times 5 = 20$
- [ ] $4 \times 6 = 24$
- [ ] $4 \times 7 = 28$
- [ ] $4 \times 8 = 32$
- [ ] $4 \times 9 = 36$
- [ ] $4 \times 10 = 40$
- [ ] $4 \times 11 = 44$
- [ ] $4 \times 12 = 48$
- [ ] $4 \times 13 = 52$
- [ ] $4 \times 14 = 56$
- [ ] $4 \times 15 = 60$

3 5s and 6s

- [ ] $5 \times 1 = 5$
- [ ] $5 \times 2 = 10$
- [ ] $5 \times 3 = 15$
- [ ] $5 \times 4 = 20$
- [ ] $5 \times 5 = 25$
- [ ] $5 \times 6 = 30$
- [ ] $5 \times 7 = 35$
- [ ] $5 \times 8 = 40$
- [ ] $5 \times 9 = 45$
- [ ] $5 \times 10 = 50$
- [ ] $5 \times 11 = 55$

- [ ] $5 \times 12 = 60$
- [ ] $5 \times 13 = 65$
- [ ] $5 \times 14 = 70$
- [ ] $5 \times 15 = 75$
- [ ] $6 \times 1 = 6$
- [ ] $6 \times 2 = 12$
- [ ] $6 \times 3 = 18$
- [ ] $6 \times 4 = 24$
- [ ] $6 \times 5 = 30$
- [ ] $6 \times 6 = 36$
- [ ] $6 \times 7 = 42$
- [ ] $6 \times 8 = 48$
- [ ] $6 \times 9 = 54$
- [ ] $6 \times 10 = 60$
- [ ] $6 \times 11 = 66$
- [ ] $6 \times 12 = 72$
- [ ] $6 \times 13 = 78$
- [ ] $6 \times 14 = 84$
- [ ] $6 \times 15 = 90$

4 7s and 8s

- [ ] $7 \times 1 = 7$
- [ ] $7 \times 2 = 14$
- [ ] $7 \times 3 = 21$
- [ ] $7 \times 4 = 28$
- [ ] $7 \times 5 = 35$
- [ ] $7 \times 6 = 42$
- [ ] $7 \times 7 = 49$
- [ ] $7 \times 8 = 56$
- [ ] $7 \times 9 = 63$
- [ ] $7 \times 10 = 70$
- [ ] $7 \times 11 = 77$
- [ ] $7 \times 12 = 84$
- [ ] $7 \times 13 = 91$
- [ ] $7 \times 14 = 98$
- [ ] $7 \times 15 = 105$
- [ ] $8 \times 1 = 8$
- [ ] $8 \times 2 = 16$

- [ ] $8 \times 3 = 24$
- [ ] $8 \times 4 = 32$
- [ ] $8 \times 5 = 40$
- [ ] $8 \times 6 = 48$
- [ ] $8 \times 7 = 56$
- [ ] $8 \times 8 = 64$
- [ ] $8 \times 9 = 72$
- [ ] $8 \times 10 = 80$
- [ ] $8 \times 11 = 88$
- [ ] $8 \times 12 = 96$
- [ ] $8 \times 13 = 104$
- [ ] $8 \times 14 = 112$
- [ ] $8 \times 15 = 120$

5 9s and 10s

- [ ] $9 \times 1 = 9$
- [ ] $9 \times 2 = 18$
- [ ] $9 \times 3 = 27$
- [ ] $9 \times 4 = 36$
- [ ] $9 \times 5 = 45$
- [ ] $9 \times 6 = 54$
- [ ] $9 \times 7 = 63$
- [ ] $9 \times 8 = 72$
- [ ] $9 \times 9 = 81$
- [ ] $9 \times 10 = 90$
- [ ] $9 \times 11 = 99$
- [ ] $9 \times 12 = 108$
- [ ] $9 \times 13 = 117$
- [ ] $9 \times 14 = 126$
- [ ] $9 \times 15 = 135$
- [ ] $10 \times 1 = 10$
- [ ] $10 \times 2 = 20$
- [ ] $10 \times 3 = 30$
- [ ] $10 \times 4 = 40$
- [ ] $10 \times 5 = 50$
- [ ] $10 \times 6 = 60$
- [ ] $10 \times 7 = 70$
- [ ] $10 \times 8 = 80$

- [ ] $10 \times 9 = 90$
- [ ] $10 \times 10 = 100$
- [ ] $10 \times 11 = 110$
- [ ] $10 \times 12 = 120$
- [ ] $10 \times 13 = 130$
- [ ] $10 \times 14 = 140$
- [ ] $10 \times 15 = 150$

6 11s and 12s

- [ ] $11 \times 1 = 11$
- [ ] $11 \times 2 = 22$
- [ ] $11 \times 3 = 33$
- [ ] $11 \times 4 = 44$
- [ ] $11 \times 5 = 55$
- [ ] $11 \times 6 = 66$
- [ ] $11 \times 7 = 77$
- [ ] $11 \times 8 = 88$
- [ ] $11 \times 9 = 99$
- [ ] $11 \times 10 = 110$
- [ ] $11 \times 11 = 121$
- [ ] $11 \times 12 = 132$
- [ ] $11 \times 13 = 143$
- [ ] $11 \times 14 = 154$
- [ ] $11 \times 15 = 165$
- [ ] $12 \times 1 = 12$
- [ ] $12 \times 2 = 24$
- [ ] $12 \times 3 = 36$
- [ ] $12 \times 4 = 48$
- [ ] $12 \times 5 = 60$
- [ ] $12 \times 6 = 72$
- [ ] $12 \times 7 = 84$
- [ ] $12 \times 8 = 96$
- [ ] $12 \times 9 = 108$
- [ ] $12 \times 10 = 120$
- [ ] $12 \times 11 = 132$
- [ ] $12 \times 12 = 144$
- [ ] $12 \times 13 = 156$
- [ ] $12 \times 14 = 168$
- [ ] $12 \times 15 = 180$

7 13s

- [ ] 13 × 1 = 13
- [ ] 13 × 2 = 26
- [ ] 13 × 3 = 39
- [ ] 13 × 4 = 52
- [ ] 13 × 5 = 65
- [ ] 13 × 6 = 78
- [ ] 13 × 7 = 91
- [ ] 13 × 8 = 104
- [ ] 13 × 9 = 117
- [ ] 13 × 10 = 130
- [ ] 13 × 11 = 143
- [ ] 13 × 12 = 156
- [ ] 13 × 13 = 169
- [ ] 13 × 14 = 182
- [ ] 13 × 15 = 195

8 14s

- [ ] 14 × 1 = 14
- [ ] 14 × 2 = 28
- [ ] 14 × 3 = 42
- [ ] 14 × 4 = 56
- [ ] 14 × 5 = 70
- [ ] 14 × 6 = 84
- [ ] 14 × 7 = 98
- [ ] 14 × 8 = 112
- [ ] 14 × 9 = 126
- [ ] 14 × 10 = 140
- [ ] 14 × 11 = 154
- [ ] 14 × 12 = 168
- [ ] 14 × 13 = 182
- [ ] 14 × 14 = 196
- [ ] 14 × 15 = 210

9 15s

- [ ] 15 × 1 = 15
- [ ] 15 × 2 = 30
- [ ] 15 × 3 = 45
- [ ] 15 × 4 = 60
- [ ] 15 × 5 = 75
- [ ] 15 × 6 = 90
- [ ] 15 × 7 = 105
- [ ] 15 × 8 = 120
- [ ] 15 × 9 = 135
- [ ] 15 × 10 = 150
- [ ] 15 × 11 = 165
- [ ] 15 × 12 = 180
- [ ] 15 × 13 = 195
- [ ] 15 × 14 = 210
- [ ] 15 × 15 = 225

10 SQUARES

- [ ] 1 × 1 = 1
- [ ] 2 × 2 = 4
- [ ] 3 × 3 = 9
- [ ] 4 × 4 = 16
- [ ] 5 × 5 = 25
- [ ] 6 × 6 = 36
- [ ] 7 × 7 = 49
- [ ] 8 × 8 = 64
- [ ] 9 × 9 = 81
- [ ] 10 × 10 = 100
- [ ] 11 × 11 = 121
- [ ] 12 × 12 = 144
- [ ] 13 × 13 = 169
- [ ] 14 × 14 = 196
- [ ] 15 × 15 = 225

11 CUBES

- [ ] 1 × 1 × 1 = 1
- [ ] 2 × 2 × 2 = 8
- [ ] 3 × 3 × 3 = 27
- [ ] 4 × 4 × 4 = 64
- [ ] 5 × 5 × 5 = 125
- [ ] 6 × 6 × 6 = 216
- [ ] 7 × 7 × 7 = 343
- [ ] 8 × 8 × 8 = 512
- [ ] 9 × 9 × 9 = 729
- [ ] 10 × 10 × 10 = 1,000
- [ ] 11 × 11 × 11 = 1,331
- [ ] 12 × 12 × 12 = 1,728
- [ ] 13 × 13 × 13 = 2,197
- [ ] 14 × 14 × 14 = 2,744
- [ ] 15 × 15 × 15 = 3,375

12 TEASPOONS AND TABLESPOONS

- [ ] 3 teaspoons equals 1 tablespoon
- [ ] 2 tablespoons equals 1 fluid ounce

13 LIQUID EQUIVALENTS

- [ ] 8 fluid ounces equals 1 cup
- [ ] 2 cups equals 1 pint
- [ ] 2 pints equals 1 quart
- [ ] 4 quarts equals 1 gallon

14 LINEAR EQUIVALENTS

- [ ] 2.54 centimeters equals 1 inch
- [ ] 12 inches equals 1 foot
- [ ] 5,280 feet equals 1 mile
- [ ] 1 kilometer equals $\frac{5}{8}$ mile

15 METRIC MEASUREMENTS

- [ ] 10 millimeters equals 1 centimeter
- [ ] 100 centimeters equals 1 meter
- [ ] 1000 meters equals 1 kilometer

16 AREA OF A RECTANGLE

- [ ] The area of a rectangle equals length times width.

17 AREA OF A SQUARE

- [ ] The area of a square equals the length of its side squared.

18 AREA OF A TRIANGLE

- [ ] The area of a triangle equals one-half base times height.

19 AREA OF A CIRCLE

- [ ] The area of a circle equals pi (3.14) times the radius squared.

20 CIRCUMFERENCE OF A CIRCLE

- [ ] The circumference of a circle equals 2 times pi (3.14) times the radius.

21 ASSOCIATIVE LAW

- [ ] The Associative Law for addition states: $(a + b) + c = a + (b + c)$
- [ ] The Associative Law for multiplication states: $(a \times b) \times c = a \times (b \times c)$

22 COMMUTATIVE LAW

- [ ] The Commutative Law for addition states: $a + b = b + a$
- [ ] The Commutative Law for multiplication states: $a \times b = b \times a$

23 DISTRIBUTIVE LAW

- [ ] The Distributive Law states: $a(b + c) = ab + ac$

24 IDENTITY LAW

- [ ] The Identity Law for addition states: $a + 0 = a$
- [ ] The Identity Law for multiplication states: $a \times 1 = a$

1 Noun Cases

- [ ] nominative—subject
- [ ] genitive—possessive
- [ ] dative—indirect object
- [ ] accusative—direct object
- [ ] ablative—object of the prep.

3 1st Declension Noun Endings

Singular	Plural
[ ] -a	[ ] -ae
[ ] -ae	[ ] -ārum
[ ] -ae	[ ] -īs
[ ] -am	[ ] -ās
[ ] -ā	[ ] -īs

5 2nd Declension Noun Endings

Singular	Plural
[ ] -us	[ ] -ī
[ ] -ī	[ ] -ōrum
[ ] -ō	[ ] -īs
[ ] -um	[ ] -ōs
[ ] -ō	[ ] -īs

7 3rd Declension Noun Endings

Singular	Plural
[ ] various	[ ] -ēs
[ ] -is	[ ] -um
[ ] -ī	[ ] -ibus
[ ] -em	[ ] -ēs
[ ] -e	[ ] -ibus

9 4th Declension Noun Endings

Singular	Plural
[ ] -us	[ ] -ūs
[ ] -ūs	[ ] -uum
[ ] -uī	[ ] -ibus
[ ] -um	[ ] -ūs
[ ] -ū	[ ] -ibus

11 5th Declension Noun Endings

Singular	Plural
[ ] -ēs	[ ] -ēs
[ ] -ēī	[ ] -ērum
[ ] -ēī	[ ] -ēbus
[ ] -em	[ ] -ēs
[ ] -ē	[ ] -ēbus

2 Noun Cases

- [ ] nominative—subject
- [ ] genitive—possessive
- [ ] dative—indirect object
- [ ] accusative—direct object
- [ ] ablative—object of the prep.

4 1st Declension Noun Endings

Singular	Plural
[ ] -a	[ ] -ae
[ ] -ae	[ ] -ārum
[ ] -ae	[ ] -īs
[ ] -am	[ ] -ās
[ ] -ā	[ ] -īs

6 2nd Declension Noun Endings

Singular	Plural
[ ] -us	[ ] -ī
[ ] -ī	[ ] -ōrum
[ ] -ō	[ ] -īs
[ ] -um	[ ] -ōs
[ ] -ō	[ ] -īs

8 3rd Declension Noun Endings

Singular	Plural
[ ] various	[ ] -ēs
[ ] -is	[ ] -um
[ ] -ī	[ ] -ibus
[ ] -em	[ ] -ēs
[ ] -e	[ ] -ibus

10 4th Declension Noun Endings

Singular	Plural
[ ] -us	[ ] -ūs
[ ] -ūs	[ ] -uum
[ ] -uī	[ ] -ibus
[ ] -um	[ ] -ūs
[ ] -ū	[ ] -ibus

12 5th Declension Noun Endings

Singular	Plural
[ ] -ēs	[ ] -ēs
[ ] -ēī	[ ] -ērum
[ ] -ēī	[ ] -ēbus
[ ] -em	[ ] -ēs
[ ] -ē	[ ] -ēbus

13	Noun Cases

- ☐ nominative—subject
- ☐ genitive—possessive
- ☐ dative—indirect object
- ☐ accusative—direct object
- ☐ ablative—object of the prep.

14	Noun Cases

- ☐ nominative—subject
- ☐ genitive—possessive
- ☐ dative—indirect object
- ☐ accusative—direct object
- ☐ ablative—object of the prep.

15	1st Declension Noun Endings

Singular	Plural
☐ -a	☐ -ae
☐ -ae	☐ -ārum
☐ -ae	☐ -īs
☐ -am	☐ -ās
☐ -ā	☐ -īs

16	1st Declension Noun Endings

Singular	Plural
☐ -a	☐ -ae
☐ -ae	☐ -ārum
☐ -ae	☐ -īs
☐ -am	☐ -ās
☐ -ā	☐ -īs

17	2nd Declension Noun Endings

Singular	Plural
☐ -us	☐ -ī
☐ -ī	☐ -ōrum
☐ -ō	☐ -īs
☐ -um	☐ -ōs
☐ -ō	☐ -īs

18	2nd Declension Noun Endings

Singular	Plural
☐ -us	☐ -ī
☐ -ī	☐ -ōrum
☐ -ō	☐ -īs
☐ -um	☐ -ōs
☐ -ō	☐ -īs

19	3rd Declension Noun Endings

Singular	Plural
☐ various	☐ -ēs
☐ -is	☐ -um
☐ -ī	☐ -ibus
☐ -em	☐ -ēs
☐ -e	☐ -ibus

20	3rd Declension Noun Endings

Singular	Plural
☐ various	☐ -ēs
☐ -is	☐ -um
☐ -ī	☐ -ibus
☐ -em	☐ -ēs
☐ -e	☐ -ibus

21	4th Declension Noun Endings

Singular	Plural
☐ -us	☐ -ūs
☐ -ūs	☐ -uum
☐ -uī	☐ -ibus
☐ -um	☐ -ūs
☐ -ū	☐ -ibus

22	4th Declension Noun Endings

Singular	Plural
☐ -us	☐ -ūs
☐ -ūs	☐ -uum
☐ -uī	☐ -ibus
☐ -um	☐ -ūs
☐ -ū	☐ -ibus

23	5th Declension Noun Endings

Singular	Plural
☐ -ēs	☐ -ēs
☐ -ēī	☐ -ērum
☐ -ēī	☐ -ēbus
☐ -em	☐ -ēs
☐ -ē	☐ -ēbus

24	5th Declension Noun Endings

Singular	Plural
☐ -ēs	☐ -ēs
☐ -ēī	☐ -ērum
☐ -ēī	☐ -ēbus
☐ -em	☐ -ēs
☐ -ē	☐ -ēbus

1 What are the classifications of living things?

- [ ] domain
- [ ] kingdom
- [ ] phylum
- [ ] class
- [ ] order
- [ ] family
- [ ] genus
- [ ] species

2 What are the kingdoms of living things?

- [ ] animalia
- [ ] plantae
- [ ] fungi
- [ ] protista
- [ ] archaea
- [ ] bacteria

3 What are some parts of an animal cell?

- [ ] nucleus
- [ ] cytoplasm
- [ ] vacuole
- [ ] mitochondria
- [ ] cell membrane
- [ ] Golgi bodies

4 What are some parts of a plant cell?

- [ ] nucleus
- [ ] cytoplasm
- [ ] vacuole
- [ ] mitochondria
- [ ] cell membrane
- [ ] cell wall
- [ ] chloroplasts
- [ ] Golgi bodies

5 What are the major groups of invertebrates?

- [ ] sponges
- [ ] stinging-cell animals
- [ ] flatworms
- [ ] roundworms
- [ ] segmented worms
- [ ] mollusks
- [ ] sea stars
- [ ] arthropods

6 What are the major groups of vertebrates?

- [ ] fish
- [ ] amphibians
- [ ] reptiles
- [ ] mammals
- [ ] birds

7 What are some ways animals reproduce?

- [ ] live birth
- [ ] eggs
- [ ] fragmentation
- [ ] budding

8 What are some types of seed plants?

- [ ] monocot
- [ ] dicot
- [ ] conifer

9 What are some parts of a plant?

- [ ] leaves
- [ ] stems
- [ ] roots

10 What are some leaf shapes?

- [ ] linear
- [ ] oval
- [ ] lobed
- [ ] cleft
- [ ] scalelike
- [ ] needlelike

11 What are some parts of a flower?

- [ ] petal
- [ ] stamen
- [ ] anther
- [ ] pistil
- [ ] sepal

12 What are some plant systems?

- [ ] photosynthesis
- [ ] respiration
- [ ] transpiration

13 What are some parts of the geosphere?

- [ ] core
- [ ] mantle
- [ ] crust
- [ ] hydrosphere
- [ ] biosphere
- [ ] atmosphere

14 What are three kinds of rock?

- [ ] sedimentary
- [ ] metamorphic
- [ ] igneous

15 What is each continent's highest mountain?

- [ ] Everest in Asia
- [ ] Aconcagua in S. America
- [ ] Denali in N. America
- [ ] Kilimanjaro in Africa
- [ ] Elbrus in Europe
- [ ] Kosciuszko in Australia
- [ ] Vinson Massif in Antarctica

16 What are four kinds of volcanoes?

- [ ] active
- [ ] intermittent
- [ ] dormant
- [ ] extinct

17 What are some parts of a volcano?

- [ ] magma
- [ ] vents
- [ ] lava
- [ ] crater
- [ ] gases

18 What are four types of ocean floor?

- [ ] continental shelf
- [ ] abyssal plain
- [ ] mid-ocean ridge
- [ ] trench

19 What are some ocean zones?

- [ ] epipelagic
- [ ] mesopelagic
- [ ] bathypelagic
- [ ] abyssalpelagic

20 What are some parts of the atmosphere?

- [ ] troposphere
- [ ] stratosphere
- [ ] mesosphere
- [ ] thermosphere
- [ ] exosphere

21 What are five circles of latitude?

- [ ] Arctic Circle
- [ ] Tropic of Cancer
- [ ] equator
- [ ] Tropic of Capricorn
- [ ] Antarctic Circle

22 What are some kinds of weather fronts?

- [ ] cold
- [ ] warm
- [ ] stationary
- [ ] occluded

23 What are some types of clouds?

- [ ] cumulonimbus
- [ ] cirrus
- [ ] stratus
- [ ] cumulus
- [ ] stratocumulus

24 What are some markings on the globe?

- [ ] latitude
- [ ] longitude
- [ ] Prime Meridian
- [ ] degrees
- [ ] Northern Hemisphere
- [ ] Southern Hemisphere

1   A PREPOSITION

☐ A **preposition** relates a noun or pronoun to another word.

2   PREPOSITIONS

☐ about
☐ above
☐ across
☐ after
☐ against

3   PREPOSITIONS

☐ along
☐ amid
☐ among
☐ around
☐ at
☐ atop

4   PREPOSITIONS

☐ before
☐ behind
☐ below
☐ beneath
☐ beside

5   PREPOSITIONS

☐ between
☐ beyond
☐ but
☐ by
☐ concerning

6   PREPOSITIONS

☐ down
☐ during
☐ except
☐ for
☐ from

7   PREPOSITIONS

☐ in
☐ inside
☐ into
☐ like
☐ near

8   PREPOSITIONS

☐ of
☐ off
☐ on
☐ onto
☐ out

9   PREPOSITIONS

☐ outside
☐ over
☐ past
☐ regarding
☐ since

10   PREPOSITIONS

☐ through
☐ throughout
☐ to
☐ toward

11   PREPOSITIONS

☐ under
☐ underneath
☐ until
☐ up
☐ upon

12   PREPOSITIONS

☐ with
☐ within
☐ without

A
B C

13 COMPOUND PREPOSITIONS

- [ ] according to
- [ ] in addition to
- [ ] except for
- [ ] in front of
- [ ] out of
- [ ] instead of

14 A HELPING VERB

- [ ] A **helping verb** helps another verb assert action, being, or existence.

15 HELPING VERBS

- [ ] do
- [ ] does
- [ ] did

16 HELPING VERBS

- [ ] has
- [ ] have
- [ ] had

17 HELPING VERBS

- [ ] may
- [ ] must
- [ ] might

18 HELPING VERBS

- [ ] should
- [ ] could
- [ ] would

19 HELPING VERBS

- [ ] shall
- [ ] will
- [ ] can

20 A LINKING VERB

- [ ] A **linking verb** makes an assertion by joining two words.

21 HELPING AND LINKING VERB: TO BE

- [ ] am
- [ ] are
- [ ] is
- [ ] was
- [ ] were
- [ ] be
- [ ] being
- [ ] been

22 LINKING VERBS

- [ ] feel
- [ ] become
- [ ] remain
- [ ] taste

23 LINKING VERBS

- [ ] seem
- [ ] appear
- [ ] look
- [ ] sound

24 LINKING VERBS

- [ ] stay
- [ ] smell
- [ ] grow

WEEK 1	1	**AGE OF ANCIENT EMPIRES**
	2	Creation and the Fall
	3	The Flood and the Tower of Babel
	4	Mesopotamia and Sumer
	5	Egyptians
	6	Indus River Valley Civilization
	7	Minoans and Mycenaeans
WEEK 2	8	Seven Wonders of the Ancient World
	9	Patriarchs of Israel
	10	Hittites and Canaanites
	11	Kush
	12	Assyrians
	13	Babylonians
	14	China's Shang Dynasty
WEEK 3	15	Hinduism in India
	16	Phoenicians and the Alphabet
	17	Olmecs of Mesoamerica
	18	Israelite Exodus and Desert Wandering
	19	Israelite Conquest and Judges
	20	Greek Dark Ages
	21	Israel's United Kingdom
WEEK 4	22	Early Native Americans
	23	Israel Divides into Two Kingdoms
	24	Homer and Hesiod
	25	Rome Founded by Romulus and Remus
	26	Israel Falls to Assyria
	27	Assyria Falls to Babylon
	28	Lao-Tzu, Confucius, Buddha

WEEK 5	29	Judah falls to Babylon, Temple Destroyed
	30	Babylon Falls to Persia
	31	Jews Return and Rebuild the Temple
	32	Roman Republic
	33	Golden Age of Greece
	34	Peloponnesian Wars
	35	Persia Falls to Alexander the Great
WEEK 6	36	India's Mauryan Empire
	37	Mayans of Mesoamerica
	38	Punic Wars
	39	Rome Conquers Greece
	40	Roman Dictator Julius Caesar
	41	Caesar Augustus and the Pax Romana
	42	John the Baptist
	43	Jesus the Messiah
	44	Pentecost and the Early Church
	45	Persecution Spreads the Gospel
WEEK 7	46	Herod's Temple Destroyed by Titus
	47	Diocletian Divides the Roman Empire
	48	Constantine Legalizes Christianity
	49	India's Gupta Dynasty
	50	Council of Nicea
	51	Augustine of Hippo
	52	Jerome Completes the Vulgate
WEEK 8	53	Visigoths Sack Rome
	54	**THE MIDDLE AGES**
	55	Council of Chalcedon
	56	Western Roman Empire Falls to Barbarians

WEEK 9	57	Byzantine Emperor Justinian
	58	Benedict and Monasticism
	59	Muhammad Founds Islam
	60	Zanj and Early Ghana in Africa
	61	Franks Defeat Muslims at the Battle of Tours
	62	Golden Age of Islam
	63	Vikings Raid and Trade
WEEK 10	64	Japan's Heian Period
	65	Charlemagne Crowned Emperor of Europe
	66	Alfred the Great of England
	67	Erik the Red and Leif Eriksson, Norse Explorers
	68	Vladimir I of Kiev
	69	Byzantine Emperor Basil II
	70	East-West Schism of the Church
WEEK 11	71	Norman Conquest and Feudalism in Europe
	72	The Crusades
	73	Zimbabwe and Early Mali in Africa
	74	Aztecs of Mesoamerica
	75	Francis of Assisi and Thomas Aquinas
	76	Japan's Shoguns
	77	Incas of South America
WEEK 12	78	Genghis Khan Rules the Mongols
	79	England's Magna Carta
	80	The Ottoman Empire
	81	Marco Polo's Journey to China
	82	The Hundred Years' War and Black Death
	83	The Renaissance
	84	China's Ming Dynasty

WEEK 24 U.S. PRESIDENTS

162		163		164		165		166		167	
	Washington		Monroe		Harrison		Fillmore		Johnson		Arthur
	Adams		Adams		Tyler		Pierce		Grant		Cleveland
	Jefferson		Jackson		Polk		Buchanan		Hayes		Harrison
	Madison		Van Buren		Taylor		Lincoln		Garfield		Cleveland

WEEK 13

☐	85 **AGE OF EXPLORATION**
☐	86 Prince Henry Founds School of Navigation
☐	87 Slave Trade in Africa
☐	88 Gutenberg's Printing Press
☐	89 Songhai in Africa
☐	90 Czar Ivan the Great of Russia
☐	91 The Spanish Inquisition

WEEK 14

☐	92 Columbus Sails to the Caribbean
☐	93 **AGE OF ABSOLUTE MONARCHS**
☐	94 Protestant Reformation
☐	95 Spanish Conquistadors in the Americas
☐	96 Calvin's *Institutes of the Christian Religion*
☐	97 Council of Trent
☐	98 Baroque Period of the Arts

WEEK 15

☐	99 Japan's Isolation
☐	100 Jamestown and Plymouth Colony Founded
☐	101 **AGE OF ENLIGHTENMENT**
☐	102 Hudson's Bay Company
☐	103 First Great Awakening
☐	104 Classical Period of the Arts
☐	105 The Seven Years' War

WEEK 16

☐	106 **AGE OF INDUSTRY**
☐	107 James Cook Sails to Australia and Antarctica
☐	108 American Revolution and General George Washington
☐	109 Madison's Constitution and the Bill of Rights
☐	110 French Revolution
☐	111 Second Great Awakening
☐	112 Louisiana Purchase and Lewis and Clark Expedition

WEEK 17

☐	113 Napoleon Crowned Emperor of France
☐	114 Liberation of South America
☐	115 The War of 1812
☐	116 The Missouri Compromise
☐	117 Immigrants Flock to America
☐	118 The Monroe Doctrine
☐	119 Romantic Period of the Arts

WEEK 18

☐	120 Cherokee Trail of Tears
☐	121 U.S. Westward Expansion
☐	122 Marx Publishes *The Communist Manifesto*
☐	123 The Compromise of 1850 and the *Dred Scott* Decision
☐	124 U.S. Restores Trade with Japan
☐	125 British Queen Victoria's Rule Over India
☐	126 Darwin Publishes *The Origin of Species*

WEEK 19

☐	127 Lincoln's War Between the States
☐	128 Reconstruction of the Southern States
☐	129 Dominion of Canada
☐	130 Otto von Bismarck Unifies Germany
☐	131 Boer Wars in Africa
☐	132 The Spanish-American War
☐	133 The Progressive Era

WEEK 20

☐	134 Australia Becomes a Commonwealth
☐	135 Mexican Revolution
☐	136 World War I and President Wilson
☐	137 Lenin and the Bolshevik Revolution in Russia
☐	138 U.S. Evangelist Billy Graham
☐	139 Modern Period of the Arts
☐	140 The Great Depression and the New Deal

WEEK 21

☐	141 World War II and President Franklin D. Roosevelt
☐	142 Stalin of the USSR and the Katyn Massacre
☐	143 The United Nations Formed
☐	144 The Cold War
☐	145 Gandhi and India's Independence
☐	146 Jewish State Established
☐	147 Mao and Communist Victory in China

WEEK 22

☐	148 North Atlantic Treaty Organization
☐	149 The Korean War
☐	150 Martin Luther King, Jr. and the Civil Rights Movement
☐	151 Jim and Elisabeth Elliot, Missionaries to Equador
☐	152 The Antarctic Treaty
☐	153 The Vietnam War
☐	154 U.S. Astronauts Walk on the Moon

WEEK 23

☐	155 **AGE OF INFORMATION AND GLOBALIZATION**
☐	156 Watergate, President Nixon Resigns
☐	157 Fall of Communism in Eastern Europe
☐	158 European Union Formed
☐	159 Apartheid Abolished in South Africa
☐	160 September 11, 2001
☐	161 Rising Tide of Freedom

168	McKinley Roosevelt Taft Wilson	169	Harding Coolidge Hoover Roosevelt	170	Truman Eisenhower Kennedy Johnson	171	Nixon Ford Carter Reagan	172	Bush Clinton Bush Obama	173	Trump

1   **Tell me about commandments 1–5.**

☐ Thou shalt …
1. have no other gods before me.
2. not make unto thee any graven image.
3. not take the name of the Lord thy God in vain.
4. remember the Sabbath day, to keep it holy.
5. honor thy father and thy mother: that thy days may be long upon the land which the Lord thy God giveth thee.

2   **Tell me about commandments 6–10.**

☐ Thou shalt …
6. not murder.
7. not commit adultery.
8. not steal.
9. not bear false witness against thy neighbor.
10. not covet.

3   **Tell me about the Greek and Roman gods.**

☐

Greek gods	Roman gods
Zeus	Jupiter
Hera	Juno
Ares	Mars
Aphrodite	Venus
Hermes	Mercury
Athena	Minerva
Poseidon	Neptune

4   **Tell me about the Seven Wonders of the Ancient World.**

☐ The Seven Wonders of the Ancient World are:
Pyramids of Giza
Hanging Gardens of Babylon
Temple of Artemis at Ephesus
Statue of Zeus at Olympia
Mausoleum at Helicarnassus
Pharos Lighthouse at Alexandria
Colossus of Rhodes

5   **Tell me about the Romans.**

☐ The Roman Republic became the Roman Empire when Augustus was crowned emperor in 27 BC. This was followed by the *Pax Romana*. In AD 286, the empire divided into the western and eastern empires until Germanic barbarians defeated the western empire in AD 476.

6   **Tell me about some ancient Greeks.**

☐ Homer, a famous poet; Pythagoras, a famous mathematician; Socrates, a famous philosopher; and Archimedes, a famous inventor, shaped Western ideas. Ancient Greek city-states were among the first democracies.

7   **Tell me about Hinduism and Buddhism in India.**

☐ Hinduism developed around 1500 BC and is known for karma, reincarnation, and the caste system.
Founded in the sixth century BC, Buddhism teaches self-denial as the path to enlightenment.

8   **Tell me about the Age of Imperialism.**

☐ During the Age of Imperialism, the British established rule over India in 1858, and Queen Victoria was declared the Empress of India in 1877.
Before his assassination in 1948, Mohandas Gandhi led the passive resistance movement, which helped win India's independence.

9   **Tell me about Lao-Tzu and Confucius in China.**

☐ Around the sixth century BC, Lao-Tzu founded Taoism, which emphasizes harmony with nature, and Confucius taught compassion and obedience.

10   **Tell me about Japan's Heian period.**

☐ Around 794, Japan's emperors moved to Heian, present-day Kyoto. The Heian period ended in the twelfth century when civil war gave control to military commanders called shoguns in a feudal system where knights called samurai protected wealthy landowners.

11   **Tell me about Emperor Constantine and the Byzantine Empire.**

☐ Emperor Constantine stopped the persecution of Christians in the Eastern Roman Empire. In AD 330, he moved the capital to Byzantium and renamed it Constantinople. Emperor Justinian's Code became a model for legal systems. The Byzantine Empire lasted until Ottoman Turks captured Constantinople in 1453.

12   **Tell me about the Muslim Empire.**

☐ In 622, Islam was founded in the Arabian Peninsula by Muhammad, who worshiped Allah. Mecca is the holy city of Islam. During the 1400s, the Ottoman Turks expanded the Muslim Empire.

13 Tell me about the Kush.

☐ The Kush mined gold along the Nile River from 2000 BC to AD 350. The Berbers traded gold, iron, and salt in the desert.

14 Tell me about trade in Africa.

☐ In 700, Ghana was known as "the land of gold." The Mali nation took control of the gold trade in 1240 and established Timbuktu as a center of trade, culture, and learning. By the mid-1400s, the wealthy and powerful Songhai Empire controlled trade in western Africa.

15 Tell me about Prince Henry of Portugal.

☐ In the 1400s, Prince Henry of Portugal founded a school of navigation. His work advanced European exploration and trade, including the slave trade.

16 Tell me about the civilizations of Mesoamerica.

☐ Three of the advanced civilizations of Mesoamerica from 1200 BC to AD 1500 were the Olmecs, the Mayans, and the Aztecs.

17 Tell me about the Aztecs.

☐ The Aztecs used pyramids in rituals of human sacrifice. Their civilization began to fall when Hernán Cortés of Spain defeated Montezuma II in 1519.

18 Tell me about the Mound Builders.

☐ Circa 1000 BC to AD 1450, three North American mound-building civilizations were the Adena, the Hopewell, and the Mississippians.

19 Tell me about the Anasazi.

☐ The Anasazi of the southwestern United States built adobe villages in caves and on the sides of cliffs from 500 BC to AD 1200.

20 Tell me about the Mexican Revolution.

☐ Circa 1910, during the Mexican Revolution, Pancho Villa and Emiliano Zapata fought the federales for "Land and Liberty."

21 Tell me about the exploration of Canada.

☐ John Cabot and Samuel de Champlain explored Canada and the St. Lawrence River. Creation of the Hudson's Bay Company, in 1670, eventually led to war between Britain and France. The maple leaf is the symbol of Canada.

22 Tell me about the British North America Act of 1867.

☐ In 1867, the British North America Act established the Dominion of Canada. The Canadians gained total independence from Britain in 1982. French is spoken in the province of Quebec.

23 Tell me about the liberation of South America.

☐ In the early 1800s, San Martín of Argentina, O'Higgins of Chile, and Bolívar of Venezuela fought to liberate South America from Spain.

24 Tell me about the Portuguese Empire.

☐ When Napoleon threatened the Portuguese Empire, King John VI fled to Brazil. His son, Dom Pedro I, declared Brazil independent in 1822.

1 FERTILE CRESCENT
- [ ] Mediterranean Sea
- [ ] Mesopotamia
- [ ] Euphrates River
- [ ] Tigris River
- [ ] Sumer

2 ASSYRIAN EMPIRE
- [ ] Red Sea
- [ ] Persian Gulf
- [ ] Caspian Sea
- [ ] Black Sea
- [ ] Babylon

3 HEBREW EMPIRE
- [ ] Judah
- [ ] Israel
- [ ] Jordan River
- [ ] Dead Sea
- [ ] Phoenicia
- [ ] Sea of Galilee

4 HITTITE EMPIRE
- [ ] Hattusa
- [ ] Asia Minor
- [ ] Arabian Desert
- [ ] Cyprus

5 EGYPTIAN EMPIRE
- [ ] Egypt
- [ ] Nile River
- [ ] Upper/Lower Egypt
- [ ] Nile River Delta

6 ANCIENT GREECE
- [ ] Greece
- [ ] Aegean Sea
- [ ] Macedonia
- [ ] Crete
- [ ] Rhodes

7 ROMAN EMPIRE
- [ ] Hispania
- [ ] Gaul
- [ ] Germania
- [ ] Alexandria
- [ ] Carthage

8 INDUS RIVER VALLEY
- [ ] Ganges River
- [ ] Himalayas
- [ ] Arabian Sea
- [ ] Bay of Bengal
- [ ] Great Indian Desert

9 CHINA
- [ ] Mongolia
- [ ] Yellow Sea
- [ ] Yellow River
- [ ] Yangtze River
- [ ] Beijing

10 JAPAN
- [ ] Kyoto
- [ ] Tokyo
- [ ] Mt. Fuji
- [ ] Pacific Ocean
- [ ] Sea of Japan

11 BYZANTINE EMPIRE
- [ ] Constantinople
- [ ] Rome
- [ ] Athens
- [ ] Ephesus
- [ ] Antioch

12 MUSLIM EMPIRE
- [ ] Mecca
- [ ] Medina
- [ ] Baghdad
- [ ] Damascus
- [ ] Tours
- [ ] Syria

13 WESTERN AFRICA
- [ ] Atlantic Ocean
- [ ] Senegal River
- [ ] Niger River
- [ ] Sahara Desert
- [ ] Ivory Coast

14 ANCIENT AFRICA
- [ ] Ancient Ghana
- [ ] Ancient Mali
- [ ] Western Sahara
- [ ] Fez
- [ ] Tangier

15 MIDDLE EAST
- [ ] Israel
- [ ] Sinai Peninsula
- [ ] Suez Canal
- [ ] Cairo
- [ ] Gaza Strip

16 AFRICAN WATERS
- [ ] Congo River
- [ ] Lake Victoria
- [ ] Zambezi River
- [ ] Orange River

17 AFRICAN COUNTRIES
- [ ] Ethiopia
- [ ] Mozambique
- [ ] Zimbabwe
- [ ] South Africa
- [ ] Madagascar

18 MESOAMERICA REGIONS
- [ ] Gulf of Mexico
- [ ] Yucatan Peninsula
- [ ] Olmec Civilization
- [ ] Maya Civilization
- [ ] Aztec Civilization

19 MESOAMERICA
- [ ] Mexico City
- [ ] Chichen Itza
- [ ] Lake Texcoco
- [ ] Mayapan
- [ ] Oaxaca

20 DOMINION OF CANADA
- [ ] Ontario
- [ ] Quebec
- [ ] New Brunswick
- [ ] Nova Scotia

21 CANADIAN WATERS
- [ ] Great Bear Lake
- [ ] Great Slave Lake
- [ ] Hudson Bay
- [ ] Baffin Bay
- [ ] Labrador Sea

22 SOUTH AMERICA (WEST)
- [ ] Venezuela
- [ ] Colombia
- [ ] Ecuador
- [ ] Peru
- [ ] Bolivia
- [ ] Chile

23 SOUTH AMERICA (EAST)
- [ ] Argentina
- [ ] Uruguay
- [ ] Paraguay
- [ ] Brazil
- [ ] French Guiana
- [ ] Suriname
- [ ] Guyana

24 NORTH ATLANTIC
- [ ] Greenland
- [ ] Iceland
- [ ] Denmark Strait
- [ ] Davis Strait

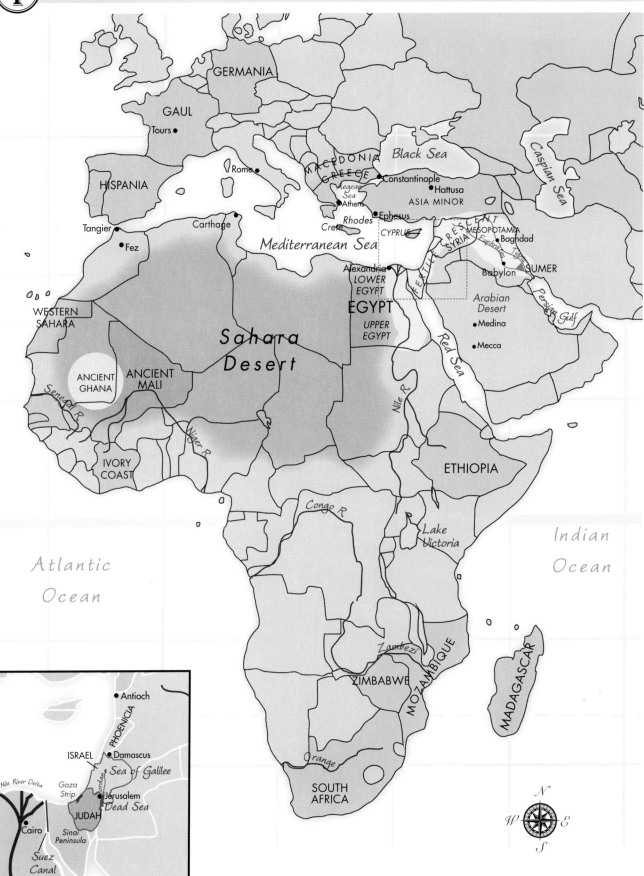

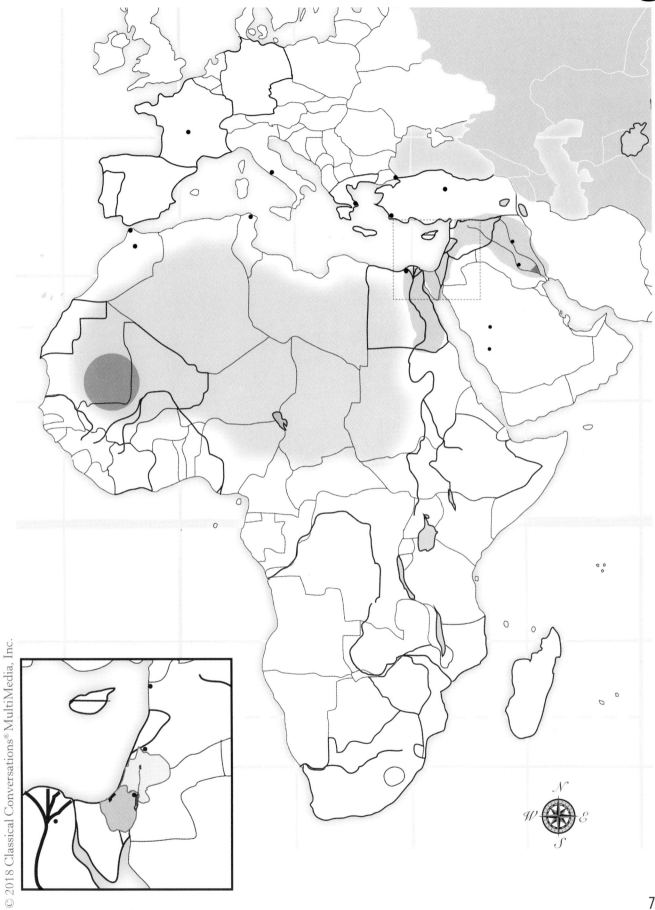

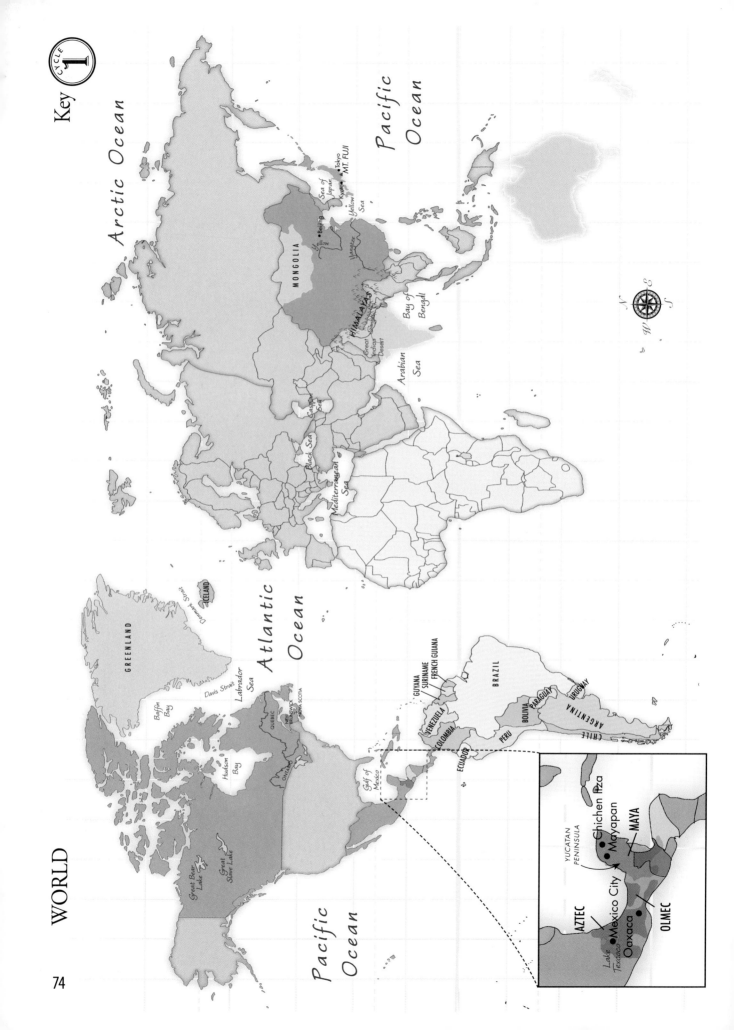

WORLD

Arctic Ocean

Pacific Ocean

Atlantic Ocean

Pacific Ocean

GREENLAND

ICELAND

Denmark Strait

Baffin Bay

Davis Strait

Labrador Sea

Great Bear Lake

Great Slave Lake

Hudson Bay

QUEBEC

Ontario

NOVA SCOTIA

NEW BRUNSWICK

Gulf of Mexico

VENEZUELA

COLOMBIA

ECUADOR

GUYANA

SURINAME

FRENCH GUIANA

BRAZIL

PERU

BOLIVIA

PARAGUAY

URUGUAY

ARGENTINA

CHILE

MONGOLIA

Beijing

Yellow

Yangtze

Sea of Japan

Kyoto

Tokyo

MT. FUJI

Yellow Sea

HIMALAYAS

Great Indian Desert

Bay of Bengal

Arabian Sea

Caspian Sea

Black Sea

Mediterranean Sea

N
W   E
S

AZTEC

Lake Texcoco

Mexico City

Oaxaca

OLMEC

YUCATAN PENINSULA

Chichen Itza

Mayapan

MAYA

WORLD

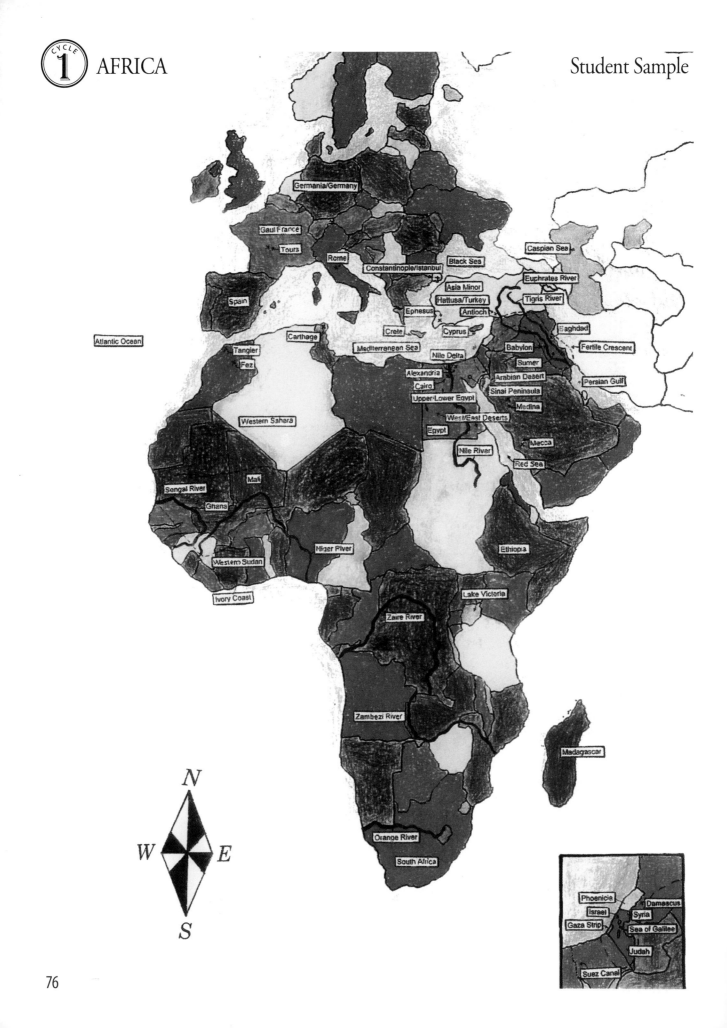

WORLD

Student Sample

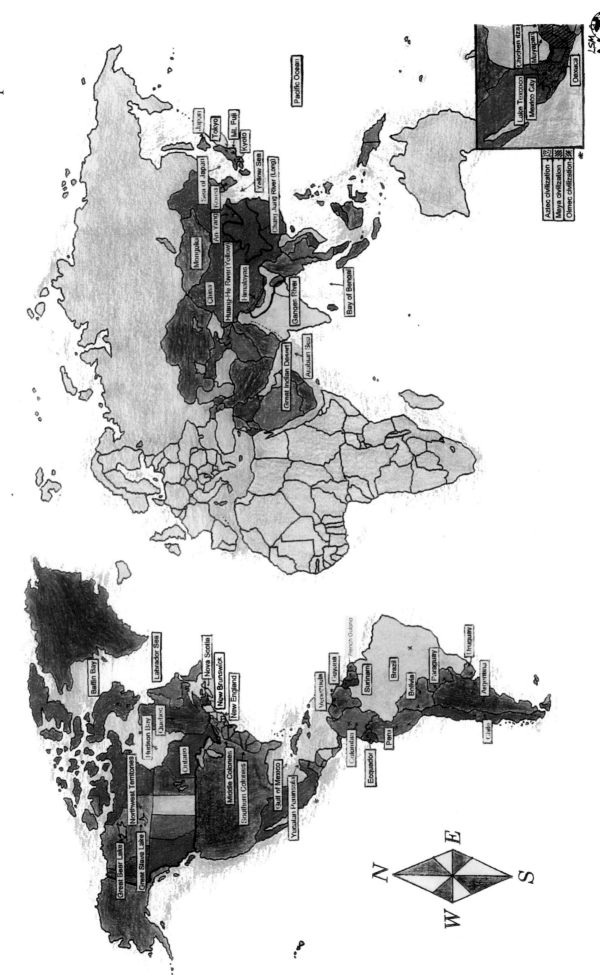

Pacific Ocean

Japan
Tokyo
Mt. Fuji
Kyoto
Korea
Sea of Japan
An Yang
Yellow Sea
Chang Jiang River (Long)
Mongolia
Huang-He River (Yellow)
China
Himalayas
Ganges River
Bay of Bengal
Great Indian Desert
Arabian Sea

Chichen Itza
Mayapan
Lake Texcoco
Mexico City
Oaxaca

Aztec civilization
Maya civilization
Olmec civilization

Baffin Bay
Labrador Sea
Nova Scotia
Hudson Bay
New Brunswick
Quebec
New England
Ontario
Northwest Territories
Middle Colonies
Southern Colonies
Gulf of Mexico
Yucatan Peninsula
Great Bear Lake
Great Slave Lake
Venezuela
Guyana
Surinam
French Guiana
Brazil
Bolivia
Paraguay
Uruguay
Argentina
Colombia
Peru
Ecuador
Chile

N E S W

THE TEN COMMANDMENTS
EXODUS 20:1–17 (KJV)

A NOTE ABOUT THIS SECTION:

We do not wish to usurp your church or family Scripture memory work. Rather, we have chosen a few designated verses per cycle to augment the **Foundations** memory work. We use the King James Version for our printed materials, but please feel free to use the translation of your choice.

¹And God spake all these words, saying,

²I am the LORD thy God, which have brought thee out of the land of Egypt, out of the house of bondage.

³Thou shalt have no other gods before me.

⁴Thou shalt not make unto thee any graven image, or any likeness of any thing that is in heaven above, or that is in the earth beneath, or that is in the water under the earth:

⁵Thou shalt not bow down thyself to them, nor serve them: for I the LORD thy God am a jealous God, visiting the iniquity of the fathers upon the children unto the third and fourth generation of them that hate me;

⁶And showing mercy unto thousands of them that love me, and keep my commandments.

⁷Thou shalt not take the name of the LORD thy God in vain; for the LORD will not hold him guiltless that taketh his name in vain.

⁸Remember the sabbath day, to keep it holy.

⁹Six days shalt thou labor, and do all thy work:

¹⁰But the seventh day is the sabbath of the LORD thy God: in it thou shalt not do any work, thou, nor thy son, nor thy daughter, thy manservant, nor thy maidservant, nor thy cattle, nor thy stranger that is within thy gates:

¹¹For in six days the LORD made heaven and earth, the sea, and all that in them is, and rested the seventh day: wherefore the LORD blessed the sabbath day, and hallowed it.

¹²Honor thy father and thy mother: that thy days may be long upon the land which the LORD thy God giveth thee.

¹³Thou shalt not kill.

¹⁴Thou shalt not commit adultery.

¹⁵Thou shalt not steal.

¹⁶Thou shalt not bear false witness against thy neighbor.

¹⁷Thou shalt not covet thy neighbor's house, thou shalt not covet thy neighbor's wife, nor his manservant, nor his maidservant, nor his ox, nor his ass, nor any thing that is thy neighbor's.

PRESENTATIONS

Let's make public speaking a pleasant part of our culture for our children. Feel free to suggest to your older child that he or she could read the IEW paper from Essentials or explain more thoroughly a *Classical Acts & Facts® Science Card*. However, if your child just wants to tell the class about their grandparent or model car, say, "Good idea! Think about what you'll say while I get a glass of iced tea." Then listen as he or she gives their story a whirl.

Remind your child to:

1. Take a clearing breath while he sees if everyone is ready to listen.
2. Introduce himself and his presentation.
3. Speak clearly and audibly and take care to look each audience member in the eye as he speaks.
4. Let the audience know he is finished by ending with, "Are there any questions?"

Just smile at your child when they present in public. And remember, ideas need time to digest and settle. Next week while listening with a glass of iced tea in your hand, ask if there's anything he wants to improve on from the previous week. Time allows ears to hear comments without taking them as criticism.

A good audience listens and participates by asking questions of other presenters. Occasionally have the students hold up eyeballs drawn on index cards and then put the card down when the presenter has caught their eye.

In community, each student presents twenty-four times a year, which provides over one hundred formal public speaking opportunities in kindergarten thru sixth grade. Success comes from consistency over many years.

More Resources to Help

Classical Conversations students exercise the skills of rhetorical presentation through all program levels, from these short presentations in Foundations to science fair, mock trial, and formal debate in Challenge. You might consider attending one of these Challenge events—this will be your child in just a few years! Additionally, we've developed some resources to serve families all the way through the high school years.

Trivium Tables®: Rhetoric

This laminated, double-sided resource has four panels on each side that describe different aspects of rhetoric—presenting—for your student to learn, review, and practice. Please see the bookstore for more information.

See our online subscription service through ClassicalConversations.com, word search: *presentation* for more ideas.

For families who subscribe, there are dozens of resources in the file-sharing area of our membership site.

Let your speech be always with grace, seasoned with salt, that ye may know how ye ought to answer every man.
—COLOSSIANS 4:6 (KJV)

Students love to dress up in character for presentations.

"Presentations are not about the material presented, they are about building the child's confidence and poise."
—LEIGH A. BORTINS
THE CORE (p. 175)

Resources

Drawing with Children, Mona Brookes (for visual game ideas, scaling of drawing projects)

Online subscription service through ClassicalConversations.com

WEEK	PROJECT
1	five elements of shape *Drawing with Children* (Mona Brookes)
2	mirror images *Drawing with Children* (Mona Brookes)
3	upside-down image
4	abstract art *Drawing with Children* (Mona Brookes)
5	perspective
6	review and final project

FINE ARTS
Drawing

For the next six weeks, we are going to practice basic drawing skills in our community. We will see firsthand that the basics used by real artists can be used by anyone, even children as young as four years old. In fact, drawing skills can be taught before handwriting skills.

For some children, the idea of "drawing for school" may be a dream come true. However, some children (and some adults) may feel apprehensive—even anxious—at being asked to draw. I imagine many of you will sympathize with this man:

> "One gentleman, shaking and sweating at the beginning of a one-day workshop, admitted to the group he was shocked to display such real fear over the idea of possibly being unable to draw. He said he was sorry he had come; he was sure he'd fail. By the end of the day, he was beaming with pride at his accomplishments and said that if he could draw, anyone could."
>
> Mona Brookes, *Drawing with Children*, (3–4)

In our culture, we tend to assume that the creative muses descend from on high only to a few, and that rest of us are doomed to stick-figure art. Nothing could be further from the truth! Classically, learning to draw is a fundamental part of a solid education. Like writing, it is a way of transmitting one's ideas to others, even if one did not become a fine artist.

In the next six weeks, we will learn the simple shapes that make up all of drawing and will practice using them. We won't achieve mastery, but it will be a good beginning. Throughout Classical Conversations, children will continue to practice these skills as they produce nature sketches, anatomy drawings, maps, and lab journal observations.

In community, you will have a lot of latitude in the drawing portion. This guide provides suggestions on teaching drawing basics; feel free to build upon these suggestions as you wish. As part of a thorough classical, Christian education, we must learn to see the world by attending to it well and learning to express it well—through both words and drawings.

In Fine Arts: Drawing, the core habits focus on *attending* while also practicing *naming* and *expressing*. The other three core habits still happen naturally through conversation on community day and at home.

Happy sketching!

WEEK ONE
Five Elements of Shape

ATTENDING

Present the five elements of shape (see page 60 of *Drawing with Children*). Draw each basic shape on the whiteboard and talk about the shapes.

What are the five elements of shape? *(OiLS)*

- **O** = circles: enclosed shapes of only curved lines that are NOT colored in
- **i** = 1. dots: enclosed shapes of only curved lines that ARE colored in
     2. straight lines
- **L** = angled lines
- **S** = curved lines that are not enclosed

Activity:

1. Let students practice drawing the five elements of shape.
2. Draw a simple animal/plant on the whiteboard.
3. Ask students to copy the animal/plant onto their paper with pencils.

Resources

Drawing with Children, Mona Brookes (the five elements of shape)
Simple picture
Whiteboard and dry-erase markers in assorted colors
Paper
Pencils (can also use colored pencils)

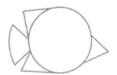 

Practice more drawing like this—as well as counting, geometry, and cursive writing—with *PreScripts® Cursive Words and Drawing: Math Terms* from Classical Conversations Books!

 Use OiLS to draw more difficult pictures (e.g., frog on a log, vase with flowers, branch with leaves, or a fruit basket).

NAMING

Sample conversation starters:

What are the similarities? How are circles similar to dots, straight lines, angled lines, curved lines?

What are the differences? How are circles different from dots, straight lines, angled lines, curved lines?

To what degree are they similar or different? How similar to or different from dots are circles? From straight lines? From angled lines? From curved lines?

EXPRESSING

1. Have students observe what they drew.
2. Hand out new pieces of paper and have students draw again.
3. Encourage students to look closely at the picture for the basic elements of shape.

WEEK TWO
Mirror Images

ATTENDING

Display pictures of half-drawn images or draw them on the whiteboard.

Sample conversation starters:

From this half-picture, can you tell what the picture is supposed to be?

What shape(s) would I need to draw to complete the picture?

Activity:

1. Draw simple symmetrical pictures (e.g., a Greek column, a vase, a face) on the whiteboard or show a simple symmetrical picture.

2. Ask students to look for the five elements of shape in the picture and begin to think which shapes could be used to complete the picture.

3. See sample mirror imaging warmup on page 67 of *Drawing with Children*.

Resources

Drawing with Children, Mona Brookes (the five elements of shape)

Various half-drawn pictures of simple symmetrical drawings (e.g., a Greek column, a vase, a face). See page 69 of *Drawing with Children* for examples.

Whiteboard and dry-erase markers in assorted colors

Paper

Pencils (can also use colored pencils)

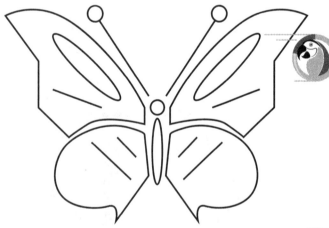

NAMING

What is a "mirror image"? A mirror image is an image that is exactly the same, but flipped, like what you see when you hold something against a mirror.

What is line of symmetry? The line of symmetry is the imaginary line down which you could fold the image and have both halves match exactly.

EXPRESSING

1. Give students half-drawn pictures.

2. Encourage students to observe the picture.

3. Allow time for students to think through what shapes they need to draw to complete the picture.

4. Using the basic elements of shape, instruct students to complete the picture.

 Offer a variety of pictures and let each student decide which pictures have a line of symmetry. Then encourage them to fold the picture in half and draw the mirror image using basic shapes.

WEEK THREE
Upside-Down Image

ATTENDING

Display simple pictures upside down or draw them on the whiteboard.

Sample conversation starters:

What shapes do you see?

Can you find a dot? A circle? A straight line? An angled line? A curved line?

Activity:

1. Let students practice finding the shapes.

2. Encourage students to draw on a sheet of paper what they see.

3. After some time drawing what they see, ask students to turn their papers right-side up.

Resources

Simple picture
Whiteboard and dry-erase markers
     in assorted colors
Paper
Pencils (can also use colored pencils)

NAMING

What is upside-down drawing? Upside-down drawing is a technique where you try to draw an image that is presented to you upside down. This technique is used to help us draw what we see and not what we think.

In the grammar of the arts, we spend a lot of time working the left side of the brain. In this section of fine arts, we spend time exercising the right side of the brain. The purpose of taking a known picture or drawing and turning it upside down is to prevent our left brain from taking over. By turning the picture upside down, students resist the temptation to draw what they "think" and focus on drawing what they actually "see."

EXPRESSING

1. Everyone observes what they drew.

2. Give students new pieces of paper and encourage them to draw again.

3. After some time drawing what they see, ask them to turn their paper right-side up.

Choose a picture that could be two different things. For example, what do you see in the picture above? Two faces, or a fancy drinking glass?

WEEK FOUR
Abstract Art

 ATTENDING

Display a variety of abstract drawings and talk about how the artist used color and basic shapes. You can even discuss the thoughts or emotions the picture inspires, or why the students think the artist put the picture together the way he or she did.

Sample conversation starters:

What colors and shapes do you see?

How does this picture make you feel?

What do you think the artist was feeling when he/she drew this?

Resources

Drawing with Children, Mona Brookes
Simple abstract art picture
Various art supplies

Activity:

1. Encourage students to draw shapes of different colors, sizes, and widths.

2. Refer to the resource *Drawing with Children* for various activity ideas.

 NAMING

What is abstract art? Abstract art is art that does not attempt a recognizable reality, but instead uses shapes, colors, forms, and textures to achieve an effect.

Optional Addition:

What are some characteristics of abstract art? Some characteristics of abstract art are indistinguishable subjects, colors, or shapes that invoke emotions, and randomness that often has meaning.

 Use more complex media for creating, like textured materials, or paint with sand or chalk.

 EXPRESSING

1. Encourage students to observe what they drew.

2. If time allows, give students new pieces of paper and encourage them to create again.

WEEK FIVE
Perspective

ATTENDING

Draw on the whiteboard a variety of one-dimensional shapes: a square, triangles, circles, and a rectangle. Ask the students to name the shapes. Then, add perspective to make these shapes look three-dimensional: The square becomes a cube, one triangle becomes a pyramid, one triangle and circle become a cone, one circle becomes a sphere, and two circles and the rectangle become a cylinder.

Sample conversation starters:

What was the difference between the first set of shapes and the second set of shapes?

Activity:

1. Encourage students to draw different one-dimensional shapes.

2. Refer back to the whiteboard and have students change their one-dimensional shapes into three-dimensional shapes.

Resources

Whiteboard and dry-erase markers in assorted colors

Paper

Pencils (can also use colored pencils)

Classical Acts & Facts® History Cards: Artists and Composers (optional)

NAMING

What is perspective? Perspective is a way of creating the illusion of depth on a flat surface.

EXPRESSING

1. Choose a *Classical Acts & Facts® Artists and Composers* card or a picture to observe.

2. Ask questions that help students discover perspective in the picture.

Sample Conversation Starters:

What do you notice about the size of the objects in the front of the picture compared with the objects in the back?

Do any of the objects in the front overlap objects in the back? This is called overlapping.

Where do the ground and sky meet? This is called the horizon.

Is there a point in this picture where parallel lines seem to come together or disappear "off in the distance" (think of staring down a long hallway)? This is called the vanishing point.

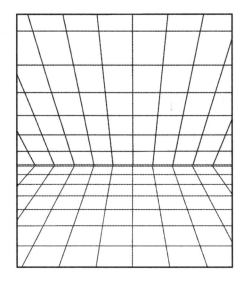

 Try to draw objects in the back that appear smaller than objects in the front, objects that overlap, a horizon, and a vanishing point.

WEEK SIX
Review and Final Project

For the next six weeks, we will learn some music theory and practice playing the tin whistle, so be sure to bring your tin whistle next week!

Resources

Whiteboard and dry-erase markers in
    assorted colors

Paper

Pencils (can also use colored pencils)

Various art supplies

Assortment of pictures

Students' previous projects

ATTENDING

Encourage students to look over their projects from the previous five weeks. Which project was their favorite? Why? Which project would they like to repeat?

Activity:

1. Encourage students to repeat the project of their choice.

EXPRESSING

1. Ask students to present their final project to you and/or other students.

2. Encourage other students to ask questions or comment on what they like about the presenter's final project.

Choose a *Classical Acts & Facts* *Artists and Composers* card and recreate its artwork on paper.

Music

Welcome to the music and tin whistle theory unit! This unit, like all other units, can be peaceful if you take a deep breath and set the right tone with your students. (Sorry, we can't help with the squeaky whistle.)

Just like each period of the Foundations morning, there will be a bit of time for review and a bit of time for new information.

It may seem strange to us, but in medieval philosophy, classical students learned music as a mathematical art. In fact, the philosopher Leibniz famously described music as "the pleasure the human mind experiences from counting without being aware that it is counting" (*Beauty for Truth's Sake*, Stratford Caldecott, 30).

For the next six weeks, we will embark on a journey through rudimentary music theory and performance on the tin whistle. In a well-rounded classical, Christian education, students will learn many languages. They will learn the language of math, formal logic, Latin, and, yes, music. We want our students to see the beauty and order of the universe and to find there the mind of their Creator.

Like all other languages, music is meant to communicate ideas. Like all other languages, it has a grammar. During the next six weeks, we will explore some basics of that grammar, including rhythm, dynamics, scales, and notation. As we expose our students to the fine arts, they need to learn to attend to art by looking at great works of art and listening to classical music. In addition, they need to name the grammar of each of these arts by naming the parts. And, they need to express great art by playing music or imitating the style of great artists.

The Foundations music theory study includes these two main parts of learning music: working hard to grasp the theory of music and experiencing the joy of playing music. As Leigh Bortins wrote in the "Fine Arts" chapter of *The Conversation*: "Students must work hard in the grammar and dialectic of learning an instrument: they must learn the names of the notes and the sounds they make, the proper handling of instruments, time signatures, and techniques. But the joy of music can be experienced as soon as a simple tune is played on a tin whistle. That joy will motivate the hard work required. That joy is the language and the rhetoric of music." (198)

In Music Theory and Practice, we focus on the core habit of expressing, and having fun playing an instrument. We will also practice some naming. This unit will lay the foundation for deeper studies of music theory and music history in the Challenge program. In addition, we hope that it whets the appetite of many budding young musicians.

Take joy in making music!

© 2018 Classical Conversations® MultiMedia, Inc.

Required Resources

A love for learning!
Tin whistle in the key of D
Reproducible handouts (see pages 88, 89, 100, 101, and 103)

Recommended Resources

Classical Music for Dummies (Pogue and Speck)
Trivium Tables®: Music
Sheet music (to practice)
Recorded music (to enjoy at home)

WEEK	LESSONS
7	parts of the tin whistle
8	dynamics
9	note values and staff
10	rhythm
11	note names and scales
12	review and celebration

The Tin Whistle

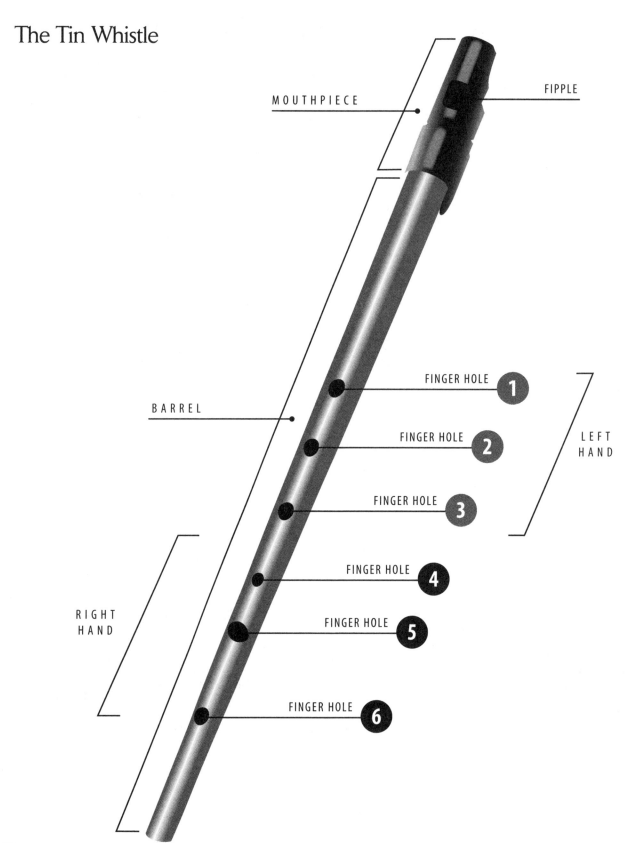

MOUTHPIECE

FIPPLE

BARREL

FINGER HOLE 1

FINGER HOLE 2

FINGER HOLE 3

LEFT HAND

FINGER HOLE 4

FINGER HOLE 5

FINGER HOLE 6

RIGHT HAND

Twinkle, Twinkle, Little Star

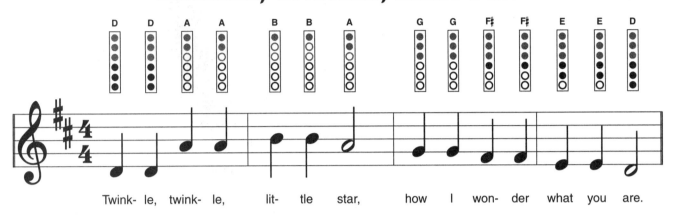

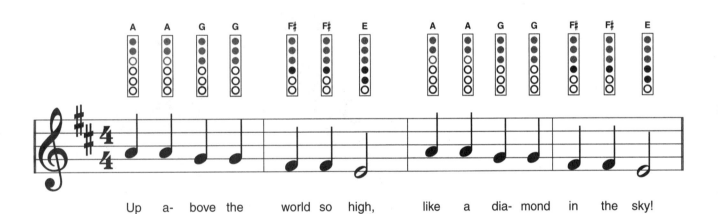

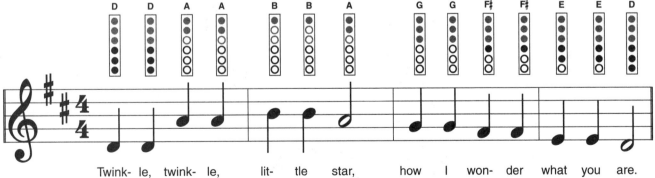

WEEK SEVEN
Parts of the Tin Whistle

Resources

Tin whistle diagram (see page 88)
Current cycle song, one copy per
   student
   Cycle 1 (page 89)
   Cycle 2 (page 181)
   Cycle 3 (page 253)
   Your child is welcome to practice
   the other cycle songs at home.

NAMING

Sing and Discuss:

1. Sing the song for the cycle (see page 89 for Cycle 1, page 181 for Cycle 2, and page 253 for Cycle 3).

2. Discuss. Ask questions like "What did we have to do to make that song?" Encourage students to realize that everyone must all sing at the same speed, start and stop at the same time, follow your lead, etc.

TIP

When you sing with the children or direct them through a tin whistle song, be sure to get them to follow your direction by counting them in with a steady beat: "1, 2, ready, sing" or "1, 2, ready, play."

EXPRESSING

1. As you **practice proper hand position, discuss the parts of the tin whistle using the terms below.**

   • **barrel**—long, cylindrical metal section

   • **finger holes**—six holes in the barrel for playing notes

   • **mouthpiece**—plastic piece at top

   • **fipple**—sharp edge on the mouthpiece hole

Have students pick up the barrel of the tin whistle without putting the fipple in their mouths. Have them place the left hand on top so that the child uses the left-hand index, middle, and ring fingers to cover the upper finger holes. The same fingers on the right hand cover the lower finger holes. It can be tempting for students to use their fingertips. Instead, demonstrate how to use the pad (fleshy part at the top of the finger) to cover the finger holes. Check each student's hand position before moving on.

TIP

If your students have trouble keeping the left hand on top, you can place a piece of masking tape labeled "top" on their left hand. If students have trouble covering the hole entirely, you can help them by covering the holes with notebook paper hole reinforcement stickers. This makes the hole smaller to help smaller fingers.

2. **Practice following the conductor** (you). Remind students that tin whistles remain in their laps until you raise your hand. Remind them that tin whistles return to the lap when you raise your hand and close your fist to indicate the end of the song.

3. **Cacophony**: Allow students to play whatever they like. ["Everyone put your tin whistle in your mouth and play whatever you like."] Let them notice how they sounded and then remind them that they will need to learn how to play the correct notes at the same speed and to stop and start together.

4. **Playing in Unison**: First model for students how to play in unison. Instruct students to cover all of the finger holes. Count them in and play four times. As they play, count 1-2-3-4 in a steady beat. Raise your fist to indicate that they should return tin whistles to their laps. Repeat. Listen to each student individually play four times (beats). Play again in unison. Repeat the process above by having the students take off one finger at a time.

 ## ATTENDING

1. Review by asking for volunteers to name the parts.

2. Encourage students to trace and label the diagram of the tin whistle, or bring copies of the diagram for them to label.

3. While students are drawing, review.

   • **cacophony**—a noise where the sounds do not work together (Allow students to display a cacophony by playing whatever they like.)

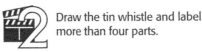

Draw the tin whistle and label more than four parts.

WEEK EIGHT
Dynamics

 NAMING

Resources

Tin whistle diagram (see page 88)

Current cycle song, one copy per
   student
   Cycle 1 (page 89)
   Cycle 2 (page 181)
   Cycle 3 (page 253)
   Your child is welcome to practice
   the other cycle songs at home.

Sing and Discuss:

1. Sing the song softly. Teach them that *piano* (*p*) means quiet or soft.

2. Sing the song again, loudly. Teach them that *forte* (*f*) means loud. Point out that the piano (instrument) was originally called pianoforte because it could easily play loudly or softly depending on how hard the player pressed the keys.

3. Sing the song again, as softly as possible. This is *pianissimo* (*pp*), which means "extremely soft."

4. Sing the song again, very loudly without yelling or straining your voices. This is *fortissimo* (*ff*), which means "extremely loud."

5. Tell students that the volume between *piano* and *forte* is medium soft and called *mezzo piano* (*mp*).

6. Tell students that the volume between *forte* and *fortissimo* is medium loud and is called *mezzo forte* (*mf*).

EXPRESSING

1. Practice proper hand position.

2. Practice following the conductor (you).

3. Practice playing different finger positions in unison. For example, cover all the holes and uncover them one at a time from the bottom to the top.

4. Listen to each student play individually with different finger positions. Students who are not playing should practice finger positions as they wait for their turns.

5. Play again as a class. Practice the new skill of dynamics once *piano*, then once *forte*.

6. Play again as a class. Practice the new skill of dynamics by playing different finger positions from *piano* to *forte* and then *forte* to *piano*.

TIP

Not all instruments are designed to play the full dynamic range from *pp* to *ff*. It is difficult to get the full range of dynamics on the tin whistle without distorting the notes. This is why we have chosen to practice the full range of dynamics during the singing portion of the lesson and to only practice *piano* and *forte* while playing the tin whistle.

ATTENDING

Conclude this part of the lesson by having students arrange the terms from softest to loudest. (*pianissimo, piano, mezzo piano, forte, mezzo forte, fortissimo*). Teach them that these terms express how loudly or quietly the music is played or sung, which is called **dynamics**. Sing the song again, pointing to the different dynamic symbols as you progress through the song. Students should vary the volume of their voices, as appropriate.

TIP

When you sing with the students or direct them through a tin whistle song, be sure to get them to follow your direction by counting them in with a steady beat: "1, 2, ready, sing" or "1, 2, ready, play."

WEEK NINE
Note Values and Staff

NAMING

Sing and Discuss:

1. Sing the cycle song together. Ask students to notice if any sounds are held longer than others.

2. Distribute copies of the cycle song. Ask students to look at the **notes** and point out differences. Just as we use ABCs to write words that we can read, we use notes to write songs that we can play.

3. Identify the staff as a group of five lines used for writing notes of a song.

3. Ask students to count the lines on the **staff** (5) and then show them how to locate the spaces.

Resources

Current cycle song, one copy per
  student
  Cycle 1 (page 89)
  Cycle 2 (page 181)
  Cycle 3 (page 253)
  Your child is welcome to practice
  the other cycle songs at home.
Blank staff paper, two copies per
  student (see page 103)

EXPRESSING

1. Practice proper hand position.

2. Practice following the conductor (you).

3. Practice playing a whole note, half note, quarter note, and eighth note.

   • Count the students in and have them play the whole note three times. As they play each note, say, "ta-ah-ah-ah, ta-ah-ah-ah, ta-ah-ah-ah."

   • Then, play the half note three times. As they play each note, say, "ta-ah, ta-ah, ta-ah."

   • Then play the quarter note three times. As they play each note, say, "ta, ta, ta."

   • Then play the eighth note three times. As they play each note, say, "tee, tee, tee," quickly. If time allows, listen to students individually.

4. Repeat using different finger positions. For example, cover all the holes and uncover them one at a time from the bottom to the top.

 ATTENDING

1. Distribute copies of blank staff paper.

2. Draw a whole note on the board. A **whole note** looks like this and is held for four counts.

3. Model using the sound "ta-ah-ah-ah" while students clap four times. Or clap four times while students say "ta-ah-ah-ah" for four counts.

4. Draw a half note on the board. A **half note** looks like this and is held for two counts: "ta-ah." Then repeat step 3 using a half note.

5. Draw a quarter note on the board. A **quarter note** looks like this and is held for one count "ta." Then repeat step 3 using a quarter note.

6. Draw an eighth note on the board. An **eighth note** looks like this and is held for half a count.

7. Model using the sound "tee" while students clap half a count. Or clap a half count while students sound "tee" for half a count.

8. Ask students to draw the different notes and label them.

9. Teach students how to draw a **treble clef** and have them draw a row of them on the staff paper (see above for an example). For abecedarians, it's easier for these very young students to start by tracing the treble clef. Draw a row of treble clefs with dashed lines for them to use.

 Practice the songs from all three cycles.

WEEK TEN
Rhythm

Resources

Current cycle song, one copy per
    student
    Cycle 1 (page 89)
    Cycle 2 (page 181)
    Cycle 3 (page 253)
    Your child is welcome to practice
    the other cycle songs at home.
Blank staff paper, one copy per
    student (see page 103)

NAMING

Sing and Discuss:

1. Pass out copies of the cycle song. Have students trace over the vertical lines as you explain these are called **bar lines**. The space between two bar lines is called a **measure**, which contains a number of beats.

   Rhythm describes the way notes form a pattern as some are played longer than others.

2. Sing the cycle song together. Ask students to notice how many beats are in a measure.

3. Go through the whole song, chanting "ta" according to the rhythm.

4. Sing the song again together. As the children sing, you chant "ta" according to the rhythm.

TIP

For the sake of simplicity, Foundations will only use the $\frac{4}{4}$ time signature.

EXPRESSING

1. Practice proper hand position.

2. Practice following the conductor (you).

3. Practice the first measure of the cycle song. Count the students in and have them play the first measure three times. As they play each note, count 1-2-3-4, 1-2-3-4, 1-2-3-4. Then, play the measure again three times. Repeat with as many measures as you have time for. If time allows, listen to students individually. Practice dynamics again by playing the first line *forte* (*f*), then the second line *piano* (*p*), then the final line *forte* (*f*).

TIP

To learn difficult passages, ask the students to "be my echo." You play the passage as they finger silently, and then they play the passage after you.

◎ ATTENDING

1. Pass out copies of staff paper. Copy the rhythm exercise (see below) on the board and have students copy these four measures on their staff paper.

2. Encourage students to copy the notes and label the rhythm. After they finish copying the notes, have students label the rhythm.

3. Clap and chant the rhythm together.

4. Give students copies of the song for this cycle. Have them label the rhythm. Chant through the song two to three times together.

5. Explain that the hole diagrams above the notes on the cycle song show students which notes to leave open (open circles) and which ones to cover (filled-in circles); the darker filled-in circles are for the right hand, and the lighter filled-in circles are for the left hand.

 Open a hymnal and practice reading time signatures, the two numbers on top of each other just to the right of the clef symbol. The top number describes the number of beats in a measure, and the bottom number tells what kind of note gets one beat.

Rhythm Exercise

WEEK ELEVEN
Note Names and Scales

Resources

Current cycle song, one copy per student
  Cycle 1 (page 89)
  Cycle 2 (page 181)
  Cycle 3 (page 253)
  Your child is welcome to practice the
  other cycle songs at home.
D scale, one copy per student (see pages
  100–101)
Blank staff paper, 1–2 copies per student
  (see page 103)

 NAMING

Sing and Discuss:

1. Sing the cycle song together.

2. Ask students how many letters are in the alphabet. [26] Tell them that there are only seven notes in the musical alphabet: A, B, C, D, E, F, and G. Just as we use ABCs to write words that we can read, we use notes to write songs that we can sing.

3. Introduce two mnemonic devices to help students remember the note names (see "Note Names" below).

Note Names

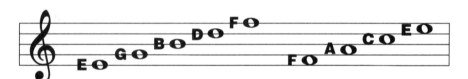

When a note is on a line,
Every **G**ood **B**oy **D**oes **F**ine.
When a note is on a space,
It spells the word **FACE**.

 EXPRESSING

1. Practice proper hand position.

2. Practice following the conductor (you).

3. Practice the cycle song one measure at a time. Count the students in (1, 2, ready, play) and have them play the first measure three times. As they play each note, count 1-2-3-4, 1-2-3-4, 1-2-3-4. Then, play the measure again three times. As they play each note, say the note names. Repeat with as many measures as you have time for.

4. Listen to students individually. As students play together and individually, you should say the note names to reinforce the note reading they have learned today. If time allows, challenge students to play the notes as you call them out by letter name. Then you play the note and they guess its name.

ATTENDING

1. Distribute the blank staff sheets and a copy of the D scale to each student.

2. A series of notes played in order with incrementally higher (or incrementally lower) sounds is called a **scale**. Study the D scale.

3. Have students draw whole notes on the lines (E–G–B–D–F). Have students draw whole notes on the spaces (F–A–C–E).

3. Since our tin whistles are in the key of D, its scale begins at D: D–E–F♯–G–A–B–C♯–D. The symbols beside the F and C are called **sharps**. Explain that a sharp (♯) slightly changes the sound of a note and gives the note a new name.

4. Using the D scale as a model, have students draw and label the D scale going up in whole notes on the page. When students are finished, have them play the D scale going up using whole notes.

5. Have students draw and label the D scale going down in whole notes on the next line of the staff. Then, play the D scale going down.

6. Distribute copies of the cycle song. Have students label the notes below each line using the guide they have just created.

Discuss how a sharp raises a note's pitch a half-step, while a flat lowers the pitch a half-step.

D SCALE (ascending)

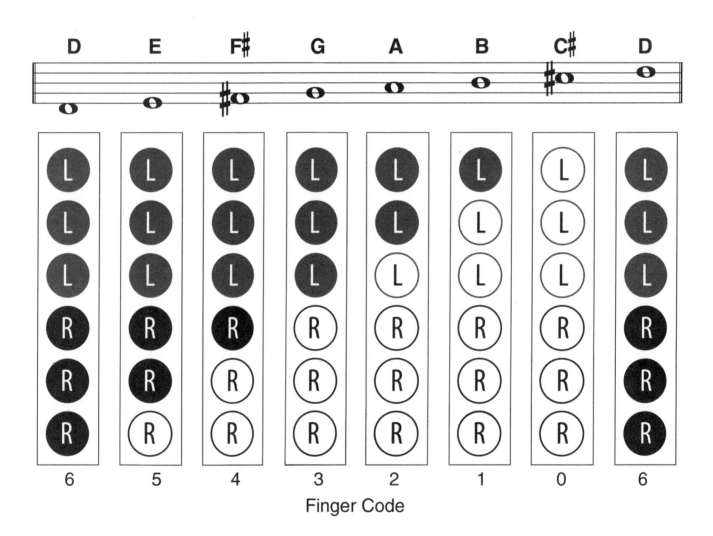

Because the tin whistle is in the key of D, it can only play F sharp rather than plain F (really known as F natural), and it can only play C sharp rather than plain C. Parents with older students can teach the students to include the sharps when drawing the scale in later weeks. It's best practice to call out "F sharp" and "C sharp" while they play, even if they don't understand fully.

D SCALE (descending)

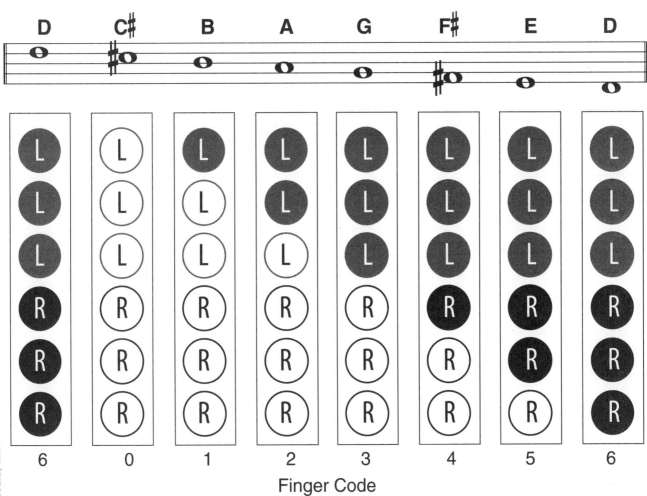

WEEK TWELVE
Review and Celebration

NAMING

Today, celebrate what you have learned and play music together. You may wish to spend five to ten minutes reviewing the music theory concepts before you play, or you may wish to spend the entire time performing.

Resources

Current cycle song, one copy per
   student
   Cycle 1 (page 89)
   Cycle 2 (page 181)
   Cycle 3 (page 253)
   Your child is welcome to practice
   the other cycle songs at home.

EXPRESSING

1. Distribute the cycle song sheet.

2. Practice proper hand position.

3. Practice following the conductor (you).

4. Play the cycle song in unison with dynamics.

5. Have individual students play the cycle song with dynamics.

ATTENDING

Encourage students to celebrate with each other as they listen and play together. Which song is their favorite? Why? What other songs inspire them to learn more?

Activity:

1. Encourage students to repeat the song of their choice.

 Have students create a short song. Pass out blank staff paper; ask them to write the notes and then play the song.

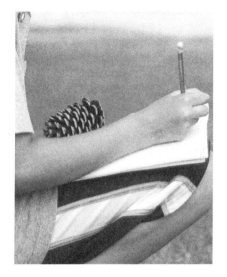

| WEEK | CYCLE 1 | | CYCLE 2 | | CYCLE 3 | |
	ARTIST	TECHNIQUE	ARTIST	TECHNIQUE	ARTIST	TECHNIQUE
13	Giotto (c. 1266–1337)	Paint (Gothic)	Rembrandt 1606–1669	Drawing (Baroque)	Grandma Moses 1860–1961	Painting Folk Art
14	Ghiberti 1378–1455	Sculpt/Relief (Renaissance)	Gainsborough 1727–1788	Drawing/Painting (Romantic)	Picasso 1881–1973	Painting Abstract
15	Angelico c. 1395–1455	Drawing (Renaissance)	Degas 1834–1917	Painting (Impressionist)	O'Keeffe 1887–1986	Watercolors Romantic
16	Dürer 1471–1528	Print (Renaissance)	Monet 1840–1926	Painting (Impressionist)	Rockwell 1895–1978	Illustration/Painting Realism
17	Michelangelo 1475–1564	Paint (Renaissance)	Morisot 1841–1895	Painting (Impressionist)	Wyeth 1917–2009	Tempera Realism
18	El Greco 1541–1614	Drawing (Baroque)	van Gogh 1853–1890	Modern Impressionist	Lichtenstein 1923–1997	Illustration Modern Pop

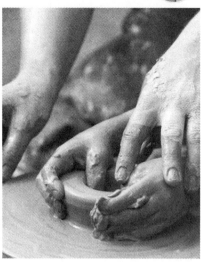

Great Artists

Resources

Discovering Great Artists (Kohl and Solga)

Classical Acts and Facts® History Cards: Artists and Composers, Set 1

Marvelous to Behold (Classical Conversations® MultiMedia)

Welcome to our six weeks of studying great artists. In this unit, we will learn some vocabulary related to creating works of art and will imitate the style of great masters. Just as your children learned to speak by hearing and imitating your speech, they will learn to draw and paint by playing with colors, shapes, and textures and by imitating great artists.

Both our ability and desire to create art stem from the fact that we are made in God's image. As such, we are re-creators: "since the beginning of time, humans have created artifacts that clearly reveal thought in the expression of form. It is one of the things that humans have in common with God: we both like to create things. God's creations are purposeful and beautiful…When humans create, we find joy in creating useful items with beautiful form." (*The Question*, 193) We begin this process by attending to the details of a piece of art and then attempting to copy the style. In Great Artists, we will focus on the core habit of **expressing** as we copy the style of famous artists. We will also practice **attending** to the colors and techniques of each artist.

By the time you and your children have completed all three cycles of the Foundations program, you will have shaken hands with the styles and techniques of eighteen of the world's great artists. This introduction will lay the foundation for future studies of great artists in the Challenge program. Perhaps some of our children will be called upon to create great works of art for use in worship like the candlesticks of the Tabernacle, the great stained glass windows of medieval cathedrals, or the Bible story paintings of the Renaissance. Others of us may simply be called to be *amateurs* (Latin for "a lover of something"). Either way, we will use our talents to glorify God.

Delight in the process of imitation and creation!

WEEK THIRTEEN
Giotto di Bondone (Egg Paint)

Resources
Discovering Great Artists (Kohl and
    Solga)
Classical Acts & Facts® History Cards:
    Artists and Composers #3 and #4
    (Giotto); #5 and #6 (Ghiberti); #8
    (Angelico)

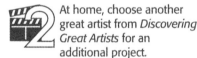 At home, choose another
great artist from *Discovering
Great Artists* for an
additional project.

 ATTENDING

At home, observe the *Classical Acts & Facts® History Cards:
Artists and Composers* cards and other artists and composers cards
from Cycle 1, Cycle 2, and Cycle 3.

Use the sample conversation starters from the list below:

What do you see in this work of art?

How is this work of art similar to others from the same time
period? Other time periods?

How is this work of art different from others from the same time
period? Other time periods?

How similar or different are these comparisons?

What was happening during the time this artwork was created?

At the same time this work of art was created, where was the
artist? Who else was there? What was happening?

What do others say about the artwork? What do you think the
artist wanted to express?

 EXPRESSING

Do the assigned project from *Discovering Great Artists*.

WEEK FOURTEEN
Lorenzo Ghiberti (Florentine Relief)

 At home, redo and improve
this week's project.

WEEK FIFTEEN
Angelico (Silver Leaf)

 Visit an art museum.

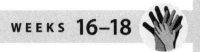

WEEK SIXTEEN
Dürer (Wood Block)

TIP

Be sure to use SOFT wood in order to make good, deep impressions.

Resources

Discovering Great Artists (Kohl and Solga)

Classical Acts & Facts® History Cards: Artists and Composers #3, #5, and #10 (Dürer); #11 (Michelangelo); #34 and #12 (El Greco)

 Watch a documentary on an ancient artist.

WEEK SEVENTEEN
Michelangelo (Fresco Plaque or Lie-Down Painting)

TIP

Practice plaster consistency the week before to ensure the proper water-to-plaster ratio.

 Visit your local artist guild and take an art class.

WEEK EIGHTEEN
El Greco (Drawing Tall Figures)

TIP

Precut photos for younger classes.

 Create an art project from items collected outside.

LESSONS		
CYCLE 1	**CYCLE 2**	**CYCLE 3**
WEEK — PROJECT	PROJECT	PROJECT
19 — Baroque and Classical Periods *Classical Music for Dummies* (Pogue and Speck)	Classical and Romantic Periods *Classical Music for Dummies* (Pogue and Speck)	Romantic and Modern Periods *Classical Music for Dummies* (Pogue and Speck)
20 — Handel: *Water Music Suite* *Classical Music for Dummies* (Pogue and Speck)	Beethoven: *Symphony no. 5* *Classical Music for Dummies* (Pogue and Speck)	Tchaikovsky: *Symphony no. 6*, Fourth Movement *(Symphony Pathétique)* *Classical Music for Dummies* (Pogue and Speck)
21 — Bach: *The Well-Tempered Clavier* Prelude and Fugue in C Major *Classical Music for Dummies* (Pogue and Speck)	Brahms: *Symphony no. 4* *Classical Music for Dummies* (Pogue and Speck)	Debussy: *La Mer* *Classical Music for Dummies* (Pogue and Speck)
22 — Mozart: *Piano Concerto no. 22 in E-flat*, Third Movement *Classical Music for Dummies* (Pogue and Speck)	Dvořák: *Serenade for Strings* *Classical Music for Dummies* (Pogue and Speck)	Stravinsky: *The Rite of Spring* *Classical Music for Dummies* (Pogue and Speck)
23 — orchestra overview *Classical Music for Dummies* (Pogue and Speck)	orchestra overview *Classical Music for Dummies* (Pogue and Speck)	orchestra overview *Classical Music for Dummies* (Pogue and Speck)
24 — review and celebration	review and celebration	review and celebration

Composers and Orchestra

The orchestra unit is designed to encourage us all to learn to sit quietly and restfully. In this quiet restfulness, we can learn to listen actively to classical music and to appreciate the beautiful symphony of instruments expressing the ideas and emotions of a composer.

There is no need to fill up this entire time slot with teaching. Instead, cultivate a restful atmosphere of quiet listening. The rest of the Foundations morning has enough busy-ness already! Depending on the age and temperament of the children in your group, you can cultivate this quiet, restful atmosphere by turning off any overhead lights; students may lay their heads on the table, or sit on carpet squares on the floor, or even lie on rest mats.

Get to know the art period by listening to all the composers' musical pieces the first week. In subsequent weeks students and parents will spend time listening to the pieces of the individual composers while a parent-tutor reads the listening outline aloud. After four weeks of directed listening, students will learn about the orchestra. We'll celebrate students' new listening skills by selecting the instruments they hear in the musical pieces.

At home the other four days, families can explore the composers' biographies, the different instruments and vocabulary associated with the orchestra, and the characteristics of each period in music history. Resources are available online within Classical Conversations' subscription site and from Classical Conversations Books to help you expound at home. Time in community should remain focused on listening to beautiful classical music. In Composers and Orchestra, we will focus on the core habit of closely **attending** as we listen to these great pieces. We will also practice **expressing** through drawing and movement.

We hope this suggestion will allow you to appreciate good music together each week.

Happy listening!

Resources

Classical Music for Dummies (Pogue and Speck)

Classical Acts & Facts® *History Cards*

Classical Acts & Facts® *History Cards: Artists and Composers*

Instrument pictures (if desired; see pages 112–116)

Foundations Audio CD (any cycle) for the *Orchestra Song*

Trivium Tables®: *Music*

WEEK NINETEEN
Introduction to Baroque and Classical Periods

Resources

Classical Music for Dummies (Pogue and Speck)

Classical Acts & Facts® History Cards #98 and #104

Classical Acts & Facts® History Cards: Artists and Composers #14 (Handel); #13 (Bach); and #15 (Mozart)

 ATTENDING

Without naming the composers, listen to pieces by Handel, Bach, and Mozart. Over the next three weeks, we will spend more time with each piece as families get to know these pieces more intimately. Each subsequent week, listen to the individual composer's piece while a parent-tutor reads the listening outline aloud. Practice cultivating restful listening in community. Here are some suggestions:

1. Turn out the lights and get students into a restful position. Have them close their eyes.

2. Turn on the lights. Have students listen again. What do they notice?

3. Listen again. Have students stand up each time the piece gets loud and sit back down when the piece gets quiet.

 EXPRESSING

Focus on active listening, not busy hands. Learn to have ears that hear. Pause music and ask questions that accompany the listening outline.

WEEK TWENTY
Handel *(Water Music Suite no. 2)*

WEEK TWENTY-ONE
Bach *(Well-Tempered Clavier)*

WEEK TWENTY-TWO
Mozart ("Piano Concerto no. 22 in E-Flat, Third Movement")

WEEK TWENTY-THREE
Orchestra Overview

ATTENDING

Teach the children the *Orchestra Song*.

EXPRESSING

1. Practice the orchestra seating chart (see *Trivium Tables®: Music*) by assigning students to be in the different instrument families (strings, woodwinds, brass, percussion). Hand out instrument pictures if desired.

2. Practice singing the orchestra song as a group while students are in the orchestra seating arrangement.

3. If students are getting to know the piece well, you can consider singing it as a round. When the first group of students finishes the violin section, group 2 starts at the beginning of the song. When group 2 finishes the violin section, group 3 starts at the beginning of the song. When a group finishes the song, they should keep singing the final lines of the song until group 3 arrives at the final line.

Your community may choose to handle this study in different ways, depending on the makeup of the group. Larger communities may opt to complete orchestra activities within individual classes during the Fine Arts component. Smaller communities may opt to do these activities as one big group, directly after morning assembly.

WEEK TWENTY-FOUR
Review and Celebration

EXPRESSING

Play *Twinkle, Twinkle, Little Star* with the whole community. Sing the *Orchestra Song* with the whole community.

Resources

Classical Music for Dummies (Pogue and Speck)
Trivium Tables®: Music
Instrument pictures if desired (see pages 112–116)
Foundations Audio CD for the *Orchestra Song*

Orchestra Song

Violins:
The violins ringing like lovely singing.
    The violins ringing like lovely song.

Clarinets:
The clarinet, the clarinet, goes doodle doodle doodle doodle dat.
The clarinet, the clarinet, goes doodle doodle doodle dat.

Trumpets:
The trumpet is braying,
Ta-ta-ta-ta TA ta-ta-ta-ta ta ta TAH.
The trumpet is braying,
Ta-ta-ta-ta TA ta-ta-ta-ta ta ta TAH.

Horns:
The horn, the horn, awakes me at morn.
The horn, the horn, awakes me at morn.

Drums:
The drum's playing two tones.
They're always the same tones.
5-1, 1-5, 5-5-5-5-1.

To which instrument family (strings, woodwinds, brass, percussion) does the violin belong? the clarinet? the trumpet? the horn? the drums?

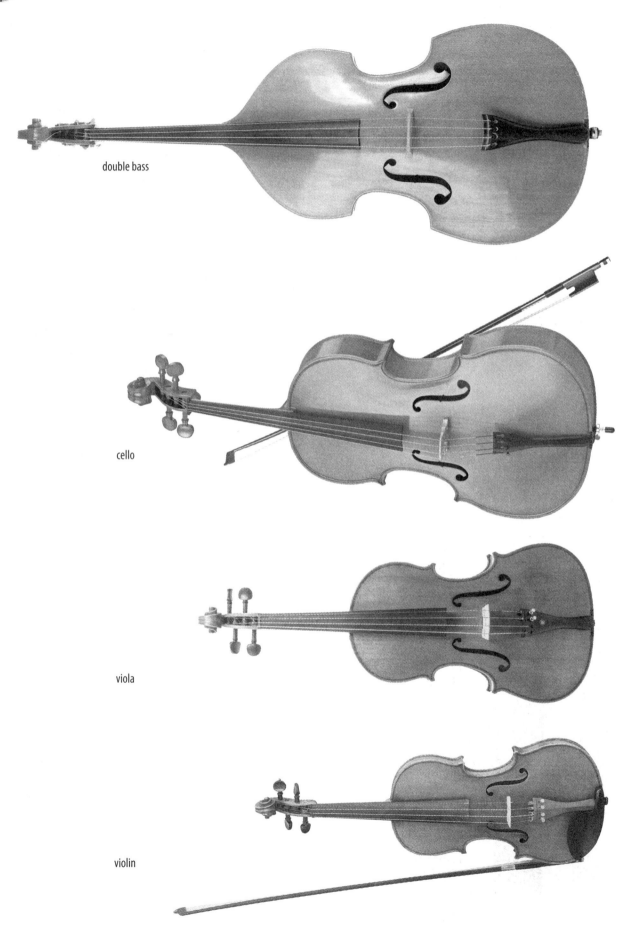

double bass

cello

viola

violin

piano

harp

Copy and cut out pictures. Students can hold up the pictures as they hear that instrument or instrument family during the listening activities, or as the students are learning the *Orchestra Song*.

113

cornet

trumpet

French horn

trombone

tuba

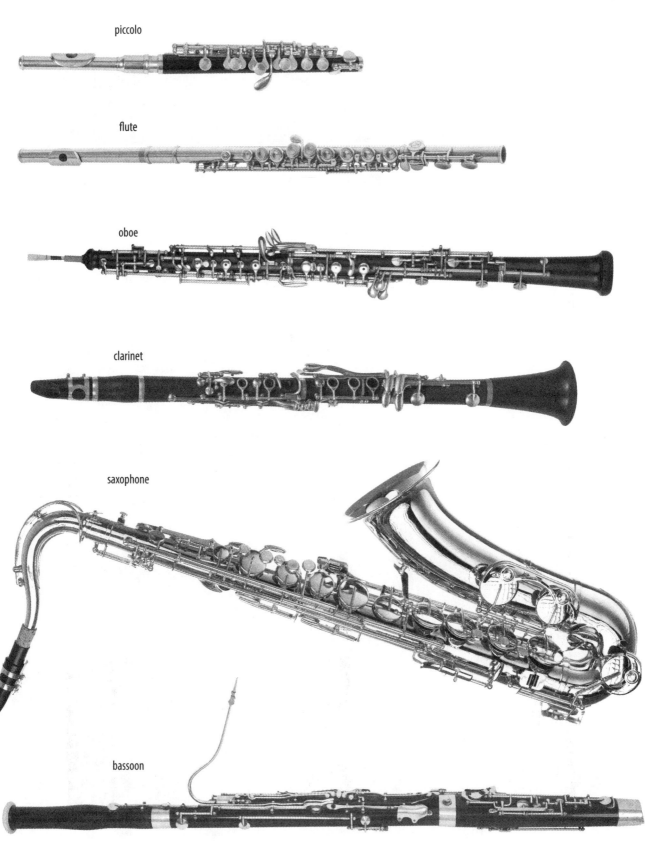

piccolo

flute

oboe

clarinet

saxophone

bassoon

bass drum

castanets

cymbals

kettle drum (timpani)

Hands-on Science

Learning science with students age four and up should be fun and hands-on. It should involve wonder and play. Small children are naturally curious about the world around them. They want to know the names of birds and trees and flowers that they see. They want to understand why the fire burns different colors. They want to fill glasses with different levels of water and play them like a xylophone. They want to turn over rocks and look at roly-polies; they want to touch them and watch them curl up. They wonder why their chest expands each time they breathe and why they can feel their heartbeat in their necks. They love to pick up earthworms and watch them wiggle. They love to draw what they see.

In Foundations, we want to capitalize on this sense of wonder with simple science activities that let children ask questions and discover answers. Along the way, we are teaching our children the core habits of **attending** with our five senses and **naming** what we observe. We don't want to fall back into the school model of telling children what to see and think. Instead, we want to draw out their observations through discussion and demonstration, awakening their sense of wonder and training their senses.

Science experiments form half of each cycle's hands-on science. These two six-week segments lay the foundation for future studies of biology, earth science, astronomy, physical science, chemistry, physics, and origins. The goal is to expose our budding scientists gently to the scientific method (see page 129) through fun and simple demonstrations. Two six-week segments of **science projects** complete each cycle. The goal is to provide students craft opportunities that relate to the science memory work for the given cycle.

As Leigh Bortins wrote in *The Core*, the goal of Foundations studies is to "teach . . . students to define the structures of the cosmos, to observe the wonders that surround them, and to develop an appreciation for all realms of scientific inquiry. . . to inspire them to explore the natural world through a variety of activities, some scheduled and academic, some real life and seren-dipitous, and all of value in developing a curious mind" (198).

Reclaim your childish sense of wonder, ask some great questions, see what happens, and reflect on it together with your community. Happy wondering!

WEEK	PROJECT
1	#45 Baby Bean*
2	#54 Telegraph Lines*
2	#56 Belly Up*
3	#57 Blending*
3	#58 Ground Temperature*
4	#62 Pollution*
5	#60 Oily Feathers*
5	#61 Tangled*
6	#65 Fooling Your Tongue*
6	#66 Trickery*
7	animal nature walk
8	plant nature walk
9	crayfish identification
10	owl pellet dissection
11	parts of a flower
12	classification: plants and animals
13	#121 Tilt*
13	#127 Sinkers*
14	#125 Spoon Pen*
14	#126 Sampler*
15	#128 Prints*
16	#130 Stretch*
16	#132 Spurt*
17	#138 Rock Bridge*
18	#140 Push Up*
18	#142 Up Draft*
19	crystals
20	layers of the geosphere
21, 22	mineral identification
23	rock structure identification
24	compass walk

* *201 Awesome, Magical, Bizarre & Incredible Experiments*

For weeks 1–6 and 13–18, see Scientific Method Discussion on page 129.

WEEK SEVEN
Animal Nature Walk

Materials

Nature Journal (per student) (See
   pages 128, 201, and 274 for
   sample nature journal pages.)
Pencil (per student)
Plastic bag to collect specimens (per
   student)
Thermometer (one per class)

 ## ATTENDING

Activity: Take a walk around outside. Although "natural" areas
are best, this activity can be done anywhere outdoors.

As students walk, ask them to identify any animals they see. This
can include any living creature: birds, insects, mammals, reptiles.

Some students may want to collect a dead bug or exoskeleton if one
can be found.

Have a conversation about what students saw and collected.

Can you identify what group of vertebrate or invertebrate you have
seen?

 ## NAMING

Name some animals you might see on this nature walk. Do you
think you might see some **vertebrates**? How about **invertebrates**?

 ## EXPRESSING

What did we use? What did we do? What did we see?

 At home, explore a variety of
areas (urban area, nature trail,
backyard) for animals. Compare
your findings.

WEEK EIGHT
Plant Nature Walk

We perish from want
of wonder, not from
want of wonders.

–G. K. CHESTERTON

ATTENDING

Activity: Take a walk outside. Although "natural" areas are best, this activity can be done anywhere outdoors.

As students walk, ask them to identify any plants they see. Ask students to collect a leaf, seed, twig, piece of bark, or anything else (non-living) that may interest them.

Have a conversation about what students saw and collected.

NAMING

Name some plants you might see on this nature walk. [*flowers, trees, weeds, grass*]

EXPRESSING

What did we use? What did we do? What did we see?

Materials
Nature Journal (per student) (See pages 128, 201, and 272 for sample nature journal page.)
Pencil (per student)
Plastic bag to collect specimens (per student)
Thermometer (one per class)

 At home, explore a variety of areas (urban area, park, nature trail, backyard) for plants. Compare your findings.

WEEK NINE
Crayfish Identification

Materials

Per student:
    Plastic gloves (optional)
    Paper and pencil
    Plastic utensil for probing crayfish

Per pair of students:
    Crayfish
    Plastic plate or tray
    Crayfish lab/Crayfish identification sheet

Many visuals can be found within Classical Conversations' online subscription service through ClassicalConversations.com or on the Internet by searching "crayfish anatomy"

 ATTENDING

Place the crayfish on the tray and have the students observe its parts. Students will identify only the outside of the crayfish. They will not dissect it.

Activity: Instruct the students to probe the crayfish gently with their plastic utensils.

Show the students any visuals of crayfish you brought while they probe and identify the parts of the crayfish.

Discuss what the students are seeing, using correct terminology.

 NAMING

Name some creatures you have seen at an aquarium or at the beach. Who has seen a crayfish?

 EXPRESSING

What did we use? What did we do? What did we see?

 Dissect the crayfish at home.

WEEK TEN
Owl Pellet Dissection

ATTENDING

Activity: Direct students to observe the owl pellet and gently break it apart with the tweezers, looking for fur, feathers, or small bones. Use the tweezers to separate any bones found.

Using the bone identification chart, try to identify some of the bones discovered in the pellet.

NAMING

What are owl pellets?

EXPRESSING

What did we use? What did we do? What did we see?

Materials
Per student:
  Plastic gloves (optional)
  Paper and pencil
Per pair of students:
  Owl pellet
  Plastic plate or tray
  Lab sheet or bone ID chart
  Tweezers
Many visuals can be found within Classical Conversations' online subscription service through ClassicalConversations.com or the Internet by searching "owl pellet diagram"

At home, take the bones found in the pellet and try to reconstruct the digested animal's skeleton.

WEEK ELEVEN
Parts of a Flower

ATTENDING

Direct students to observe the flower and all of its parts carefully.

Activity: Using a flower parts diagram, have the students locate the various parts of the flower.

Materials

Per student:
    Pencil
Per pair of students:
    Real flowers, if possible
    Flower ID guide
    Flower part ID guide

NAMING

Can you tell me some parts of a flower? [*Week 11 memory work*]

EXPRESSING

What did we use? What did we do? What did we see?

 Visit a local horticulture center.

WEEK TWELVE
Plants and Animals Classification

ATTENDING

Observe: Direct students to find pictures using the Kingdoms of Living Things chart and memory work from weeks 1–2, 5–6, and 8.

Activity: Direct students to cut out pictures of plants, animals, etc. and sort/classify the pictures that correspond to the Kingdoms of Living Things chart.

NAMING

Have students select pictures for their charts, naming the animals or plants as they go.

EXPRESSING

What did we use? What did we do? What did we see?

Materials
Pictures of plants and animals
Poster board (younger students may create one poster as a group; older students may create posters in pairs)
Kingdoms of Living Things chart

Kingdoms of Living Things

Animalia	vertebrate	fish, amphibians, reptiles, mammals, birds
	invertebrate	sponges, stinging-cell animals, flatworms, roundworms, segmented worms, mollusks, sea stars, arthropods
Plantae	seed bearing	monocots, dicots, conifers
	non-seed bearing	green algae, liverworts, mosses, club mosses/ground pines, horsetails, ferns
Fungi	no chlorophyll	yeasts, lichens, and truffles; mushrooms, shelf fungi, puffballs, rusts, smuts; penicillin; bread mold; others
Protista	everything that isn't animals, plants, or fungi	some algae, molds, and mildew
Archaea	micro-organisms that live in harsh climates	
Bacteria	micro-organisms that live everywhere	

 Encourage older students to use OiLS to draw pictures of plants and animals instead of cutting them out.

© 2018 Classical Conversations® MultiMedia, Inc.

123

WEEK NINETEEN
Crystals

Materials

Epsom salts

Liquid dish soap

Warm water

4-cup jar, bowl, or measuring cup

Stirring tool

Magnifying glass

Cloth

Glass surface or mirror

ATTENDING

1. Stir together ⅓ cup of Epsom salts with ½ cup warm water until dissolved.

2. Stir 1–2 drops of dish soap into the mixture.

3. Apply the solution with the cloth to a glass window or mirror.

4. Clean away any excess or drips.

5. Let dry.

6. Have students look at the design with the magnifying glass.

NAMING

Discuss some crystal formations (e.g., snowflakes, table salt, some rocks, diamonds, ice, sugar).

EXPRESSING

What did we use? What did we do? What did we see?

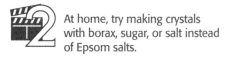 At home, try making crystals with borax, sugar, or salt instead of Epsom salts.

WEEK TWENTY
Layers of the Geosphere

ATTENDING

Discuss a geosphere diagram (can be found online) with the students, and an atmosphere diagram (found online), if needed.

Activity:

Option 1: Direct students to draw large concentric circles on half of the styrofoam ball, starting at the center (inner core) and moving to the outside (crust) of the half. (See Week 13 memory work.)

Option 2: Direct students to use different colored Play-Doh,® layered one on top of the other, to represent the different layers of the geosphere. (See Week 13 memory work.)

Option 3: Students can depict the layers of the geosphere and the layers of the atmosphere on paper using different colored crayons or pencils. (See Weeks 13 and 20 memory work.)

Materials
Option 1
Styrofoam ball (half per student)

Option 2
Play-Doh® to share among students

Option 3
Paper
Crayons or pencils

Diagrams of the geosphere can be
found on the *Classical Acts &
Facts® Science Cards Cycle 1*,
second edition or on the Internet

NAMING

What are some parts of the geosphere? [*Week 13 memory work*]

EXPRESSING

What did we use? What did we do? What did we see?

At home, do all three activity
options and compare.

WEEKS TWENTY-ONE AND TWENTY-TWO
Mineral Identification

Materials

Lab sheet, one per student (included in kit)

Mineral Identification Kit, one per class or share a few among all classes

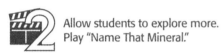

Allow students to explore more. Play "Name That Mineral."

 ATTENDING

Follow the instructions in the Mineral Identification Kit.

 NAMING

Students will have the opportunity to work with the various mineral substances and their properties.

 EXPRESSING

What did we use? What did we do? What did we see?

WEEK TWENTY-THREE
Rock Structure Identification

Materials

Lab sheet, one per student (included in kit)

Rock Structure Identification Kit, one per class

Encourage students to compare rocks and minerals.

 ATTENDING

Follow the instructions in the Rock Structure Identification Kit.

 NAMING

Display and discuss some well-known rocks or rocks you have found.

 EXPRESSING

What did we use? What did we do? What did we see?

WEEK TWENTY-FOUR
Compass Walk

NAMING

Using a map (world, city) discuss the cardinal directions and compass rose. Discuss directions for getting from one place to another.

With younger students discuss N, S, E, W, and maybe NE, NW, SE, SW. With older students, discuss these plus the degree circle.

ATTENDING

With young students, call out simple directions and a number of steps, and have students walk following your directions.

With older students, create a "course" and create a series of directions ahead of time that students can follow, possibly working in pairs.

EXPRESSING

What did we use? What did we do? What did we see?

Materials

Compass, one per student

Inside or outside "course" (plan ahead of time)

 Encourage students to create their own compass walk or course.

SAMPLE JOURNAL ENTRY

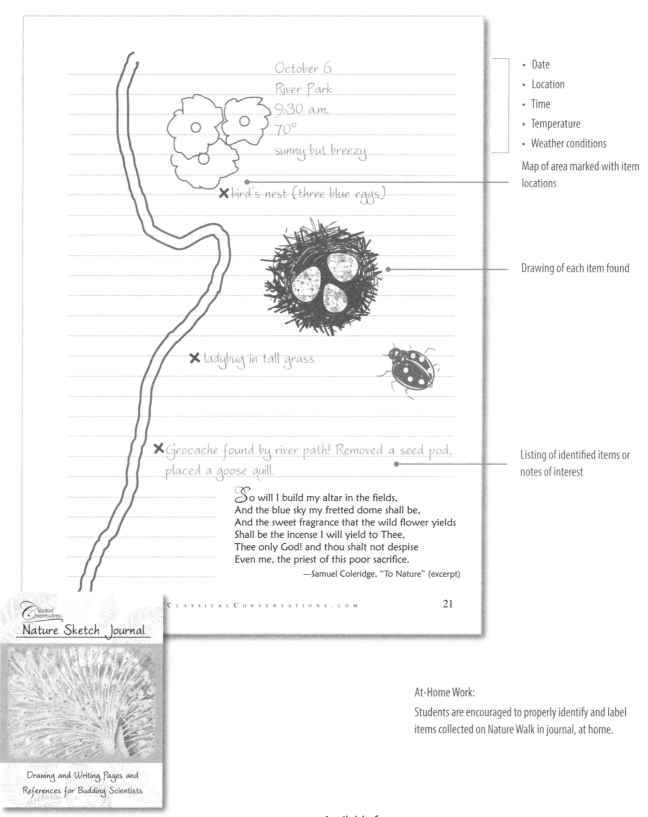

October 6
River Park
9:30 a.m.
70°
sunny but breezy

✗ bird's nest (three blue eggs)

✗ ladybug in tall grass

✗ Geocache found by river path! Removed a seed pod,
placed a goose quill.

So will I build my altar in the fields,
And the blue sky my fretted dome shall be,
And the sweet fragrance that the wild flower yields
Shall be the incense I will yield to Thee,
Thee only God! and thou shalt not despise
Even me, the priest of this poor sacrifice.

—Samuel Coleridge, "To Nature" (excerpt)

CLASSICALCONVERSATIONS.COM

21

- • Date
- • Location
- • Time
- • Temperature
- • Weather conditions

Map of area marked with item
locations

Drawing of each item found

Listing of identified items or
notes of interest

Nature Sketch Journal

Drawing and Writing Pages and
References for Budding Scientists

At-Home Work:

Students are encouraged to properly identify and label
items collected on Nature Walk in journal, at home.

SCIENTIFIC METHOD DISCUSSION

_____ _____
TITLE   DATE

1. **QUESTION** (Look around you: what questions do you wonder about?)

2. **RESEARCH** (What do you or your parents already know and what do you need to find out?)

3. **HYPOTHESIS** (What do you think is the answer to your question?)

4. **EXPERIMENT** (How can you discover if your answer is true/correct/right? What materials do you need to test your answer? What will you do with the materials?)

5. **ANALYSIS** (What happened when you tested your idea/answer? What did you see?)

6. **CONCLUSION** (What did you learn about your question and answer?)

RISING TO THE CHALLENGE

TEACHER CERTIFICATE

Congratulations

FOR SUCCESSFULLY
COMPLETING

CYCLE
1

IN YOUR HOME
SCHOOL

Parents' Names

Classical Conversations® honors your commitment to learn alongside
your children and values your service to family and community.

Classical Conversations recognizes your achievements as parents who completed Foundations Cycle 1. You
have taught your children and continued your own education by leading others through the grammar of math,
Latin, science, English, history, geography, art, and music. This Cycle 1 knowledge, enhanced by weekly
community training in the classical model, has equipped you to homeschool with confidence during the exciting
high school years ahead. You are prepared to consider future roles tutoring the Foundations, Essentials, and
Challenge programs.

Licensed Classical Conversations® Community Name

Director Signature

Date

*It is the glory of God to
conceal a thing; but the
honour of kings is to search
out a matter.*
Proverbs 25:2

CYCLE

2

Through wisdom is an house builded; and by understanding it is established:
And by knowledge shall the chambers be filled with all precious and pleasant riches.

—PROVERBS 24:3–4

A CYCLE 2 MEMORY MASTER KNOWS...

MEDIEVAL TO MODERN

161 EVENTS AND PEOPLE
in a chronological timeline

HISTORY SENTENCES **24**
add depth to the timeline

100 GEOGRAPHIC FEATURES
and political locations, primarily in Europe

24 SCIENCE FACTS
including biomes, planets, laws of motion, and laws of thermodynamics

U.S. PRESIDENTS **45**

1st CONJUGATION LATIN
verb endings in both singular and plural

MULTIPLICATION TABLES **15s**
as well as common squares and cubes, basic geometry formulas, and unit conversions

65 PRONOUNS
along with other grammar facts, including 8 parts of speech and 4 purposes of a sentence

For practice on the go, download our mobile app!

132

not to mention drawing techniques, music theory, and tin whistle, 6 great artists and related projects, introduction to orchestra and 3 classical composers, 12 science experiments, 12 science projects, and 24 oral presentations!

THAT'S OVER **500** pieces of information **in one year!**

CYCLE 2

WEEK	MATH	LATIN	SCIENCE	ENGLISH	TIMELINE	HISTORY	GEOGRAPHY	PROJECTS	FINE ARTS
1	1s and 2s	1st conjugation present tense	days of creation	8 parts of speech	1–7	Charlemagne	continents and oceans	2 Shaded 17 Same Place	5 elements of shape
2	3s and 4s		land biomes	pronouns	8–14	William the Conqueror	European waters	24 Mirage 26 Distortion	mirror images
3	5s and 6s	1st conjugation imperfect tense	consumers	pronoun order	15–21	The Crusades	Western Euro. countries	9 See Through	upside-down
4	7s and 8s		food chain	nominative pronouns	22–28	Magna Carta	European rivers	11 On the Move 12 Speedy	abstract
5	9s and 10s	1st conjugation future tense	natural cycles	objective pronouns	29–35	Hundred Years' War	European cities	13 Expanding 16 In and Out	perspective
6	11s and 12s		reaction to environment	possessive pronouns	36–42	Renaissance	European mountains	3 Cover Up 4 Thick	final project
7	13s	1st conjugation perfect tense	pollution	possessive pro. adjectives	43–49	Reformation	European peninsulas	sun prints	tin whistle
8	14s		aquatic biomes	reflexive pronouns	50–56	European Explorers	Mid-Atlantic world	proportional solar system	dynamics
9	15s	1st conjugation pluperfect tense	parts of sun	interrogative pronouns	57–63	Absolute Monarchs	Caribbean	rockets	note values and staff
10	squares		names of planets	demonstrative pronouns	64–70	History of Russia	Southwest Asia	facility clean-up	rhythm
11	cubes	1st conjugation future perfect tense	phases of moon	indefinite pronouns	71–77	French Revolution	Europe and Asia	solar system model	note name and scales
12	tsp. and tbsp.		bodies in solar system	indefinite pronouns	78–84	Battle of Waterloo	Eastern European seas	constellations	review and celebration
13	liquid equivalents	1st conjugation present tense	U.S. space missions	indefinite pronouns	85–91	Industrial Revolution	N. European countries	161 Spoon Bell 162 Humming Glass	Rembrandt
14	linear equivalents		states of matter	adverb	92–98	World War I Leaders	Baltic Europe	165 Cold Foot 171 Pepper Run	Gainsborough
15	metric measurements	1st conjugation imperfect tense	forms of energy	4 sentence purposes	99–105	World War I Countries	The Levant	164 Bottle Organ	Degas
16	area rectangle		Newton's first law of motion	verb	106–112	How World War II Began	Balkans	189 Shape Up 190 Breakthrough	Monet
17	area square	1st conjugation future tense	Newton's second law of motion	noun	113–119	World War II Leaders	Central European countries	174 Energy Change 177 Snap!	Morisot
18	area triangle		Newton's third law of motion	5 cases of nouns	120–126	United Nations	More Central European countries	184 Lifter 185 Ramp	van Gogh
19	area circle	1st conjugation perfect tense	first law of thermodynamics	gerund	127–133	Korean War	Southeast Asia	paper airplanes	Classical and Romantic
20	circumference		second law of thermodynamics	appositive	134–140	Vietnam War	South Central Asia	straw bridge	Beethoven
21	Associative Law	1st conjugation pluperfect tense	third law of thermodynamics	conjunction	141–147	End of the Cold War	Central America	tower construction	Brahms
22	Commutative Law		ways light observed	coordinating conjunctions	148–154	Fall of Communism	Oceania	popsicle stick catapult	Dvořák
23	Distributive Law	1st conjugation future perfect tense	heat flow	adjective	155–161	Gulf War	Central Asia	egg protector	orchestra
24	Identity Law		units of electricity	interjection	U. S. Presidents	End of Apartheid	Southern Africa	outdoor contest	review

 MATH

MULTIPLICATION TABLES
1s and 2s

1 × 1 = 1	2 × 1 = 2
1 × 2 = 2	2 × 2 = 4
1 × 3 = 3	2 × 3 = 6
1 × 4 = 4	2 × 4 = 8
1 × 5 = 5	2 × 5 = 10
1 × 6 = 6	2 × 6 = 12
1 × 7 = 7	2 × 7 = 14
1 × 8 = 8	2 × 8 = 16
1 × 9 = 9	2 × 9 = 18
1 × 10 = 10	2 × 10 = 20
1 × 11 = 11	2 × 11 = 22
1 × 12 = 12	2 × 12 = 24
1 × 13 = 13	2 × 13 = 26
1 × 14 = 14	2 × 14 = 28
1 × 15 = 15	2 × 15 = 30

 ENGLISH

PARTS OF SPEECH

noun
pronoun
verb
adverb
conjunction
interjection
preposition
adjective

 HISTORY 65

Tell me about Charlemagne.
In 800, during the medieval period, Pope Leo III crowned Charlemagne Holy Roman Emperor of Europe.

 LATIN

FIRST CONJUGATION ENDINGS
PRESENT TENSE

SINGULAR
___ ō	I ___
___ s	you ___
___ t	he, she, it ___

PLURAL
___ mus	we ___
___ tis	you ___
___ nt	they ___

TIMELINE

Classical Acts & Facts® History Cards

1. **AGE OF ANCIENT EMPIRES**
2. Creation and the Fall
3. The Flood and the Tower of Babel
4. Mesopotamia and Sumer
5. Egyptians
6. Indus River Valley Civilization
7. Minoans and Mycenaeans

 GEOGRAPHY

CONTINENTS / OCEANS

North America	Indian Ocean
South America	Arctic Ocean
Europe	Atlantic Ocean
Asia	Pacific Ocean
Africa	Southern
Australia	Ocean
Antarctica	

 SCIENCE

Classical Acts & Facts® Science Cycle 2

What occurred on each day of creation?
DAY
1. earth, space, time, light
2. atmosphere
3. dry land, plants
4. sun, moon, stars
5. fish, sea creatures, birds
6. land animals, Adam, Eve

PRESENTATION NOTES

 Recite math memory work in speed rounds.

 HANDS-ON

FINE ARTS

Drawing Introduction (see page 80)
Five Elements of Shape (see page 81)

SCIENCE

Shaded (#2)
Same Place (#17)

 *Memoria*

CYCLE 2

  MATH

MULTIPLICATION TABLES
3s and 4s

3 × 1 = 3	4 × 1 = 4
3 × 2 = 6	4 × 2 = 8
3 × 3 = 9	4 × 3 = 12
3 × 4 = 12	4 × 4 = 16
3 × 5 = 15	4 × 5 = 20
3 × 6 = 18	4 × 6 = 24
3 × 7 = 21	4 × 7 = 28
3 × 8 = 24	4 × 8 = 32
3 × 9 = 27	4 × 9 = 36
3 × 10 = 30	4 × 10 = 40
3 × 11 = 33	4 × 11 = 44
3 × 12 = 36	4 × 12 = 48
3 × 13 = 39	4 × 13 = 52
3 × 14 = 42	4 × 14 = 56
3 × 15 = 45	4 × 15 = 60

  ENGLISH

A PRONOUN
A **pronoun** replaces a noun in order to avoid repetition.

  LATIN

FIRST CONJUGATION ENDINGS
PRESENT TENSE

SINGULAR
____ ō	I ____
____ s	you ____
____ t	he, she, it ____

PLURAL
____ mus	we ____
____ tis	you ____
____ nt	they ____

TIMELINE

Classical Acts & Facts® History Cards

8	Seven Wonders of the Ancient World
9	Patriarchs of Israel
10	Hittites and Canaanites
11	Kush
12	Assyrians
13	Babylonians
14	China's Shang Dynasty

 **SCIENCE**

Classical Acts & Facts® Science Cycle 2

What are some land biomes?
- grassland
- desert
- scrubland
- tundra
- deciduous forest
- coniferous forest
- tropical rainforest

PRESENTATION NOTES

Set a goal of drawing one map a day.

  HISTORY   70

71

Tell me about William the Conqueror.

In 1054, the church split into Roman Catholic and Eastern Orthodox. William the Conqueror defeated King Harold of England in 1066 and started feudalism.

 **GEOGRAPHY**

EUROPEAN WATERS
North Sea
Baltic Sea
Adriatic Sea
English Channel
Mediterranean Sea

HANDS-ON

FINE ARTS
Mirror Images (see page 82)

SCIENCE
Mirage (#24)
Distortion (#26)

Memoria
What are some outside activities you enjoy at night?

 MATH

MULTIPLICATION TABLES
5s and 6s

5 × 1 = 5	6 × 1 = 6
5 × 2 = 10	6 × 2 = 12
5 × 3 = 15	6 × 3 = 18
5 × 4 = 20	6 × 4 = 24
5 × 5 = 25	6 × 5 = 30
5 × 6 = 30	6 × 6 = 36
5 × 7 = 35	6 × 7 = 42
5 × 8 = 40	6 × 8 = 48
5 × 9 = 45	6 × 9 = 54
5 × 10 = 50	6 × 10 = 60
5 × 11 = 55	6 × 11 = 66
5 × 12 = 60	6 × 12 = 72
5 × 13 = 65	6 × 13 = 78
5 × 14 = 70	6 × 14 = 84
5 × 15 = 75	6 × 15 = 90

 ENGLISH

PRONOUN ORDER

singular	plural
first person	first person
second person	second person
third person	third person

 LATIN

FIRST CONJUGATION ENDINGS
IMPERFECT TENSE

SINGULAR

____ bam	I was ____ing
____ bās	you were ____ing
____ bat	he, she, it was ____ing

PLURAL

____ bāmus	we were ____ing
____ bātis	you were ____ing
____ bant	they were ____ing

TIMELINE

Classical Acts & Facts® History Cards

15 Hinduism in India
16 Phoenicians and the Alphabet
17 Olmecs of Mesoamerica
18 Israelite Exodus and Desert Wandering
19 Israelite Conquest and Judges
20 Greek Dark Ages
21 Israel's United Kingdom

 SCIENCE 5

Classical Acts & Facts® Science Cycle 2

What are three types of consumers?
herbivore
carnivore
omnivore

PRESENTATION NOTES

 Review Cycle 3 history.

 **HISTORY** 72

Tell me about the Crusades.

Richard the Lion-Hearted, son of Eleanor of Aquitaine, fought the Turks for Jerusalem during the time of the Crusades, from 1095 to 1291.

 GEOGRAPHY

WESTERN EUROPEAN COUNTRIES
Ireland
England
Portugal
Spain
France

HANDS-ON

FINE ARTS
Upside-down image (see page 83)

SCIENCE
See Through (#9)

Memoria

 MATH

MULTIPLICATION TABLES
7s and 8s

7 × 1 = 7	8 × 1 = 8
7 × 2 = 14	8 × 2 = 16
7 × 3 = 21	8 × 3 = 24
7 × 4 = 28	8 × 4 = 32
7 × 5 = 35	8 × 5 = 40
7 × 6 = 42	8 × 6 = 48
7 × 7 = 49	8 × 7 = 56
7 × 8 = 56	8 × 8 = 64
7 × 9 = 63	8 × 9 = 72
7 × 10 = 70	8 × 10 = 80
7 × 11 = 77	8 × 11 = 88
7 × 12 = 84	8 × 12 = 96
7 × 13 = 91	8 × 13 = 104
7 × 14 = 98	8 × 14 = 112
7 × 15 = 105	8 × 15 = 120

 ENGLISH

NOMINATIVE PRONOUNS

	singular	plural
first	I	we
second	you	you
third	he/she/it	they

 HISTORY 79

Tell me about the Magna Carta.
English King John signed the Magna Carta in 1215, limiting the king's power. Later, England's King Edward III claimed to be king of France and began the Hundred Years' War in 1337.

 LATIN

FIRST CONJUGATION ENDINGS
IMPERFECT TENSE

SINGULAR

____	bam	I was ____ing
____	bās	you were ____ing
____	bat	he, she, it was ____ing

PLURAL

____	bāmus	we were ____ing
____	bātis	you were ____ing
____	bant	they were ____ing

TIMELINE

Classical Acts & Facts® History Cards

22	Early Native Americans
23	Israel Divides into Two Kingdoms
24	Homer and Hesiod
25	Rome Founded by Romulus and Remus
26	Israel Falls to Assyria
27	Assyria Falls to Babylon
28	Lao-Tzu, Confucius, Buddha

 GEOGRAPHY

EUROPEAN RIVERS
Seine River
Rhine River
Elbe River
Po River
Danube River
Volga River

 SCIENCE CYCLE 2 6

Classical Acts & Facts® Science Cycle 2

What are some parts of the food chain?
producer
consumer
decomposer

PRESENTATION NOTES

 Review Cycle 3 English.

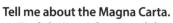 **HANDS-ON**

FINE ARTS

Abstract Art (see page 84)

SCIENCE

On the Move (#11)
Speedy (#12)

What are you praying for?

MATH

MULTIPLICATION TABLES
9s and 10s

9 × 1 = 9	10 × 1 = 10
9 × 2 = 18	10 × 2 = 20
9 × 3 = 27	10 × 3 = 30
9 × 4 = 36	10 × 4 = 40
9 × 5 = 45	10 × 5 = 50
9 × 6 = 54	10 × 6 = 60
9 × 7 = 63	10 × 7 = 70
9 × 8 = 72	10 × 8 = 80
9 × 9 = 81	10 × 9 = 90
9 × 10 = 90	10 × 10 = 100
9 × 11 = 99	10 × 11 = 110
9 × 12 = 108	10 × 12 = 120
9 × 13 = 117	10 × 13 = 130
9 × 14 = 126	10 × 14 = 140
9 × 15 = 135	10 × 15 = 150

 ENGLISH

OBJECTIVE PRONOUNS

	singular	plural
first	me	us
second	you	you
third	him/her/it	them

LATIN

FIRST CONJUGATION ENDINGS
FUTURE TENSE

SINGULAR
____	bō	I shall ____
____	bis	you will ____
____	bit	he, she, it will ____

PLURAL
____	bimus	we shall ____
____	bitis	you will ____
____	bunt	they will ____

TIMELINE

Classical Acts & Facts® History Cards

29	Judah falls to Babylon, Temple Destroyed
30	Babylon Falls to Persia
31	Jews Return and Rebuild the Temple
32	Roman Republic
33	Golden Age of Greece
34	Peloponnesian Wars
35	Persia Falls to Alexander the Great

SCIENCE

Classical Acts & Facts® Science Cycle 2

What are some cycles in nature?
water cycle
carbon and oxygen cycle
nitrogen cycle

PRESENTATION NOTES

 Recite Cycle 2 Latin conjugations in speed rounds.

HISTORY

 82

Tell me about the Hundred Years' War.

During the Hundred Years' War, Joan of Arc and King Charles VII led the French to defeat the English at the Siege of Orleans. In the late 1340s, fleas on rats carried the plague, which killed one out of three Europeans.

GEOGRAPHY

EUROPEAN CITIES

London
Paris
Rome
Barcelona
Orleans

HANDS-ON

FINE ARTS

Perspective (see page 85)

SCIENCE

Expanding (#13)
In and Out (#16)

Memoria

MATH

MULTIPLICATION TABLES
11s and 12s

11 × 1 = 11	12 × 1 = 12
11 × 2 = 22	12 × 2 = 24
11 × 3 = 33	12 × 3 = 36
11 × 4 = 44	12 × 4 = 48
11 × 5 = 55	12 × 5 = 60
11 × 6 = 66	12 × 6 = 72
11 × 7 = 77	12 × 7 = 84
11 × 8 = 88	12 × 8 = 96
11 × 9 = 99	12 × 9 = 108
11 × 10 = 110	12 × 10 = 120
11 × 11 = 121	12 × 11 = 132
11 × 12 = 132	12 × 12 = 144
11 × 13 = 143	12 × 13 = 156
11 × 14 = 154	12 × 14 = 168
11 × 15 = 165	12 × 15 = 180

ENGLISH

POSSESSIVE PRONOUNS

	singular	plural
first	mine	ours
second	yours	yours
third	his/hers/its	theirs

LATIN

FIRST CONJUGATION ENDINGS
FUTURE TENSE

SINGULAR
____ bō — I shall ____
____ bis — you will ____
____ bit — he, she, it will ____

PLURAL
____ bimus — we shall ____
____ bitis — you will ____
____ bunt — they will ____

TIMELINE

Classical Acts & Facts® History Cards

36 India's Mauryan Empire
37 Mayans of Mesoamerica
38 Punic Wars
39 Rome Conquers Greece
40 Roman Dictator Julius Caesar
41 Caesar Augustus and the *Pax Romana*
42 John the Baptist

SCIENCE

Classical Acts & Facts® Science Cycle 2

How do animals react to environmental change?
adapt
migrate
hibernate

PRESENTATION NOTES

HISTORY

Tell me about the Renaissance.
During the Renaissance period, from 1350 to 1600, Leonardo da Vinci was a famous inventor, Shakespeare was a famous playwright, Michelangelo was a famous artist, and Copernicus was a famous scientist.

GEOGRAPHY

EUROPEAN MOUNTAINS
Pyrenees
Alps
Carpathians
Caucasus
Ural
Matterhorn

HANDS-ON

FINE ARTS

Drawing Review and Final Project (see page 86)

SCIENCE

Cover Up (#3)
Thick (#4)

What do you want to do differently next week?

 MATH

MULTIPLICATION TABLES

13s

$13 \times 1 = 13$
$13 \times 2 = 26$
$13 \times 3 = 39$
$13 \times 4 = 52$
$13 \times 5 = 65$
$13 \times 6 = 78$
$13 \times 7 = 91$
$13 \times 8 = 104$
$13 \times 9 = 117$
$13 \times 10 = 130$
$13 \times 11 = 143$
$13 \times 12 = 156$
$13 \times 13 = 169$
$13 \times 14 = 182$
$13 \times 15 = 195$

 ENGLISH

POSSESSIVE PRONOUN ADJECTIVES

	singular	plural
first	my	our
second	your	your
third	his/her/its	their

 HISTORY

Tell me about the Reformation.

In 1517, Martin Luther began the Protestant Reformation by printing the *Ninety-five Theses* that made Pope Leo X excommunicate him. Later, John Calvin joined the Reformation.

 LATIN

FIRST CONJUGATION ENDINGS
PERFECT TENSE

SINGULAR

____ ī	I have ____ed
____ istī	you have ____ed
____ it	he, she, it has ____ed

PLURAL

____ imus	we have ____ed
____ istis	you have ____ed
____ ērunt	they have ____ed

TIMELINE

Classical Acts & Facts® History Cards

43   Jesus the Messiah
44   Pentecost and the Early Church
45   Persecution Spreads the Gospel
46   Herod's Temple Destroyed by Titus
47   Diocletian Divides the Roman Empire
48   Constantine Legalizes Christianity
49   India's Gupta Dynasty

 **GEOGRAPHY**

EUROPEAN PENINSULAS

Iberian Peninsula
Balkan Peninsula
Scandinavian Peninsula
Apennine Peninsula

 SCIENCE   9

Classical Acts & Facts® Science Cycle 2

What are six forms of pollution?

noise
air
water
land
thermal
radioactive

PRESENTATION NOTES

 Choose a *Classical Acts & Facts® History Card* at random and recite cards that come after.

 HANDS-ON

FINE ARTS

Music Theory and Practice Introduction (see page 87)
Parts of the Tin Whistle (see pages 88, 90–91)

SCIENCE

Sun Prints (see page 189)

Memoria

MATH

MULTIPLICATION TABLES
14s

$14 \times 1 = 14$
$14 \times 2 = 28$
$14 \times 3 = 42$
$14 \times 4 = 56$
$14 \times 5 = 70$
$14 \times 6 = 84$
$14 \times 7 = 98$
$14 \times 8 = 112$
$14 \times 9 = 126$
$14 \times 10 = 140$
$14 \times 11 = 154$
$14 \times 12 = 168$
$14 \times 13 = 182$
$14 \times 14 = 196$
$14 \times 15 = 210$

 ENGLISH

REFLEXIVE PRONOUNS

	singular	plural
first	myself	ourselves
second	yourself	yourselves
third	himself/ herself/ itself	themselves

 LATIN

FIRST CONJUGATION ENDINGS
PERFECT TENSE

SINGULAR
_____ ī — I have _____ed
_____ istī — you have _____ed
_____ it — he, she, it has _____ed

PLURAL
_____ imus — we have _____ed
_____ istis — you have _____ed
_____ ērunt — they have _____ed

TIMELINE

Classical Acts & Facts® History Cards

50 Council of Nicea
51 Augustine of Hippo
52 Jerome Completes the Vulgate
53 Visigoths Sack Rome
54 THE MIDDLE AGES
55 Council of Chalcedon
56 Western Roman Empire Falls to Barbarians

 Refer to *Trivium Tables®: Rhetoric* to enhance your presentation this week.

SCIENCE

Classical Acts & Facts® Science Cycle 2

What are some aquatic biomes?
ponds and lakes
streams and rivers
wetlands and estuaries
oceans and seas

PRESENTATION NOTES

 HISTORY 85

Tell me about European explorers.
Between the late 1400s and the mid-1500s, Dias rounded the Cape of Good Hope, Amerigo Vespucci sailed to the Americas, Balboa crossed Central America to the Pacific, Magellan's crew sailed around the globe, and Coronado explored the American Southwest.

 **GEOGRAPHY**

MID-ATLANTIC WORLD
Cape of Good Hope
Strait of Magellan
Canary Islands
Treaty of Tordesillas

HANDS-ON

FINE ARTS
Dynamics (see pages 92–93)

SCIENCE
Proportional Solar System (see page 190)

 *Memoria*
What new discovery about God's world brought you joy?

 MATH

MULTIPLICATION TABLES
15s
15 × 1 = 15
15 × 2 = 30
15 × 3 = 45
15 × 4 = 60
15 × 5 = 75
15 × 6 = 90
15 × 7 = 105
15 × 8 = 120
15 × 9 = 135
15 × 10 = 150
15 × 11 = 165
15 × 12 = 180
15 × 13 = 195
15 × 14 = 210
15 × 15 = 225

 ENGLISH

INTERROGATIVE PRONOUNS
who
whom
whose
which
what

 HISTORY 93

Tell me about some absolute monarchs.

Between the 1500s and 1800s, Henry VIII of England, Louis XIV of France, Philip II of Spain, Peter the Great of Russia, and Frederick the Great of Prussia ruled during the age of absolute monarchs.

 LATIN

FIRST CONJUGATION ENDINGS PLUPERFECT TENSE

SINGULAR
____ eram — I had ____ed
____ erās — you had ____ed
____ erat — he, she, it had ____ed

PLURAL
____ erāmus — we had ____ed
____ erātis — you had ____ed
____ erant — they had ____ed

TIMELINE

Classical Acts & Facts® History Cards

57 Byzantine Emperor Justinian
58 Benedict and Monasticism
59 Muhammad Founds Islam
60 Zanj and Early Ghana in Africa
61 Franks Defeat Muslims at the Battle of Tours
62 Golden Age of Islam
63 Vikings Raid and Trade

 GEOGRAPHY

CARIBBEAN
Cuba
Jamaica
Haiti
Dominican Republic
Puerto Rico

 SCIENCE 16

Classical Acts & Facts® Science Cycle 2

What are some parts of the sun?
core
radiative zone
convective zone
sunspots
photosphere
solar flare
corona

PRESENTATION NOTES

Review Cycle 3 science.

 **HANDS-ON**

FINE ARTS
Note Values and Staff (see pages 94–95)

SCIENCE
Rockets (see page 191)

 Memoria

MATH

SQUARES
$1 \times 1 = 1$
$2 \times 2 = 4$
$3 \times 3 = 9$
$4 \times 4 = 16$
$5 \times 5 = 25$
$6 \times 6 = 36$
$7 \times 7 = 49$
$8 \times 8 = 64$
$9 \times 9 = 81$
$10 \times 10 = 100$
$11 \times 11 = 121$
$12 \times 12 = 144$
$13 \times 13 = 169$
$14 \times 14 = 196$
$15 \times 15 = 225$

 ENGLISH

DEMONSTRATIVE PRONOUNS
this
that
these
those

 LATIN

FIRST CONJUGATION ENDINGS
PLUPERFECT TENSE

SINGULAR	____ eram	I had ____ed
	____ erās	you had ____ed
	____ erat	he, she, it had ____ed
PLURAL	____ erāmus	we had ____ed
	____ erātis	you had ____ed
	____ erant	they had ____ed

TIMELINE

Classical Acts & Facts® History Cards

64 Japan's Heian Period
65 Charlemagne Crowned Emperor of Europe
66 Alfred the Great of England
67 Erik the Red and Leif Eriksson, Norse Explorers
68 Vladimir I of Kiev
69 Byzantine Emperor Basil II
70 East-West Schism of the Church

 SCIENCE 17

Classical Acts & Facts® Science Cycle 2

What are the names of the planets?
Mercury
Venus
Earth
Mars
Jupiter
Saturn
Uranus
Neptune

PRESENTATION NOTES

 Review Cycle 3 geography.

 HISTORY 68

Tell me about the history of Russia. 90
Vladimir I brought Christianity to Russia in the 900s. In the 1500s, Czar Ivan the Terrible unified Russia. Peter the Great and Catherine the Great expanded and Westernized Russia in the 1700s.

 GEOGRAPHY

SOUTHWEST ASIA
Afghanistan
Pakistan
India
Kolkata
Arabian Sea

HANDS-ON

FINE ARTS
Rhythm (see pages 96–97)

SCIENCE
Facility Clean-up or Community Service (see page 192)

Share some details from a field trip.

 MATH

CUBES

$1 \times 1 \times 1 = 1$
$2 \times 2 \times 2 = 8$
$3 \times 3 \times 3 = 27$
$4 \times 4 \times 4 = 64$
$5 \times 5 \times 5 = 125$
$6 \times 6 \times 6 = 216$
$7 \times 7 \times 7 = 343$
$8 \times 8 \times 8 = 512$
$9 \times 9 \times 9 = 729$
$10 \times 10 \times 10 = 1{,}000$
$11 \times 11 \times 11 = 1{,}331$
$12 \times 12 \times 12 = 1{,}728$
$13 \times 13 \times 13 = 2{,}197$
$14 \times 14 \times 14 = 2{,}744$
$15 \times 15 \times 15 = 3{,}375$

 ENGLISH

INDEFINITE PRONOUNS

all
another
any
anybody
anyone
anything
both
each
either

 HISTORY 110

Tell me about the French Revolution.
In 1789, the French Revolution began when citizens stormed the Bastille and fought for the Declaration of the Rights of Man. Later, during the Reign of Terror, the aristocrats' heads were removed by the guillotine.

 LATIN

FIRST CONJUGATION ENDINGS FUTURE PERFECT TENSE

SINGULAR		
____ erō	I shall have ____ed
____ eris	you will have ____ed
____ erit	he, she, it had ____ed

PLURAL		
____ erimus	we shall have ____ed
____ eritis	you will have ____ed
____ erint	they will have ____ed

 **TIMELINE**

Classical Acts & Facts® History Cards

71 Norman Conquest and Feudalism in Europe
72 The Crusades
73 Zimbabwe and Early Mali in Africa
74 Aztecs of Mesoamerica
75 Francis of Assisi and Thomas Aquinas
76 Japan's Shoguns
77 Incas of South America

 GEOGRAPHY

EUROPE AND ASIA

Moscow
Kiev
Russia
Siberia
Ukraine

 SCIENCE 18

Classical Acts & Facts® Science Cycle 2

What are the phases of the moon?
new
crescent
quarter
gibbous
full

PRESENTATION NOTES

 Recite timeline backwards *and* forwards.

 HANDS-ON

FINE ARTS

Note Names and Scales (see pages 98–101)

SCIENCE

Solar System Model (see page 193)

 *Memoria*

MATH

TEASPOONS AND TABLESPOONS

3 teaspoons (tsp.) =
1 tablespoon (tbsp.)

2 tablespoons (tbsp.) =
1 fluid ounce (fl. oz.)

 LATIN

FIRST CONJUGATION ENDINGS
FUTURE PERFECT TENSE

SINGULAR

_____ erō	I shall have _____ed
_____ eris	you will have _____ed
_____ erit	he, she, it had _____ed

PLURAL

_____ erimus	we shall have _____ed
_____ eritis	you will have _____ed
_____ erint	they will have _____ed

 SCIENCE 19

Classical Acts & Facts® Science Cycle 2

What are some other bodies in our solar system?

asteroids
meteoroids
meteorites
comets

 ENGLISH

INDEFINITE PRONOUNS

everybody
everyone
everything
few
many
more
most
neither

TIMELINE

Classical Acts & Facts® History Cards

78 Genghis Khan Rules the Mongols
79 England's Magna Carta
80 Ottoman Empire
81 Marco Polo's Journey to China
82 The Hundred Years' War and Black Death
83 The Renaissance
84 China's Ming Dynasty

PRESENTATION NOTES

 Choose a series of history sentences and create a history story.

 HISTORY 113

Tell me about the Battle of Waterloo.

Napoleon Bonaparte of the French Empire was defeated at the Battle of Waterloo by British General Wellington and his allies soon after the War of 1812 in the United States.

 GEOGRAPHY

EASTERN EUROPEAN SEAS

White Sea
Barents Sea
Black Sea
Caspian Sea
Aral Sea

 HANDS-ON

FINE ARTS

Review and Celebration (see pages 102–103)

SCIENCE

Constellations (see page 194)

Memoria
Who are some mentors you value?

WEEK 13

MATH

LIQUID EQUIVALENTS
8 fluid ounces (fl. oz.) = 1 cup (c.)

2 cups (c.) = 1 pint (pt.)

2 pints (pt.) = 1 quart (qt.)

4 quarts (qt.) = 1 gallon (gal.)

LATIN

**FIRST CONJUGATION ENDINGS
PRESENT TENSE**

SINGULAR
____ ō   I ____
____ s   you ____
____ t   he, she, it ____

PLURAL
____ mus   we ____
____ tis   you ____
____ nt   they ____

SCIENCE   20

Classical Acts & Facts® Science Cycle 2

What are some names of U.S. space missions?
Mercury
Gemini
Apollo
Shuttle

ENGLISH

INDEFINITE PRONOUNS
nobody
none
one
other
several
some
somebody
someone
such

 TIMELINE

Classical Acts & Facts® History Cards

85   AGE OF EXPLORATION
86   Prince Henry Founds School of Navigation
87   Slave Trade in Africa
88   Gutenberg's Printing Press
89   Songhai in Africa
90   Czar Ivan the Great of Russia
91   The Spanish Inquisition

PRESENTATION NOTES

 Use a highlighter to mark nouns in the history sentences.

HISTORY   106

Tell me about the Industrial Revolution.
Watt's steam engine, Cartwright's power loom, and Whitney's cotton gin spurred the Industrial Revolution that began in the 1760s.

GEOGRAPHY

NORTHERN EUROPEAN COUNTRIES
Norway
Sweden
Finland
Denmark

HANDS-ON   16

FINE ARTS
Introduction to Great Artists (see pages 104–105, 182)
Rembrandt (see page 183)

SCIENCE
Spoon Bell (#161)
Humming Glass (#162)

Memoria

MATH

LINEAR EQUIVALENTS
2.54 centimeters (cm) = 1 inch (in.)

12 inches (in.) = 1 foot (ft.)

5,280 feet (ft.) = 1 mile (mi.)

1 kilometer (km) = ⅝ mile (mi.)

 LATIN

FIRST CONJUGATION ENDINGS
PRESENT TENSE

SINGULAR
_____ ō   I _____
_____ s   you _____
_____ t   he, she, it _____

PLURAL
_____ mus   we _____
_____ tis   you _____
_____ nt   they _____

 SCIENCE

Classical Acts & Facts® Science Cycle 2

What are the states of matter?
solid
liquid
gas
plasma

 ENGLISH

AN ADVERB
An **adverb** modifies a verb, adjective, or another adverb—and answers the questions:
How? When? Where? and Why?

TIMELINE

Classical Acts & Facts® History Cards

92   Columbus Sails to the Caribbean
93   AGE OF ABSOLUTE MONARCHS
94   Protestant Reformation
95   Spanish Conquistadors in the Americas
96   Calvin's *Institutes of the Christian Religion*
97   Council of Trent
98   Baroque Period of the Arts

PRESENTATION NOTES

 Review Cycle 3 Latin.

 HISTORY 136

Tell me about World War I leaders.
Clemenceau of France, Lloyd George of England, Nicholas II of Russia, Wilhelm II of Germany, and Wilson of the United States were leaders during World War I, which started in 1914 and ended in 1918.

 **GEOGRAPHY**

BALTIC EUROPE
Estonia
Latvia
Lithuania
Poland
Belarus

 HANDS-ON 18

FINE ARTS
Gainsborough (see page 183)

SCIENCE
Cold Foot (#165)
Pepper Run (#171)

 *Memoria*
Describe God's goodness to your family.

WEEK 15

MEMORY WORK

 MATH

METRIC MEASUREMENTS

10 millimeters (mm) = 1 centimeter (cm)

100 centimeters (cm) = 1 meter (m)

1,000 meters (m) = 1 kilometer (km)

 LATIN

FIRST CONJUGATION ENDINGS IMPERFECT TENSE

SINGULAR
- ____ bam — I was ____ing
- ____ bās — you were ____ing
- ____ bat — he, she, it was ____ing

PLURAL
- ____ bāmus — we were ____ing
- ____ bātis — you were ____ing
- ____ bant — they were ____ing

 SCIENCE 23

Classical Acts & Facts® Science Cycle 2

What are two forms of energy?
kinetic
potential

 ENGLISH

FOUR PURPOSES OF SENTENCES
declarative
exclamatory
interrogative
imperative

TIMELINE

Classical Acts & Facts® History Cards

99 Japan's Isolation
100 Jamestown and Plymouth Colony Founded
101 AGE OF ENLIGHTENMENT
102 Hudson's Bay Company
103 First Great Awakening
104 Classical Period of the Arts
105 The Seven Years' War

PRESENTATION NOTES

 Review Cycle 1 history.

 HISTORY 136

Tell me about World War I countries.
During World War I, Great Britain, France, and Russia were Allies and fought against Austria-Hungary and Germany, which were called the Central Powers. In 1917, the United States entered the war, assisting the Allies.

 GEOGRAPHY

THE LEVANT
Turkey
Cyprus
Syria
Iraq
Iran

 HANDS-ON 26

FINE ARTS
Degas (see page 183)

SCIENCE
Bottle Organ (#164)

Memoria

MATH

AREA OF A RECTANGLE

The area of a rectangle equals length times width.

 LATIN

FIRST CONJUGATION ENDINGS
IMPERFECT TENSE

SINGULAR	____ bam	I was ____ing
	____ bās	you were ____ing
	____ bat	he, she, it was ____ing
PLURAL	____ bāmus	we were ____ing
	____ bātis	you were ____ing
	____ bant	they were ____ing

 SCIENCE 25

Classical Acts & Facts® Science Cycle 2

What is Newton's first law of motion?
Newton's first law of motion states that an object at rest tends to remain at rest and an object in motion tends to continue moving in a straight line at constant speed unless an outside force acts upon it.

 ENGLISH

A VERB

A **verb** is a word that asserts an action, shows a state of being, links two words together, or helps another verb.

TIMELINE

Classical Acts & Facts® History Cards

106 AGE OF INDUSTRY
107 James Cook Sails to Australia and Antarctica
108 American Revolution and Gen. George Washington
109 Madison's Constitution and the Bill of Rights
110 French Revolution
111 Second Great Awakening
112 Louisiana Purchase and Lewis and Clark Expedition

PRESENTATION NOTES

 Categorize timeline cards by continent.

 HISTORY 141

Tell me about how World War II began.
World War II began in 1939 when Hitler invaded Poland. Two engagements that helped the United States win the Pacific front were defeating Japan at the Battle of Midway and dropping atomic bombs on Hiroshima and Nagasaki in 1945.

GEOGRAPHY

BALKANS
Greece
Albania
Bulgaria
Slovenia
Romania

HANDS-ON 28

FINE ARTS
Monet (see page 184)

SCIENCE
Shape Up (#189)
Breakthrough (#190)

What are you learning about yourself?

MATH

AREA OF A SQUARE
The area of a square equals length of its side squared.

LATIN

FIRST CONJUGATION ENDINGS FUTURE TENSE

SINGULAR	____ bō	I shall ____
	____ bis	you will ____
	____ bit	he, she, it will ____
PLURAL	____ bimus	we shall ____
	____ bitis	you will ____
	____ bunt	they will ____

SCIENCE

Classical Acts & Facts® Science Cycle 2

What is Newton's second law of motion?
Newton's second law of motion states that force equals mass times acceleration.

$$F = ma$$

ENGLISH

A NOUN
A **noun** names a person, place, thing, activity, or idea.

TIMELINE

Classical Acts & Facts® History Cards

113 Napoleon Crowned Emperor of France
114 Liberation of South America
115 The War of 1812
116 The Missouri Compromise
117 Immigrants Flock to America
118 The Monroe Doctrine
119 Romantic Period of the Arts

PRESENTATION NOTES

 In ten minutes, draw as much of the world as you can remember, with locations and features.

HISTORY 141

Tell me about World War II leaders.
World War II AXIS leaders were: Hitler of Germany, Tojo of Japan, and Mussolini of Italy. World War II Allied leaders were: Churchill of England, Roosevelt, Eisenhower, and MacArthur of the United States, and Stalin of the USSR.

GEOGRAPHY

CENTRAL EUROPEAN COUNTRIES
Netherlands
Belgium
Luxembourg
Germany
Switzerland

HANDS-ON 30

FINE ARTS
Morisot (see page 184)

SCIENCE
Energy Change (#174)
Snap! (#177)

Memoria

MATH

AREA OF A TRIANGLE
The area of a triangle equals one-half base times height.

 LATIN

FIRST CONJUGATION ENDINGS
FUTURE TENSE

SINGULAR	____ bō	I shall ____
	____ bis	you will ____
	____ bit	he, she, it will ____
PLURAL	____ bimus	we shall ____
	____ bitis	you will ____
	____ bunt	they will ____

 SCIENCE CYCLE 2 27

Classical Acts & Facts® Science Cycle 2

What is Newton's third law of motion?
Newton's third law of motion states that for every action, there is an equal and opposite reaction.

 ENGLISH

FIVE CASES OF NOUNS
subject
direct object
indirect object
object of the preposition
possessive

 TIMELINE

Classical Acts & Facts® History Cards

120 Cherokee Trail of Tears
121 U.S. Westward Expansion
122 Marx Publishes *The Communist Manifesto*
123 The Compromise of 1850 and the *Dred Scott* Decision
124 U.S. Restores Trade with Japan
125 British Queen Victoria's Rule Over India
126 Darwin Publishes *The Origin of Species*

PRESENTATION NOTES

 Recite Latin endings by recalling with a pronoun (e.g., first conjugation imperfect tense singular he, she, it).

 HISTORY 143

Tell me about the United Nations.
In 1945, after the League of Nations failed to prevent World War II, American President Roosevelt, British Prime Minister Churchill, and Soviet Premier Stalin began the United Nations.

 GEOGRAPHY

MORE CENTRAL EUROPEAN COUNTRIES
Italy
Austria
Hungary
Czechia
Slovakia

HANDS-ON 34

FINE ARTS
van Gogh (see page 184)

SCIENCE
Lifter (#184)
Ramp (#185)

Memoria
How did your parents contribute to your success?

MATH

AREA OF A CIRCLE
The area of a circle equals pi (3.14) times the radius squared.

LATIN

FIRST CONJUGATION ENDINGS PERFECT TENSE

SINGULAR	____ ī	I have ____ed
	____ istī	you have ____ed
	____ it	he, she, it has ____ed
PLURAL	____ imus	we have ____ed
	____ istis	you have ____ed
	____ ērunt	they have ____ed

SCIENCE

Classical Acts & Facts® Science Cycle 2

What is the first law of thermodynamics?
The first law of thermodynamics states that energy cannot be created or destroyed.

ENGLISH

A GERUND
A **gerund** is a present participle verb form used as a noun.

TIMELINE

Classical Acts & Facts® History Cards

127   Lincoln's War Between the States
128   Reconstruction of the Southern States
129   Dominion of Canada
130   Otto von Bismarck Unifies Germany
131   Boer Wars in Africa
132   The Spanish-American War
133   The Progressive Era

PRESENTATION NOTES

 Review Cycle 1 science.

HISTORY
 149

Tell me about the Korean War.
In 1950, General Douglas MacArthur led United Nations forces to stop communist North Korea from capturing all of South Korea during the Korean War.

GEOGRAPHY

SOUTHEASTERN ASIA
North Korea
South Korea
Taiwan
Philippines
Guam

HANDS-ON
 104

FINE ARTS
119
Composers and Orchestra Introduction (see pages 108–109, 185)
Classical and Romantic Periods (see page 186)

SCIENCE
Paper Airplanes (see page 195)

Memoria

MATH

CIRCUMFERENCE OF A CIRCLE
The circumference of a circle equals two times pi (3.14) times the radius.

LATIN

FIRST CONJUGATION ENDINGS
PERFECT TENSE

SINGULAR	____ ī	I have ____ed
	____ istī	you have ____ed
	____ it	he, she, it has ____ed
PLURAL	____ imus	we have ____ed
	____ istis	you have ____ed
	____ ērunt	they have ____ed

SCIENCE

Classical Acts & Facts® Science Cycle 2

What is the second law of thermodynamics?
Often called the law of entropy, the second law of thermodynamics explains why heat flows from an area of higher temperature to an area of lower temperature.

ENGLISH

AN APPOSITIVE
An **appositive** is a noun or pronoun directly beside another noun that explains or identifies it.

TIMELINE

Classical Acts & Facts® History Cards

134 Australia Becomes a Commonwealth
135 Mexican Revolution
136 World War I and President Wilson
137 Lenin and the Bolshevik Revolution in Russia
138 U.S. Evangelist Billy Graham
139 Modern Period of the Arts
140 The Great Depression and the New Deal

PRESENTATION NOTES

 Review Cycle 1 English.

HISTORY 153

Tell me about the Vietnam War.
In 1965, President Johnson sent U.S. troops to stop communist North Vietnam from capturing all of South Vietnam during the Vietnam War.

GEOGRAPHY

SOUTH CENTRAL ASIA
Laos
Thailand
Cambodia
North Vietnam
South Vietnam

HANDS-ON 21

FINE ARTS

Beethoven *Symphony no. 5* (see page 186)

SCIENCE

Straw Bridge Construction (see page 196)

Memoria
What did you struggle with this week?

MATH

The Associative Law for addition states:
$(a + b) + c = a + (b + c)$

The Associative Law for multiplication states:
$(a \times b) \times c = a \times (b \times c)$

LATIN

FIRST CONJUGATION ENDINGS PLUPERFECT TENSE

SINGULAR
____ eram	I had ____ed
____ erās	you had ____ed
____ erat	he, she, it had ____ed

PLURAL
____ erāmus	we had ____ed
____ erātis	you had ____ed
____ erant	they had ____ed

SCIENCE

Classical Acts & Facts® Science Cycle 2

What is the third law of thermodynamics?
The third law of thermodynamics explains that it is impossible to reach the state of absolute zero temperature.

ENGLISH

A CONJUNCTION
A **conjunction** is a word used to connect words, phrases, or clauses together.

TIMELINE

Classical Acts & Facts® History Cards

141 World War II and President Franklin D. Roosevelt
142 Stalin of the USSR and the Katyn Massacre
143 The United Nations Formed
144 The Cold War
145 Gandhi and India's Independence
146 Jewish State Established
147 Mao and Communist Victory in China

PRESENTATION NOTES

 Review Cycle 1 geography.

HISTORY

 144

Tell me about the end of the Cold War.
In the 1980s, British Prime Minister Margaret Thatcher and American President Ronald Reagan worked together to end the Cold War, lessen big government, and strengthen the conservative movement.

GEOGRAPHY

CENTRAL AMERICA
Guatemala
Belize
El Salvador
Honduras
Nicaragua

HANDS-ON 25

FINE ARTS

Brahms *Symphony no. 4* (see page 186)

SCIENCE

Tower Construction (see page 197)

Memoria

MATH

The Commutative Law
for addition states:
$a + b = b + a$

The Commutative Law
for multiplication states:
$a \times b = b \times a$

LATIN

FIRST CONJUGATION ENDINGS
PLUPERFECT TENSE

SINGULAR	____ eram	I had ____ed
	____ erās	you had ____ed
	____ erat	he, she, it had ____ed
PLURAL	____ erāmus	we had ____ed
	____ erātis	you had ____ed
	____ erant	they had ____ed

SCIENCE

CYCLE 2   32

Classical Acts & Facts® Science Cycle 2

What are some ways light is observed?
reflection
refraction
spectrum
wave
particle

ENGLISH

COORDINATING CONJUNCTIONS

F	for
A	and
N	nor
B	but
O	or
Y	yet
S	so

TIMELINE

Classical Acts & Facts® History Cards

148   North Atlantic Treaty Organization
149   The Korean War
150   Martin Luther King, Jr. and the Civil Rights Movement
151   Jim and Elisabeth Elliot, Missionaries to Ecuador
152   The Antarctic Treaty
153   The Vietnam War
154   U.S. Astronauts Walk on the Moon

PRESENTATION NOTES

 Substitute different numbers in the equation and calculate to prove commutative laws.

HISTORY   157

Tell me about the fall of communism.
In 1989, the communist dictators began to fall in Eastern Europe when Soviet General Secretary Gorbachev refused to send them military aid.

GEOGRAPHY

OCEANIA
Australia
Great Barrier Reef
New Zealand
Papua New Guinea
Indonesia

HANDS-ON   29

FINE ARTS

Dvořák "Serenade for Strings" (see page 186)

SCIENCE

Popsicle Stick Catapult (see page 198)

Memoria
How did your family grow this year?

MATH

The Distributive Law states:
$$a(b + c) = ab + ac$$

 LATIN

FIRST CONJUGATION ENDINGS
FUTURE PERFECT TENSE

SINGULAR	____ erō	I shall have ____ed
	____ eris	you will have ____ed
	____ erit	he, she, it had ____ed
PLURAL	____ erimus	we shall have ____ed
	____ eritis	you will have ____ed
	____ erint	they will have ____ed

 SCIENCE 33 CYCLE 2

Classical Acts & Facts® Science Cycle 2

How does heat flow?
radiation
conduction
convection

 ENGLISH

AN ADJECTIVE
An **adjective** modifies a noun or pronoun by describing, qualifying, or limiting—and answers the questions: What kind? How many? Which? Whose?

TIMELINE

Classical Acts & Facts® History Cards

155 AGE OF INFORMATION AND GLOBALIZATION
156 Watergate, President Nixon Resigns
157 Fall of Communism in Eastern Europe
158 European Union Formed
159 Apartheid Abolished in South Africa
160 September 11, 2001
161 Rising Tide of Freedom

PRESENTATION NOTES

 Review Cycle 1 Latin.

 HISTORY

Tell me about the Gulf War.
In 1990, President George H. W. Bush sent troops to the Persian Gulf to expel Iraqi leader Saddam Hussein from Kuwait during the Gulf War.

GEOGRAPHY

CENTRAL ASIA
Kazakhstan
Uzbekistan
Turkmenistan
Tajikistan
Kyrgyzstan

HANDS-ON

FINE ARTS
Orchestra Overview (see page 187)

SCIENCE
Egg Protector (see page 199)

MATH

The Identity Law
for addition states:
$$a + 0 = a$$

The Identity Law
for multiplication states:
$$a \times 1 = a$$

LATIN

FIRST CONJUGATION ENDINGS
FUTURE PERFECT TENSE

SINGULAR
____ erō	I shall have ____ed
____ eris	you will have ____ed
____ erit	he, she, it had ____ed

PLURAL
____ erimus	we shall have ____ed
____ eritis	you will have ____ed
____ erint	they will have ____ed

SCIENCE

Classical Acts & Facts® Science Cycle 2

What units are used to measure electricity?
ohms measure resistance
volts measure voltage
amps measure current
watts measure power

ENGLISH

AN INTERJECTION
An **interjection** is a word or phrase used as a strong expression of feeling or emotion.

TIMELINE

Classical Acts & Facts® History Cards

U.S. Presidents:
Washington, Adams, Jefferson, Madison, Monroe, Adams, Jackson, Van Buren, Harrison, Tyler, Polk, Taylor, Fillmore, Pierce, Buchanan, Lincoln, Johnson, Grant, Hayes, Garfield, Arthur, Cleveland, Harrison, Cleveland, McKinley, Roosevelt, Taft, Wilson, Harding, Coolidge, Hoover, Roosevelt, Truman, Eisenhower, Kennedy, Johnson, Nixon, Ford, Carter, Reagan, Bush, Clinton, Bush, Obama, Trump

PRESENTATION NOTES

Recite each president's first *and* last name. List the political party of each president. List the state in which each president was born.

HISTORY
 159

Tell me about the end of apartheid.
In 1994, South African President de Klerk allowed free elections. Nelson Mandela became South Africa's first black president, demonstrating apartheid was ending.

GEOGRAPHY

SOUTHERN AFRICA
South Africa
Lesotho
Botswana
Mozambique
Namibia

HANDS-ON

FINE ARTS
Orchestra Review and Celebration (see page 187)

SCIENCE
Outdoor Contest (see page 200)

Memoria
Celebrate!

1 1s and 2s

- $1 \times 1 = 1$
- $1 \times 2 = 2$
- $1 \times 3 = 3$
- $1 \times 4 = 4$
- $1 \times 5 = 5$
- $1 \times 6 = 6$
- $1 \times 7 = 7$
- $1 \times 8 = 8$
- $1 \times 9 = 9$
- $1 \times 10 = 10$
- $1 \times 11 = 11$
- $1 \times 12 = 12$
- $1 \times 13 = 13$
- $1 \times 14 = 14$
- $1 \times 15 = 15$
- $2 \times 1 = 2$
- $2 \times 2 = 4$
- $2 \times 3 = 6$
- $2 \times 4 = 8$
- $2 \times 5 = 10$
- $2 \times 6 = 12$
- $2 \times 7 = 14$
- $2 \times 8 = 16$
- $2 \times 9 = 18$
- $2 \times 10 = 20$
- $2 \times 11 = 22$
- $2 \times 12 = 24$
- $2 \times 13 = 26$
- $2 \times 14 = 28$
- $2 \times 15 = 30$

2 3s and 4s

- $3 \times 1 = 3$
- $3 \times 2 = 6$
- $3 \times 3 = 9$
- $3 \times 4 = 12$
- $3 \times 5 = 15$
- $3 \times 6 = 18$
- $3 \times 7 = 21$
- $3 \times 8 = 24$
- $3 \times 9 = 27$
- $3 \times 10 = 30$
- $3 \times 11 = 33$
- $3 \times 12 = 36$
- $3 \times 13 = 39$
- $3 \times 14 = 42$
- $3 \times 15 = 45$
- $4 \times 1 = 4$
- $4 \times 2 = 8$
- $4 \times 3 = 12$
- $4 \times 4 = 16$
- $4 \times 5 = 20$
- $4 \times 6 = 24$
- $4 \times 7 = 28$
- $4 \times 8 = 32$
- $4 \times 9 = 36$
- $4 \times 10 = 40$
- $4 \times 11 = 44$
- $4 \times 12 = 48$
- $4 \times 13 = 52$
- $4 \times 14 = 56$
- $4 \times 15 = 60$

3 5s and 6s

- $5 \times 1 = 5$
- $5 \times 2 = 10$
- $5 \times 3 = 15$
- $5 \times 4 = 20$
- $5 \times 5 = 25$
- $5 \times 6 = 30$
- $5 \times 7 = 35$
- $5 \times 8 = 40$
- $5 \times 9 = 45$
- $5 \times 10 = 50$
- $5 \times 11 = 55$
- $5 \times 12 = 60$
- $5 \times 13 = 65$
- $5 \times 14 = 70$
- $5 \times 15 = 75$
- $6 \times 1 = 6$
- $6 \times 2 = 12$
- $6 \times 3 = 18$
- $6 \times 4 = 24$
- $6 \times 5 = 30$
- $6 \times 6 = 36$
- $6 \times 7 = 42$
- $6 \times 8 = 48$
- $6 \times 9 = 54$
- $6 \times 10 = 60$
- $6 \times 11 = 66$
- $6 \times 12 = 72$
- $6 \times 13 = 78$
- $6 \times 14 = 84$
- $6 \times 15 = 90$

4 7s and 8s

- $7 \times 1 = 7$
- $7 \times 2 = 14$
- $7 \times 3 = 21$
- $7 \times 4 = 28$
- $7 \times 5 = 35$
- $7 \times 6 = 42$
- $7 \times 7 = 49$
- $7 \times 8 = 56$
- $7 \times 9 = 63$
- $7 \times 10 = 70$
- $7 \times 11 = 77$
- $7 \times 12 = 84$
- $7 \times 13 = 91$
- $7 \times 14 = 98$
- $7 \times 15 = 105$
- $8 \times 1 = 8$
- $8 \times 2 = 16$
- $8 \times 3 = 24$
- $8 \times 4 = 32$
- $8 \times 5 = 40$
- $8 \times 6 = 48$
- $8 \times 7 = 56$
- $8 \times 8 = 64$
- $8 \times 9 = 72$
- $8 \times 10 = 80$
- $8 \times 11 = 88$
- $8 \times 12 = 96$
- $8 \times 13 = 104$
- $8 \times 14 = 112$
- $8 \times 15 = 120$

5 9s and 10s

- $9 \times 1 = 9$
- $9 \times 2 = 18$
- $9 \times 3 = 27$
- $9 \times 4 = 36$
- $9 \times 5 = 45$
- $9 \times 6 = 54$
- $9 \times 7 = 63$
- $9 \times 8 = 72$
- $9 \times 9 = 81$
- $9 \times 10 = 90$
- $9 \times 11 = 99$
- $9 \times 12 = 108$
- $9 \times 13 = 117$
- $9 \times 14 = 126$
- $9 \times 15 = 135$
- $10 \times 1 = 10$
- $10 \times 2 = 20$
- $10 \times 3 = 30$
- $10 \times 4 = 40$
- $10 \times 5 = 50$
- $10 \times 6 = 60$
- $10 \times 7 = 70$
- $10 \times 8 = 80$
- $10 \times 9 = 90$
- $10 \times 10 = 100$
- $10 \times 11 = 110$
- $10 \times 12 = 120$
- $10 \times 13 = 130$
- $10 \times 14 = 140$
- $10 \times 15 = 150$

6 11s and 12s

- $11 \times 1 = 11$
- $11 \times 2 = 22$
- $11 \times 3 = 33$
- $11 \times 4 = 44$
- $11 \times 5 = 55$
- $11 \times 6 = 66$
- $11 \times 7 = 77$
- $11 \times 8 = 88$
- $11 \times 9 = 99$
- $11 \times 10 = 110$
- $11 \times 11 = 121$
- $11 \times 12 = 132$
- $11 \times 13 = 143$
- $11 \times 14 = 154$
- $11 \times 15 = 165$
- $12 \times 1 = 12$
- $12 \times 2 = 24$
- $12 \times 3 = 36$
- $12 \times 4 = 48$
- $12 \times 5 = 60$
- $12 \times 6 = 72$
- $12 \times 7 = 84$
- $12 \times 8 = 96$
- $12 \times 9 = 108$
- $12 \times 10 = 120$
- $12 \times 11 = 132$
- $12 \times 12 = 144$
- $12 \times 13 = 156$
- $12 \times 14 = 168$
- $12 \times 15 = 180$

7 · 13s

- [ ] $13 \times 1 = 13$
- [ ] $13 \times 2 = 26$
- [ ] $13 \times 3 = 39$
- [ ] $13 \times 4 = 52$
- [ ] $13 \times 5 = 65$
- [ ] $13 \times 6 = 78$
- [ ] $13 \times 7 = 91$
- [ ] $13 \times 8 = 104$
- [ ] $13 \times 9 = 117$
- [ ] $13 \times 10 = 130$
- [ ] $13 \times 11 = 143$
- [ ] $13 \times 12 = 156$
- [ ] $13 \times 13 = 169$
- [ ] $13 \times 14 = 182$
- [ ] $13 \times 15 = 195$

8 · 14s

- [ ] $14 \times 1 = 14$
- [ ] $14 \times 2 = 28$
- [ ] $14 \times 3 = 42$
- [ ] $14 \times 4 = 56$
- [ ] $14 \times 5 = 70$
- [ ] $14 \times 6 = 84$
- [ ] $14 \times 7 = 98$
- [ ] $14 \times 8 = 112$
- [ ] $14 \times 9 = 126$
- [ ] $14 \times 10 = 140$
- [ ] $14 \times 11 = 154$
- [ ] $14 \times 12 = 168$
- [ ] $14 \times 13 = 182$
- [ ] $14 \times 14 = 196$
- [ ] $14 \times 15 = 210$

9 · 15s

- [ ] $15 \times 1 = 15$
- [ ] $15 \times 2 = 30$
- [ ] $15 \times 3 = 45$
- [ ] $15 \times 4 = 60$
- [ ] $15 \times 5 = 75$
- [ ] $15 \times 6 = 90$
- [ ] $15 \times 7 = 105$
- [ ] $15 \times 8 = 120$
- [ ] $15 \times 9 = 135$
- [ ] $15 \times 10 = 150$
- [ ] $15 \times 11 = 165$
- [ ] $15 \times 12 = 180$
- [ ] $15 \times 13 = 195$
- [ ] $15 \times 14 = 210$
- [ ] $15 \times 15 = 225$

10 · SQUARES

- [ ] $1 \times 1 = 1$
- [ ] $2 \times 2 = 4$
- [ ] $3 \times 3 = 9$
- [ ] $4 \times 4 = 16$
- [ ] $5 \times 5 = 25$
- [ ] $6 \times 6 = 36$
- [ ] $7 \times 7 = 49$
- [ ] $8 \times 8 = 64$
- [ ] $9 \times 9 = 81$
- [ ] $10 \times 10 = 100$
- [ ] $11 \times 11 = 121$
- [ ] $12 \times 12 = 144$
- [ ] $13 \times 13 = 169$
- [ ] $14 \times 14 = 196$
- [ ] $15 \times 15 = 225$

11 · CUBES

- [ ] $1 \times 1 \times 1 = 1$
- [ ] $2 \times 2 \times 2 = 8$
- [ ] $3 \times 3 \times 3 = 27$
- [ ] $4 \times 4 \times 4 = 64$
- [ ] $5 \times 5 \times 5 = 125$
- [ ] $6 \times 6 \times 6 = 216$
- [ ] $7 \times 7 \times 7 = 343$
- [ ] $8 \times 8 \times 8 = 512$
- [ ] $9 \times 9 \times 9 = 729$
- [ ] $10 \times 10 \times 10 = 1,000$
- [ ] $11 \times 11 \times 11 = 1,331$
- [ ] $12 \times 12 \times 12 = 1,728$
- [ ] $13 \times 13 \times 13 = 2,197$
- [ ] $14 \times 14 \times 14 = 2,744$
- [ ] $15 \times 15 \times 15 = 3,375$

12 · TEASPOONS AND TABLESPOONS

- [ ] 3 teaspoons equals 1 tablespoon
- [ ] 2 tablespoons equals 1 fluid ounce

13 · LIQUID EQUIVALENTS

- [ ] 8 fluid ounces equals 1 cup
- [ ] 2 cups equals 1 pint
- [ ] 2 pints equals 1 quart
- [ ] 4 quarts equals 1 gallon

14 · LINEAR EQUIVALENTS

- [ ] 2.54 centimeters equals 1 inch
- [ ] 12 inches equals 1 foot
- [ ] 5,280 feet equals 1 mile
- [ ] 1 kilometer equals ⅝ mile

15 · METRIC MEASUREMENTS

- [ ] 10 millimeters equals 1 centimeter
- [ ] 100 centimeters equals 1 meter
- [ ] 1000 meters equals 1 kilometer

16 · AREA OF A RECTANGLE

- [ ] The area of a rectangle equals length times width.

17 · AREA OF A SQUARE

- [ ] The area of a square equals the length of its side squared.

18 · AREA OF A TRIANGLE

- [ ] The area of a triangle equals one-half base times height.

19 · AREA OF A CIRCLE

- [ ] The area of a circle equals pi (3.14) times the radius squared.

20 · CIRCUMFERENCE OF A CIRCLE

- [ ] The circumference of a circle equals 2 times pi (3.14) times the radius.

21 · ASSOCIATIVE LAW

- [ ] The Associative Law for addition states: $(a + b) + c = a + (b + c)$
- [ ] The Associative Law for multiplication states: $(a \times b) \times c = a \times (b \times c)$

22 · COMMUTATIVE LAW

- [ ] The Commutative Law for addition states: $a + b = b + a$
- [ ] The Commutative Law for multiplication states: $a \times b = b \times a$

23 · DISTRIBUTIVE LAW

- [ ] The Distributive Law states: $a(b + c) = ab + ac$

24 · IDENTITY LAW

- [ ] The Identity Law for addition states: $a + 0 = a$
- [ ] The Identity Law for multiplication states: $a \times 1 = a$

1–2	FIRST CONJUGATION ENDINGS PRESENT TENSE	
☐	SINGULAR	____ ō
☐		____ s
☐		____ t
☐	PLURAL	____ mus
☐		____ tis
☐		____ nt

3–4	FIRST CONJUGATION ENDINGS IMPERFECT TENSE	
☐	SINGULAR	____ bam
☐		____ bās
☐		____ bat
☐	PLURAL	____ bāmus
☐		____ bātis
☐		____ bant

5–6	FIRST CONJUGATION ENDINGS FUTURE TENSE	
☐	SINGULAR	____ bō
☐		____ bis
☐		____ bit
☐	PLURAL	____ bimus
☐		____ bitis
☐		____ bunt

7–8	FIRST CONJUGATION ENDINGS PERFECT TENSE	
☐	SINGULAR	____ ī
☐		____ istī
☐		____ it
☐	PLURAL	____ imus
☐		____ istis
☐		____ ērunt

9–10	FIRST CONJUGATION ENDINGS PLUPERFECT TENSE	
☐	SINGULAR	____ eram
☐		____ erās
☐		____ erat
☐	PLURAL	____ erāmus
☐		____ erātis
☐		____ erant

11–12	FIRST CONJUGATION ENDINGS FUTURE PERFECT TENSE	
☐	SINGULAR	____ erō
☐		____ eris
☐		____ erit
☐	PLURAL	____ erimus
☐		____ eritis
☐		____ erint

13–14	FIRST CONJUGATION ENDINGS PRESENT TENSE
☐	SINGULAR ____ ō
☐	____ s
☐	____ t
☐	PLURAL ____ mus
☐	____ tis
☐	____ nt

15–16	FIRST CONJUGATION ENDINGS IMPERFECT TENSE
☐	SINGULAR ____ bam
☐	____ bās
☐	____ bat
☐	PLURAL ____ bāmus
☐	____ bātis
☐	____ bant

17–18	FIRST CONJUGATION ENDINGS FUTURE TENSE
☐	SINGULAR ____ bō
☐	____ bis
☐	____ bit
☐	PLURAL ____ bimus
☐	____ bitis
☐	____ bunt

19–20	FIRST CONJUGATION ENDINGS PERFECT TENSE
☐	SINGULAR ____ ī
☐	____ istī
☐	____ it
☐	PLURAL ____ imus
☐	____ istis
☐	____ ērunt

21–22	FIRST CONJUGATION ENDINGS PLUPERFECT TENSE
☐	SINGULAR ____ eram
☐	____ erās
☐	____ erat
☐	PLURAL ____ erāmus
☐	____ erātis
☐	____ erant

23–24	FIRST CONJUGATION ENDINGS FUTURE PERFECT TENSE
☐	SINGULAR ____ erō
☐	____ eris
☐	____ erit
☐	PLURAL ____ erimus
☐	____ eritis
☐	____ erint

1 What occurred on each day of creation?

- [ ] 1 earth, space, time, light
- [ ] 2 atmosphere
- [ ] 3 dry land, plants
- [ ] 4 sun, moon, stars
- [ ] 5 fish, sea creatures, birds
- [ ] 6 land animals, Adam, Eve

2 What are some land biomes?

- [ ] grassland
- [ ] desert
- [ ] scrubland
- [ ] tundra
- [ ] deciduous forest
- [ ] coniferous forest
- [ ] tropical rainforest

3 What are three types of consumers?

- [ ] herbivore
- [ ] carnivore
- [ ] omnivore

4 What are some parts of the food chain?

- [ ] producer
- [ ] consumer
- [ ] decomposer

5 What are some cycles in nature?

- [ ] water cycle
- [ ] carbon and oxygen cycle
- [ ] nitrogen cycle

6 How do animals react to environmental change?

- [ ] adapt
- [ ] migrate
- [ ] hibernate

7 What are six forms of pollution?

- [ ] noise
- [ ] air
- [ ] water
- [ ] land
- [ ] thermal
- [ ] radioactive

8 What are some aquatic biomes?

- [ ] ponds and lakes
- [ ] streams and rivers
- [ ] wetlands and estuaries
- [ ] oceans and seas

9 What are some parts of the sun?

- [ ] core
- [ ] radiative zone
- [ ] convective zone
- [ ] sunspots
- [ ] photosphere
- [ ] solar flare
- [ ] corona

10 What are the names of the planets?

- [ ] Mercury
- [ ] Venus
- [ ] Earth
- [ ] Mars
- [ ] Jupiter
- [ ] Saturn
- [ ] Uranus
- [ ] Neptune

11 What are the phases of the moon?

- [ ] new
- [ ] crescent
- [ ] quarter
- [ ] gibbous
- [ ] full

12 What are some other bodies in our solar system?

- [ ] asteroids
- [ ] meteroids
- [ ] meteorites
- [ ] comets

13 What are some names of U.S. space missions?

☐ Mercury

☐ Gemini

☐ Apollo

☐ Shuttle

14 What are the states of matter?

☐ solid

☐ liquid

☐ gas

☐ plasma

15 What are two forms of energy?

☐ kinetic

☐ potential

16 What is Newton's first law of motion?

☐ Newton's first law of motion states that an object at rest tends to remain at rest and an object in motion tends to continue moving in a straight line at constant speed unless an outside force acts upon it.

17 What is Newton's second law of motion?

☐ Newton's second law of motion states that force equals mass times acceleration.
$$F = ma$$

18 What is Newton's third law of motion?

☐ Newton's third law of motion states that for every action, there is an equal and opposite reaction.

19 What is the first law of thermodynamics?

☐ The first law of thermodynamics states that energy cannot be created or destroyed.

20 What is the second law of thermodynamics?

☐ Often called the law of entropy, the second law of thermodynamics explains why heat flows from an area of higher temperature to an area of lower temperature.

21 What is the third law of thermodynamics?

☐ The third law of thermodynamics explains that it is impossible to reach the state of absolute zero temperature.

22 What are some ways light is observed?

☐ reflection

☐ refraction

☐ spectrum

☐ wave

☐ particle

23 How does heat flow?

☐ radiation

☐ conduction

☐ convection

24 What units are used to measure electricity?

☐ ohms measure resistance

☐ volts measure voltage

☐ amps measure current

☐ watts measure power

1 PARTS OF SPEECH

- [ ] noun
- [ ] pronoun
- [ ] verb
- [ ] adverb
- [ ] conjunction
- [ ] interjection
- [ ] preposition
- [ ] adjective

2 A PRONOUN

- [ ] A **pronoun** replaces a noun in order to avoid repetition.

3 PRONOUN ORDER

- [ ] 1st person singular
- [ ] 2nd person singular
- [ ] 3rd person singular
- [ ] 1st person plural
- [ ] 2nd person plural
- [ ] 3rd person plural

4 NOMINATIVE PRONOUNS

- [ ] I
- [ ] you
- [ ] he/she/it
- [ ] we
- [ ] you
- [ ] they

5 OBJECTIVE PRONOUNS

- [ ] me
- [ ] you
- [ ] him/her/it
- [ ] us
- [ ] you
- [ ] them

6 POSSESSIVE PRONOUNS

- [ ] mine
- [ ] yours
- [ ] his/hers/its
- [ ] ours
- [ ] yours
- [ ] theirs

7 POSSESSIVE PRONOUN ADJECTIVES

- [ ] my
- [ ] your
- [ ] his/her/its
- [ ] our
- [ ] your
- [ ] their

8 REFLEXIVE PRONOUNS

- [ ] myself
- [ ] yourself
- [ ] himself/herself/itself
- [ ] ourselves
- [ ] yourselves
- [ ] themselves

9 INTERROGATIVE PRONOUNS

- [ ] who
- [ ] whom
- [ ] whose
- [ ] which
- [ ] what

10 DEMONSTRATIVE PRONOUNS

- [ ] this
- [ ] that
- [ ] these
- [ ] those

11 INDEFINITE PRONOUNS

- [ ] all
- [ ] another
- [ ] any
- [ ] anybody
- [ ] anyone
- [ ] anything
- [ ] both
- [ ] each
- [ ] either

12 INDEFINITE PRONOUNS

- [ ] everybody
- [ ] everyone
- [ ] everything
- [ ] few
- [ ] many
- [ ] more
- [ ] most
- [ ] neither

13 INDEFINITE PRONOUNS

☐ nobody

☐ none

☐ one

☐ other

☐ several

☐ some

☐ somebody

☐ someone

☐ such

14 AN ADVERB

☐ An **adverb** modifies a verb, adjective, or another adverb—and answers the questions: How? When? Where? and Why?

15 FOUR PURPOSES OF SENTENCES

☐ declarative

☐ exclamatory

☐ interrogative

☐ imperative

16 A VERB

☐ A **verb** is a word that asserts an action, shows a state of being, links two words together, or helps another verb.

17 A NOUN

☐ A **noun** names a person, place, thing, activity, or idea.

18 FIVE CASES OF NOUNS

☐ subject

☐ direct object

☐ indirect object

☐ object of the preposition

☐ possessive

19 A GERUND

☐ A **gerund** is a present participle verb form used as a noun.

20 AN APPOSITIVE

☐ An **appositive** is a noun or pronoun directly beside another noun that explains or identifies it.

21 A CONJUNCTION

☐ A **conjunction** is a word used to connect words, phrases, or clauses together.

22 COORDINATING CONJUNCTIONS

☐ **F** for

☐ **A** and

☐ **N** nor

☐ **B** but

☐ **O** or

☐ **Y** yet

☐ **S** so

23 AN ADJECTIVE

☐ An **adjective** modifies a noun or pronoun by describing, qualifying, or limiting—and answers the questions: What kind? How many? Which? Whose?

24 AN INTERJECTION

☐ An **interjection** is a word or phrase used as a strong expression of feeling or emotion.

WEEK 1	☐ 1	**AGE OF ANCIENT EMPIRES**
	☐ 2	Creation and the Fall
	☐ 3	The Flood and the Tower of Babel
	☐ 4	Mesopotamia and Sumer
	☐ 5	Egyptians
	☐ 6	Indus River Valley Civilization
	☐ 7	Minoans and Mycenaeans
WEEK 2	☐ 8	Seven Wonders of the Ancient World
	☐ 9	Patriarchs of Israel
	☐ 10	Hittites and Canaanites
	☐ 11	Kush
	☐ 12	Assyrians
	☐ 13	Babylonians
	☐ 14	China's Shang Dynasty
WEEK 3	☐ 15	Hinduism in India
	☐ 16	Phoenicians and the Alphabet
	☐ 17	Olmecs of Mesoamerica
	☐ 18	Israelite Exodus and Desert Wandering
	☐ 19	Israelite Conquest and Judges
	☐ 20	Greek Dark Ages
	☐ 21	Israel's United Kingdom
WEEK 4	☐ 22	Early Native Americans
	☐ 23	Israel Divides into Two Kingdoms
	☐ 24	Homer and Hesiod
	☐ 25	Rome Founded by Romulus and Remus
	☐ 26	Israel Falls to Assyria
	☐ 27	Assyria Falls to Babylon
	☐ 28	Lao-Tzu, Confucius, Buddha

WEEK 5	☐ 29	Judah falls to Babylon, Temple Destroyed
	☐ 30	Babylon Falls to Persia
	☐ 31	Jews Return and Rebuild the Temple
	☐ 32	Roman Republic
	☐ 33	Golden Age of Greece
	☐ 34	Peloponnesian Wars
	☐ 35	Persia Falls to Alexander the Great
WEEK 6	☐ 36	India's Mauryan Empire
	☐ 37	Mayans of Mesoamerica
	☐ 38	Punic Wars
	☐ 39	Rome Conquers Greece
	☐ 40	Roman Dictator Julius Caesar
	☐ 41	Caesar Augustus and the Pax Romana
	☐ 42	John the Baptist
WEEK 7	☐ 43	Jesus the Messiah
	☐ 44	Pentecost and the Early Church
	☐ 45	Persecution Spreads the Gospel
	☐ 46	Herod's Temple Destroyed by Titus
	☐ 47	Diocletian Divides the Roman Empire
	☐ 48	Constantine Legalizes Christianity
	☐ 49	India's Gupta Dynasty
WEEK 8	☐ 50	Council of Nicea
	☐ 51	Augustine of Hippo
	☐ 52	Jerome Completes the Vulgate
	☐ 53	Visigoths Sack Rome
	☐ 54	**THE MIDDLE AGES**
	☐ 55	Council of Chalcedon
	☐ 56	Western Roman Empire Falls to Barbarians

WEEK 9	☐ 57	Byzantine Emperor Justinian
	☐ 58	Benedict and Monasticism
	☐ 59	Muhammad Founds Islam
	☐ 60	Zanj and Early Ghana in Africa
	☐ 61	Franks Defeat Muslims at the Battle of Tours
	☐ 62	Golden Age of Islam
	☐ 63	Vikings Raid and Trade
WEEK 10	☐ 64	Japan's Heian Period
	☐ 65	Charlemagne Crowned Emperor of Europe
	☐ 66	Alfred the Great of England
	☐ 67	Erik the Red and Leif Eriksson, Norse Explorers
	☐ 68	Vladimir I of Kiev
	☐ 69	Byzantine Emperor Basil II
	☐ 70	East-West Schism of the Church
WEEK 11	☐ 71	Norman Conquest and Feudalism in Europe
	☐ 72	The Crusades
	☐ 73	Zimbabwe and Early Mali in Africa
	☐ 74	Aztecs of Mesoamerica
	☐ 75	Francis of Assisi and Thomas Aquinas
	☐ 76	Japan's Shoguns
	☐ 77	Incas of South America
WEEK 12	☐ 78	Genghis Khan Rules the Mongols
	☐ 79	England's Magna Carta
	☐ 80	The Ottoman Empire
	☐ 81	Marco Polo's Journey to China
	☐ 82	The Hundred Years' War and Black Death
	☐ 83	The Renaissance
	☐ 84	China's Ming Dynasty

WEEK 24 U.S. PRESIDENTS

162	Washington Adams Jefferson Madison	163	Monroe Adams Jackson Van Buren	164	Harrison Tyler Polk Taylor	165	Fillmore Pierce Buchanan Lincoln	166	Johnson Grant Hayes Garfield	167	Arthur Cleveland Harrison Cleveland

WEEK 13

- ☐ 85 **AGE OF EXPLORATION**
- ☐ 86 Prince Henry Founds School of Navigation
- ☐ 87 Slave Trade in Africa
- ☐ 88 Gutenberg's Printing Press
- ☐ 89 Songhai in Africa
- ☐ 90 Czar Ivan the Great of Russia
- ☐ 91 The Spanish Inquisition

WEEK 14

- ☐ 92 Columbus Sails to the Caribbean
- ☐ 93 **AGE OF ABSOLUTE MONARCHS**
- ☐ 94 Protestant Reformation
- ☐ 95 Spanish Conquistadors in the Americas
- ☐ 96 Calvin's *Institutes of the Christian Religion*
- ☐ 97 Council of Trent
- ☐ 98 Baroque Period of the Arts

WEEK 15

- ☐ 99 Japan's Isolation
- ☐ 100 Jamestown and Plymouth Colony Founded
- ☐ 101 **AGE OF ENLIGHTENMENT**
- ☐ 102 Hudson's Bay Company
- ☐ 103 First Great Awakening
- ☐ 104 Classical Period of the Arts
- ☐ 105 The Seven Years' War

WEEK 16

- ☐ 106 **AGE OF INDUSTRY**
- ☐ 107 James Cook Sails to Australia and Antarctica
- ☐ 108 American Revolution and General George Washington
- ☐ 109 Madison's Constitution and the Bill of Rights
- ☐ 110 French Revolution
- ☐ 111 Second Great Awakening
- ☐ 112 Louisiana Purchase and Lewis and Clark Expedition

WEEK 17

- ☐ 113 Napoleon Crowned Emperor of France
- ☐ 114 Liberation of South America
- ☐ 115 The War of 1812
- ☐ 116 The Missouri Compromise
- ☐ 117 Immigrants Flock to America
- ☐ 118 The Monroe Doctrine
- ☐ 119 Romantic Period of the Arts

WEEK 18

- ☐ 120 Cherokee Trail of Tears
- ☐ 121 U.S. Westward Expansion
- ☐ 122 Marx Publishes *The Communist Manifesto*
- ☐ 123 The Compromise of 1850 and the *Dred Scott* Decision
- ☐ 124 U.S. Restores Trade with Japan
- ☐ 125 British Queen Victoria's Rule Over India
- ☐ 126 Darwin Publishes *The Origin of Species*

WEEK 19

- ☐ 127 Lincoln's War Between the States
- ☐ 128 Reconstruction of the Southern States
- ☐ 129 Dominion of Canada
- ☐ 130 Otto von Bismarck Unifies Germany
- ☐ 131 Boer Wars in Africa
- ☐ 132 The Spanish-American War
- ☐ 133 The Progressive Era

WEEK 20

- ☐ 134 Australia Becomes a Commonwealth
- ☐ 135 Mexican Revolution
- ☐ 136 World War I and President Wilson
- ☐ 137 Lenin and the Bolshevik Revolution in Russia
- ☐ 138 U.S. Evangelist Billy Graham
- ☐ 139 Modern Period of the Arts
- ☐ 140 The Great Depression and the New Deal

WEEK 21

- ☐ 141 World War II and President Franklin D. Roosevelt
- ☐ 142 Stalin of the USSR and the Katyn Massacre
- ☐ 143 The United Nations Formed
- ☐ 144 The Cold War
- ☐ 145 Gandhi and India's Independence
- ☐ 146 Jewish State Established
- ☐ 147 Mao and Communist Victory in China

WEEK 22

- ☐ 148 North Atlantic Treaty Organization
- ☐ 149 The Korean War
- ☐ 150 Martin Luther King, Jr. and the Civil Rights Movement
- ☐ 151 Jim and Elisabeth Elliot, Missionaries to Equador
- ☐ 152 The Antarctic Treaty
- ☐ 153 The Vietnam War
- ☐ 154 U.S. Astronauts Walk on the Moon

WEEK 23

- ☐ 155 **AGE OF INFORMATION AND GLOBALIZATION**
- ☐ 156 Watergate, President Nixon Resigns
- ☐ 157 Fall of Communism in Eastern Europe
- ☐ 158 European Union Formed
- ☐ 159 Apartheid Abolished in South Africa
- ☐ 160 September 11, 2001
- ☐ 161 Rising Tide of Freedom

168	McKinley Roosevelt Taft Wilson	169	Harding Coolidge Hoover Roosevelt	170	Truman Eisenhower Kennedy Johnson	171	Nixon Ford Carter Reagan	172	Bush Clinton Bush Obama	173	Trump

1   **Tell me about Charlemagne.**

☐ In 800, during the medieval period, Pope Leo III crowned Charlemagne Holy Roman Emperor of Europe.

2   **Tell me about William the Conqueror.**

☐ In 1054, the church split into Roman Catholic and Eastern Orthodox. William the Conqueror defeated King Harold of England in 1066 and started feudalism.

3   **Tell me about the Crusades.**

☐ Richard the Lion-Hearted, son of Eleanor of Aquitaine, fought the Turks for Jerusalem during the time of the Crusades, from 1095 to 1291.

4   **Tell me about the Magna Carta.**

☐ English King John signed the Magna Carta in 1215, limiting the king's power. Later, England's King Edward III claimed to be king of France and began the Hundred Years' War in 1337.

5   **Tell me about the Hundred Years' War.**

☐ During the Hundred Years' War, Joan of Arc and King Charles VII led the French to defeat the English at the Siege of Orleans. In the late 1340s, fleas on rats carried the plague, which killed one out of three Europeans.

6   **Tell me about the Renaissance.**

☐ During the Renaissance period, from 1350 to 1600, Leonardo da Vinci was a famous inventor, Shakespeare was a famous playwright, Michelangelo was a famous artist, and Copernicus was a famous scientist.

7   **Tell me about the Reformation.**

☐ In 1517, Martin Luther began the Protestant Reformation by printing the *Ninety-five Theses* that made Pope Leo X excommunicate him. Later, John Calvin joined the Reformation.

8   **Tell me about European explorers.**

☐ Between the late 1400s and the mid-1500s, Dias rounded the Cape of Good Hope, Amerigo Vespucci sailed to the Americas, Balboa crossed Central America to the Pacific, Magellan's crew sailed around the globe, and Coronado explored the American Southwest.

9   **Tell me about some absolute monarchs.**

☐ Between the 1500s and 1800s, Henry VIII of England, Louis XIV of France, Philip II of Spain, Peter the Great of Russia, and Frederick the Great of Prussia ruled during the age of absolute monarchs.

10   **Tell me about the history of Russia.**

☐ Vladimir I brought Christianity to Russia in the 900s. In the 1500s, Czar Ivan the Terrible unified Russia. Peter the Great and Catherine the Great expanded and Westernized Russia in the 1700s.

11   **Tell me about the French Revolution.**

☐ In 1789, the French Revolution began when citizens stormed the Bastille and fought for the Declaration of the Rights of Man. Later, during the Reign of Terror, the aristocrats' heads were removed by the guillotine.

12   **Tell me about the Battle of Waterloo.**

☐ Napoleon Bonaparte of the French Empire was defeated at the Battle of Waterloo by British General Wellington and his allies soon after the War of 1812 in the United States.

13   Tell me about the Industrial Revolution.

☐   Watt's steam engine, Cartwright's power loom, and Whitney's cotton gin spurred the Industrial Revolution that began in the 1760s.

14   Tell me about World War I leaders.

☐   Clemenceau of France, Lloyd George of England, Nicholas II of Russia, Wilhelm II of Germany, and Wilson of the United States were leaders during World War I, which started in 1914 and ended in 1918.

15   Tell me about World War I countries.

☐   During World War I, Great Britain, France, and Russia were Allies and fought against Austria-Hungary and Germany, which were called the Central Powers. In 1917, the United States entered the war, assisting the Allies.

16   Tell me about how World War II began.

☐   World War II began in 1939 when Hitler invaded Poland. Two engagements that helped the United States win the Pacific front were defeating Japan at the Battle of Midway and dropping atomic bombs on Hiroshima and Nagasaki in 1945.

17   Tell me about World War II leaders.

☐   World War II AXIS leaders were: Hitler of Germany, Tojo of Japan, and Mussolini of Italy. World War II Allied leaders were: Churchill of England, Roosevelt, Eisenhower, and MacArthur of the United States, and Stalin of the USSR.

18   Tell me about the United Nations.

☐   In 1945, after the League of Nations failed to prevent World War II, American President Roosevelt, British Prime Minister Churchill, and Soviet Premier Stalin began the United Nations.

19   Tell me about the Korean War.

☐   In 1950, General Douglas MacArthur led United Nations forces to stop communist North Korea from capturing all of South Korea during the Korean War.

20   Tell me about the Vietnam War.

☐   In 1965, President Johnson sent U.S. troops to stop communist North Vietnam from capturing all of South Vietnam during the Vietnam War.

21   Tell me about the end of the Cold War.

☐   In the 1980s, British Prime Minister Margaret Thatcher and American President Ronald Reagan worked together to end the Cold War, lessen big government, and strengthen the conservative movement.

22   Tell me about the fall of communism.

☐   In 1989, the communist dictators began to fall in Eastern Europe when Soviet General Secretary Gorbachev refused to send them military aid.

23   Tell me about the Gulf War.

☐   In 1990, President George H. W. Bush sent troops to the Persian Gulf to expel Iraqi leader Saddam Hussein from Kuwait during the Gulf War.

24   Tell me about the end of apartheid.

☐   In 1994, South African President de Klerk allowed free elections. Nelson Mandela became South Africa's first black president, demonstrating apartheid was ending.

1 CONTINENTS/ OCEANS

- [ ] North America
- [ ] South America
- [ ] Europe
- [ ] Asia
- [ ] Africa
- [ ] Australia
- [ ] Antarctica
- [ ] Indian Ocean
- [ ] Arctic Ocean
- [ ] Atlantic Ocean
- [ ] Pacific Ocean
- [ ] Southern Ocean

2 EUROPEAN WATERS

- [ ] North Sea
- [ ] Baltic Sea
- [ ] Adriatic Sea
- [ ] English Channel
- [ ] Mediterranean Sea

3 WESTERN EUROPEAN COUNTRIES

- [ ] Ireland
- [ ] England
- [ ] Portugal
- [ ] Spain
- [ ] France

4 EUROPEAN RIVERS

- [ ] Seine River
- [ ] Rhine River
- [ ] Elbe River
- [ ] Po River
- [ ] Danube River
- [ ] Volga River

5 EUROPEAN CITIES

- [ ] London
- [ ] Paris
- [ ] Rome
- [ ] Barcelona
- [ ] Orleans

6 EUROPEAN MOUNTAINS

- [ ] Pyrenees
- [ ] Alps
- [ ] Carpathians
- [ ] Caucasus
- [ ] Ural
- [ ] Matterhorn

7 EUROPEAN PENINSULAS

- [ ] Iberian Peninsula
- [ ] Balkan Peninsula
- [ ] Scandinavian Peninsula
- [ ] Apennine Peninsula

8 MID-ATLANTIC WORLD

- [ ] Cape of Good Hope
- [ ] Strait of Magellan
- [ ] Canary Islands
- [ ] Treaty of Tordesillas

9 CARIBBEAN

- [ ] Cuba
- [ ] Jamaica
- [ ] Haiti
- [ ] Dominican Republic
- [ ] Puerto Rico

10 SOUTHWEST ASIA

- [ ] Afghanistan
- [ ] Pakistan
- [ ] India
- [ ] Kolkata
- [ ] Arabian Sea

11 EUROPE AND ASIA

- [ ] Moscow
- [ ] Kiev
- [ ] Russia
- [ ] Siberia
- [ ] Ukraine

12 EASTERN EUROPEAN SEAS

- [ ] White Sea
- [ ] Barents Sea
- [ ] Black Sea
- [ ] Caspian Sea
- [ ] Aral Sea

13 NORTHERN EUROPEAN COUNTRIES
- [ ] Norway
- [ ] Sweden
- [ ] Finland
- [ ] Denmark

14 BALTIC EUROPE
- [ ] Estonia
- [ ] Latvia
- [ ] Lithuania
- [ ] Poland
- [ ] Belarus

15 THE LEVANT
- [ ] Turkey
- [ ] Cyprus
- [ ] Syria
- [ ] Iraq
- [ ] Iran

16 BALKANS
- [ ] Greece
- [ ] Albania
- [ ] Bulgaria
- [ ] Slovenia
- [ ] Romania

17 CENTRAL EUROPEAN COUNTRIES
- [ ] Netherlands
- [ ] Belgium
- [ ] Luxembourg
- [ ] Germany
- [ ] Switzerland

18 MORE CENTRAL EUROPEAN COUNTRIES
- [ ] Italy
- [ ] Austria
- [ ] Hungary
- [ ] Czechia
- [ ] Slovakia

19 SOUTHEASTERN ASIA
- [ ] North Korea
- [ ] South Korea
- [ ] Taiwan
- [ ] Philippines
- [ ] Guam

20 SOUTH CENTRAL ASIA
- [ ] Laos
- [ ] Thailand
- [ ] Cambodia
- [ ] North Vietnam
- [ ] South Vietnam

21 CENTRAL AMERICA
- [ ] Guatemala
- [ ] Belize
- [ ] El Salvador
- [ ] Honduras
- [ ] Nicaragua

22 OCEANIA
- [ ] Australia
- [ ] Great Barrier Reef
- [ ] New Zealand
- [ ] Papua New Guinea
- [ ] Indonesia

23 CENTRAL ASIA
- [ ] Kazakhstan
- [ ] Uzbekistan
- [ ] Turkmenistan
- [ ] Tajikistan
- [ ] Kyrgyzstan

24 SOUTHERN AFRICA
- [ ] South Africa
- [ ] Lesotho
- [ ] Botswana
- [ ] Mozambique
- [ ] Namibia

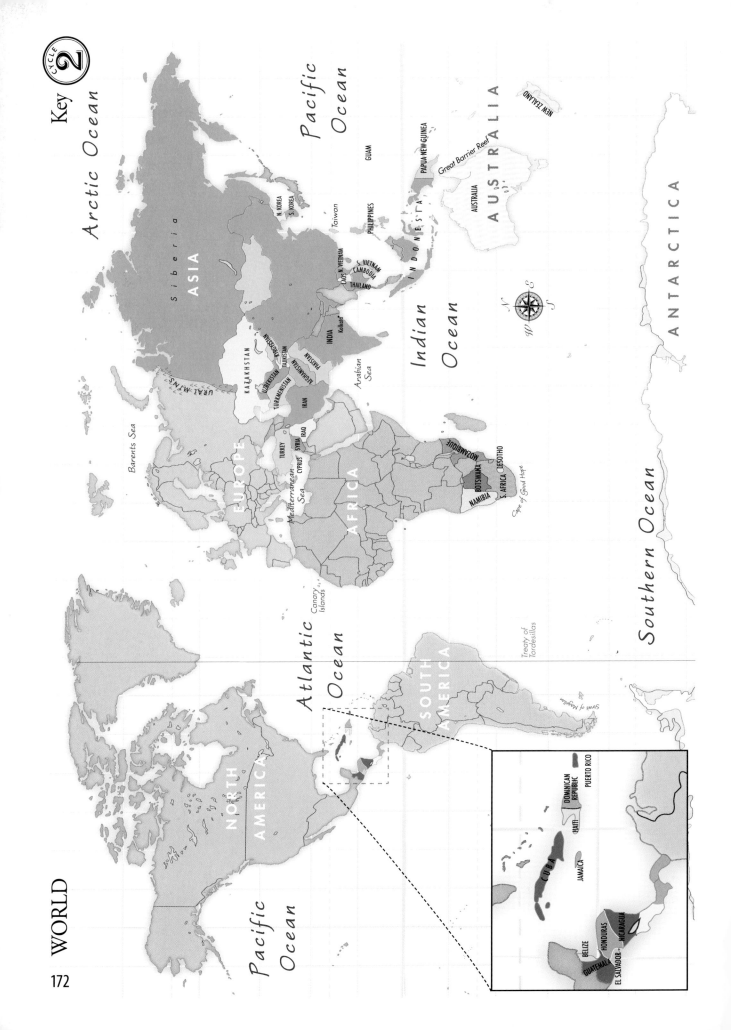

WORLD

Arctic Ocean

Pacific Ocean

Pacific Ocean

NORTH AMERICA

Atlantic Ocean

SOUTH AMERICA

EUROPE

Barents Sea

URAL MTNS.

Siberia

ASIA

KAZAKHSTAN

UZBEKISTAN

TURKMENISTAN

TAJIKISTAN

KYRGYZSTAN

AFGHANISTAN

PAKISTAN

IRAN

IRAQ

TURKEY

SYRIA

CYPRUS

Mediterranean Sea

AFRICA

Arabian Sea

Indian Ocean

INDIA

Kolkata

N. KOREA

S. KOREA

Taiwan

LAOS N. VIETNAM

S. VIETNAM

CAMBODIA

THAILAND

PHILIPPINES

INDONESIA

GUAM

PAPUA NEW GUINEA

Great Barrier Reef

AUSTRALIA

AUSTRALIA

NEW ZEALAND

ANTARCTICA

Southern Ocean

MOZAMBIQUE

BOTSWANA

NAMIBIA

S. AFRICA

LESOTHO

Cape of Good Hope

Canary Islands

Treaty of Tordesillas

Strait of Magellan

CUBA

JAMAICA

DOMINICAN REPUBLIC

HAITI

PUERTO RICO

BELIZE

GUATEMALA

EL SALVADOR

HONDURAS

NICARAGUA

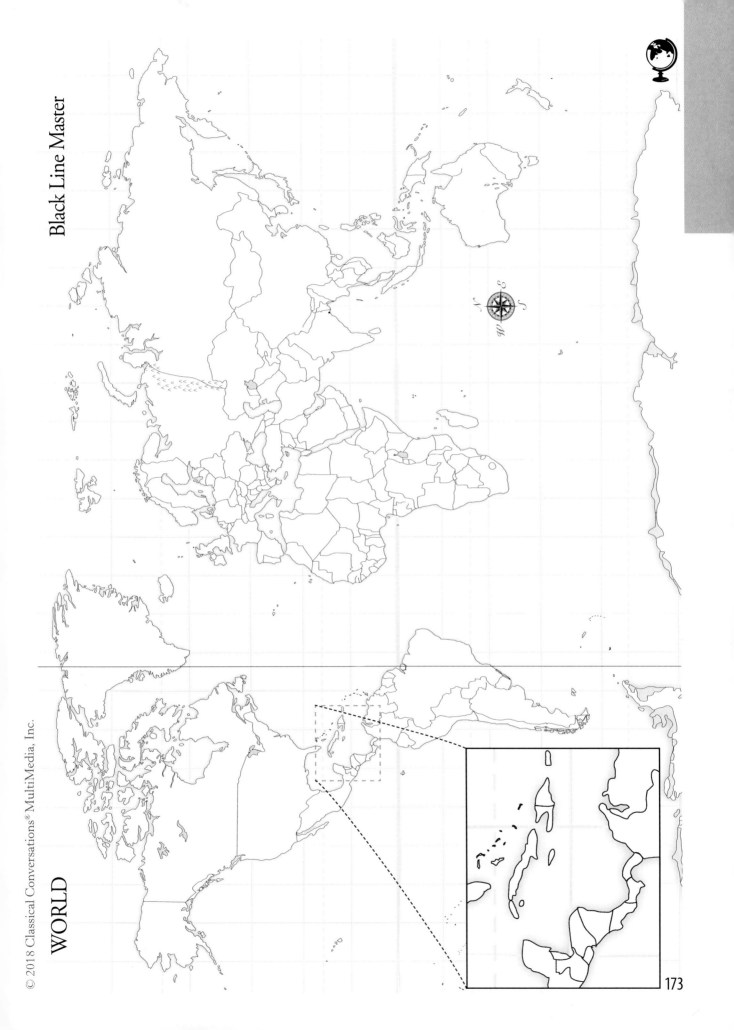

WORLD

EUROPE

Key

CYCLE ②

174

Atlantic Ocean

ICELAND

IRELAND

ENGLAND
London
English Channel

North Sea

NETHERLANDS
BELGIUM
Paris
Orleans
FRANCE
Pyrenees Mtns.
Barcelona
SPAIN
IBERIAN PENINSULA
PORTUGAL

Rhine R.
Seine R.
Elbe R.
GERMANY
DENMARK
LUX.

SWITZERLAND
ALPS
Matterhorn
Po R.
AUSTRIA
SLOVENIA
CROATIA
Rome
ITALY
APENNINE PENINSULA
Adriatic Sea

NORWAY
SCANDINAVIAN PENINSULA
SWEDEN

Baltic Sea

FINLAND

ESTONIA
LATVIA
LITHUANIA

POLAND

CZECHIA
SLOVAKIA
HUNGARY
Carpathian Mtns.
Danube R.
ROMANIA
BULGARIA
GREECE
ALBANIA
BALKAN PENINSULA

Mediterranean Sea

AFRICA

BELARUS

UKRAINE
Kiev

Moscow

White Sea

Barents Sea

RUSSIA

Volga R.

Ural Mountains

Siberia

ASIA

Aral Sea

Caspian Sea

Caucasus Mtns.

Black Sea

N
W E
S

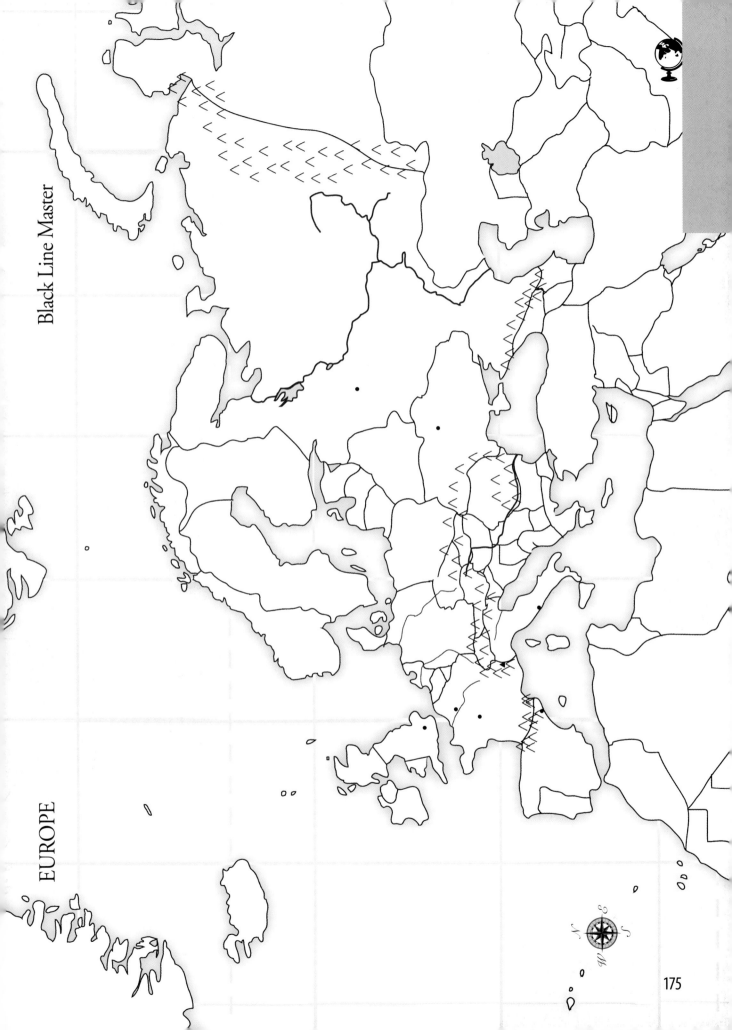

EUROPE

CYCLE 2

Arctic

Hudson Bay

Massachusetts Bay Colony

N. America

Cuba

Haiti

Dominican Republic

Puerto Rico

Jamaica

Honduras

El Salvador

Nicaragua

Costa Rica

Panama

Incas

S. America

Strait of Magellan

Treaty of Tordesillas

Atlantic

Canary Islands

Portugal

Europe

Africa

Namibia

Botswana

South Africa

Lesotho

Mozambique

Cape of Good Hope

Antarctica

Indian

Arabian Sea

Kazakhstan

Uzbekistan

Turkmenistan

Afghanistan

Pakistan

India

Calcutta

Asia

China

North Vietnam

Laos

Thailand

Cambodia

South Vietnam

Taiwan

Philippines

Guam

North Korea

South Korea

Pacific

Australia

N

E

S

W

L.S.M. o

EUROPE

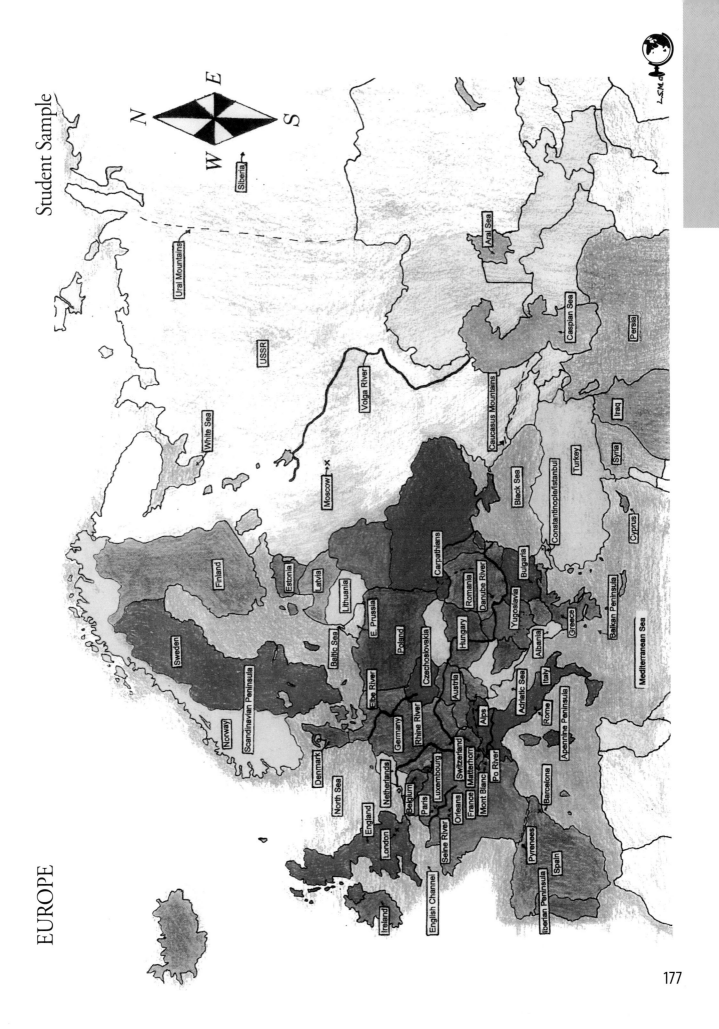

CREATION
GENESIS 1:1–27 (KJV)

[1] In the beginning God created the heaven and the earth.

[2] And the earth was without form, and void; and darkness was upon the face of the deep. And the Spirit of God moved upon the face of the waters.

[3] And God said, Let there be light: and there was light. [4] And God saw the light, that it was good: and God divided the light from the darkness.

[5] And God called the light Day, and the darkness he called Night. And the evening and the morning were the first day.

[6] And God said, Let there be a firmament in the midst of the waters, and let it divide the waters from the waters.

[7] And God made the firmament, and divided the waters which were under the firmament from the waters which were above the firmament: and it was so.

[8] And God called the firmament Heaven. And the evening and the morning were the second day.

[9] And God said, Let the waters under the heaven be gathered together unto one place, and let the dry land appear: and it was so.

[10] And God called the dry land Earth; and the gathering together of the waters called he Seas: and God saw that it was good.

[11] And God said, Let the earth bring forth grass, the herb yielding seed, and the fruit tree yielding fruit after his kind, whose seed is in itself, upon the earth: and it was so.

[12] And the earth brought forth grass, and herb yielding seed after his kind, and the tree yielding fruit, whose seed was in itself, after his kind: and God saw that it was good. [13] And the evening and the morning were the third day.

[14] And God said, Let there be lights in the firmament of the heaven to divide the day from the night; and let them be for signs, and for seasons, and for days, and years:

[15] And let them be for lights in the firmament of the heaven to give light upon the earth: and it was so.

[16] And God made two great lights; the greater light to rule the day, and the lesser light to rule the night: he made the stars also.

[17] And God set them in the firmament of the heaven to give light upon the earth, [18] And to rule over the day and over the night, and to divide the light from the darkness: and God saw that it was good.

[19] And the evening and the morning were the fourth day.

[20] And God said, Let the waters bring forth abundantly the moving creature that hath life, and fowl that may fly above the earth in the open firmament of heaven.

[21] And God created great whales, and every living creature that moveth, which the waters brought forth abundantly, after their kind, and every winged fowl after his kind: and God saw that it was good.

[22] And God blessed them, saying, Be fruitful, and multiply, and fill the waters in the seas, and let fowl multiply in the earth.

[23] And the evening and the morning were the fifth day.

> A NOTE ABOUT THIS SECTION:
>
> We do not wish to usurp your church or family Scripture memory work. Rather, we have chosen a few designated verses per cycle to augment the **Foundations** memory work. We use the King James Version for our printed materials, but please feel free to use the translation of your choice.

[24] And God said, Let the earth bring forth the living creature after his kind, cattle, and creeping thing, and beast of the earth after his kind: and it was so.

[25] And God made the beast of the earth after his kind, and cattle after their kind, and every thing that creepeth upon the earth after his kind: and God saw that it was good.

[26] And God said, Let us make man in our image, after our likeness: and let them have dominion over the fish of the sea, and over the fowl of the air, and over the cattle, and over all the earth, and over every creeping thing that creepeth upon the earth.

[27] So God created man in his own image, in the image of God created he him; male and female created he them.

PRESENTATIONS

Let's make public speaking a pleasant part of our culture for our children. Feel free to suggest to your older child that he or she could read the IEW paper from Essentials or explain more thoroughly a *Classical Acts & Facts® Science Card*. However, if your child just wants to tell the class about their grandparent or model car, say, "Good idea! Think about what you'll say while I get a glass of iced tea." Then listen as he or she gives their story a whirl.

Remind your child to:

1. Take a clearing breath while he sees if everyone is ready to listen.
2. Introduce himself and his presentation.
3. Speak clearly and audibly and take care to look each audience member in the eye as he speaks.
4. Let the audience know he is finished by ending with, "Are there any questions?"

Just smile at your child when they present in public. And remember, ideas need time to digest and settle. Next week while listening with a glass of iced tea in your hand, ask if there's anything he wants to improve on from the previous week. Time allows ears to hear comments without taking them as criticism.

A good audience listens and participates by asking questions of other presenters. Occasionally have the students hold up eyeballs drawn on index cards and then put the card down when the presenter has caught their eye.

In community, each student presents twenty-four times a year, which provides over one hundred formal public speaking opportunities in kindergarten thru sixth grade. Success comes from consistency over many years.

More Resources to Help

Classical Conversations students exercise the skills of rhetorical presentation through all program levels, from these short presentations in Foundations to science fair, mock trial, and formal debate in Challenge. You might consider attending one of these Challenge events—this will be your child in just a few years! Additionally, we've developed some resources to serve families all the way through the high school years.

Trivium Tables®: Rhetoric
This laminated, double-sided resource has four panels on each side that describe different aspects of rhetoric—presenting—for your student to learn, review, and practice. Please see the bookstore for more information.

See our online subscription service at ClassicalConversations. com, word search: *presentation* for more ideas.

For families who subscribe, there are dozens of resources in the file-sharing area of our membership site.

Let your speech be always with grace, seasoned with salt, that ye may know how ye ought to answer every man.
—COLOSSIANS 4:6 (KJV)

Students love to dress up in character for presentations.

"Presentations are not about the material presented, they are about building the child's confidence and poise."
—LEIGH A. BORTINS
THE CORE (p. 175)

Resources

Drawing with Children, Mona
Brookes (for visual game
ideas, scaling of drawing
projects)

Classical Conversations online
subscription services through
ClassicalConversations.com

WEEK	PROJECT
1	five elements of shape *Drawing with Children* (Mona Brookes)
2	mirror images *Drawing with Children* (Mona Brookes)
3	upside-down image *Drawing with Children* (Mona Brookes)
4	abstract art *Drawing with Children* (Mona Brookes)
5	perspective *Drawing with Children* (Mona Brookes)
6	review and final project

Required Resources

Tin whistle in the key of D
Reproducible handouts included
in this curriculum (see pages 88,
100, 101, 103, 181)

Recommended Resources

Classical Music for Dummies (Pogue
and Speck)
Sheet music (to practice)
Recorded music (to enjoy at home)

FINE ARTS
Drawing

In Weeks 1 through 6, students practice various drawing techniques using the
OiLS technique from *Drawing with Children*. For the full text on these weeks'
study, please refer to Cycle 1 (pages 80–86).

Music

In Weeks 7 through 12, we introduce very basic music theory while students
learn a tune on the tin whistle. For the full text on these weeks' study, please
refer to Cycle 1 (pages 87–103).

Mary Had a Little Lamb

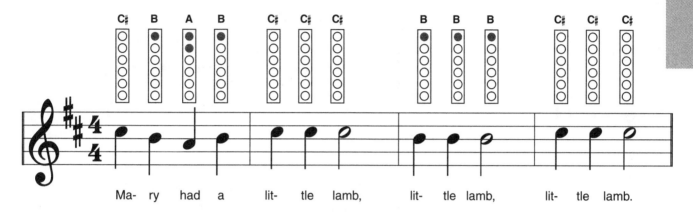

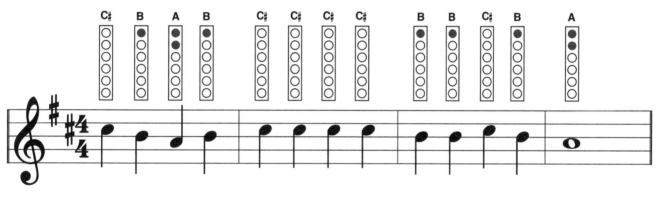

Resources

Discovering Great Artists (Kohl and Solga)

Classical Acts and Facts® History Cards: Artists and Composers, Sets 2 and 3

Marvelous to Behold (Classical Conversations® MultiMedia)

Great Artists

In Weeks 13 through 18, we learn about six artists from the Baroque, Romantic, and Modern periods. For the full introductory text on these weeks' study, please refer to Cycle 1 (pages 104–105).

WEEK	CYCLE 1		CYCLE 2		CYCLE 3	
	ARTIST	TECHNIQUE	ARTIST	TECHNIQUE	ARTIST	TECHNIQUE
13	Giotto (c. 1266–1337)	Paint (Gothic)	Rembrandt 1606–1669	Drawing (Baroque)	Grandma Moses 1860–1961	Painting Folk Art
14	Ghiberti 1378–1455	Sculpt/Relief (Renaissance)	Gainsborough 1727–1788	Drawing/Painting (Romantic)	Picasso 1881–1973	Painting Abstract
15	Angelico c. 1395–1455	Drawing (Renaissance)	Degas 1834–1917	Painting (Impressionist)	O'Keeffe 1887–1986	Watercolors Romantic
16	Dürer 1471–1528	Print (Renaissance)	Monet 1840–1926	Painting (Impressionist)	Rockwell 1895–1978	Illustration/ Painting Realism
17	Michelangelo 1475–1564	Paint (Renaissance)	Morisot 1841–1895	Painting (Impressionist)	Wyeth 1917–2009	Tempera Realism
18	El Greco 1541–1614	Drawing (Baroque)	van Gogh 1853–1890	Modern Impressionist	Lichtenstein 1923–1997	Illustration Modern Pop

WEEK THIRTEEN
Rembrandt van Rijn (Making Faces!)

ATTENDING

At home, observe the *Classical Acts & Facts® History Cards: Artists and Composers* card #16 and other artists and composers cards from Cycle 2, Cycle 1, and Cycle 3.

Use the sample conversation starters from the list below.

Sample conversation starters:

What do you see in this work of art?

How is this work of art similar to others from the same time period? Other time periods?

How is this work of art different from others from the same time period? Other time periods?

How similar or different are these comparisons?

What was happening during the time this artwork was created?

At the same time this work of art was created, where was the artist? Who else was there? What was happening?

What do others say about the artwork? What do you think the artist wanted to express?

Resources

Discovering Great Artists (Kohl and Solga)

Classical Acts & Facts® History Cards #98

Classical Acts & Facts® History Cards: Artists and Composers #16 (Rembrandt); #18 (Gainsborough); and #26 (Degas)

 At home, choose another great artist for an additional project from *Discovering Great Artists.*

EXPRESSING

Do the assigned project from *Discovering Great Artists.*

WEEK FOURTEEN
Thomas Gainsborough (Portrait on Landscape)

TIP

For younger students, consider using pre-cut pictures from magazines.

 At home, redo and improve this week's project.

WEEK FIFTEEN
Edgar Degas (Resist in Motion or Chalk on Cloth)

TIP

Parents may help with the ironing.

 Visit an art museum.

WEEK SIXTEEN
Claude Monet (Dabble in Paint)

Resources
Discovering Great Artists (Kohl and
    Solga)
*Classical Acts & Facts® History
    Cards: Artists and Composers* #28
    (Monet); #30 (Morisot); and #34
    (van Gogh)

 Watch a documentary on a
classical artist.

TIP

For younger students, use smaller paper (e.g., blank index
cards) and cotton swabs for painting "impressions."

WEEK SEVENTEEN
Berthe Morisot (Texture Paints)

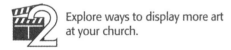 Explore ways to display more art
at your church.

WEEK EIGHTEEN
Vincent van Gogh (Impasto or Starry Night)

 Create an art project from
recycled clothes.

Composers and Orchestra

In weeks 19 through 24, students practice listening skills using music and listening guides from *Classical Music for Dummies*. For the full text on these weeks' study, please refer to Cycle 1 (pages 108–109).

Resources

Classical Music for Dummies (Pogue and Speck)

Classical Acts & Facts® History Cards

Classical Acts & Facts® History Cards: *Artists and Composers*

Instrument pictures (if desired; see pages 112–116)

Foundations Audio CD for Orchestra Song

	LESSONS		
	CYCLE 1	CYCLE 2	CYCLE 3
WEEK	PROJECT	PROJECT	PROJECT
19	Baroque and Classical Periods *Classical Music for Dummies* (Pogue and Speck)	**Classical and Romantic Periods** *Classical Music for Dummies* (Pogue and Speck)	Romantic and Modern Periods *Classical Music for Dummies* (Pogue and Speck)
20	Handel: *Water Music Suite* *Classical Music for Dummies* (Pogue and Speck)	Beethoven: *Symphony no. 5* *Classical Music for Dummies* (Pogue and Speck)	Tchaikovsky: *Symphony no. 6*, Fourth Movement *(Symphony Pathétique)* *Classical Music for Dummies* (Pogue and Speck)
21	Bach: *The Well-Tempered Clavier* Prelude and Fugue in C Major *Classical Music for Dummies* (Pogue and Speck)	Brahms: *Symphony no. 4* *Classical Music for Dummies* (Pogue and Speck)	Debussy: *La Mer* *Classical Music for Dummies* (Pogue and Speck)
22	Mozart: *Piano Concerto no. 22 in E-flat*, Third Movement *Classical Music for Dummies* (Pogue and Speck)	Dvořák: *Serenade for Strings* *Classical Music for Dummies* (Pogue and Speck)	Stravinsky: *The Rite of Spring* *Classical Music for Dummies* (Pogue and Speck)
23	orchestra overview *Classical Music for Dummies* (Pogue and Speck)	orchestra overview *Classical Music for Dummies* (Pogue and Speck)	orchestra overview *Classical Music for Dummies* (Pogue and Speck)
24	review and celebration	review and celebration	review and celebration

WEEK NINETEEN
Classical and Romantic Periods

Resources

Classical Music for Dummies (Pogue and Speck)

Classical Acts & Facts® *History Cards* 104 and 119

Classical Acts & Facts® *History Cards: Artists and Composers* #21 (Beethoven); #25 (Brahms); and #29 (Dvořák)

 At home, listen to Rossini's *The William Tell Overture* and Saint-Saëns' *The Carnival of the Animals*.

 ## ATTENDING

Without naming the composers, listen to pieces by Beethoven, Brahms, and Dvořák. Over the next three weeks, we will spend more time with each piece as families get to know these pieces more intimately. Each subsequent week, listen to the individual composer's piece while a parent-tutor reads the listening outline aloud. Practice cultivating restful listening in community.

Here are some suggestions:

1. Turn out the lights and have students get into a restful position. Have them close their eyes and listen to the music as you read the listening outline.

2. Turn on the lights. Have students listen again. What do they notice?

3. Listen again. Have students stand up each time the piece gets loud and sit back down when the piece gets quiet.

 ## EXPRESSING

Focus on active listening, not busy hands. Learn to have ears that hear. Pause music and ask questions that accompany the listening outline.

WEEK TWENTY
Beethoven *(Symphony no. 5)*

WEEK TWENTY-ONE
Brahms *(Symphony no. 4)*

WEEK TWENTY-TWO
Dvořák ("Serenade for Strings")

WEEK TWENTY-THREE
Orchestra Overview

ATTENDING

Teach the children the *Orchestra Song.*

EXPRESSING

1. Practice the orchestra seating chart (see *Trivium Tables®: Music*) by assigning students to be in the different instrument families (strings, woodwinds, brass, percussion). Hand out instrument pictures if desired.

2. Practice singing the orchestra song as a group while students are in the orchestra seating arrangement.

3. If students are getting to know the piece well, you can consider singing it as a round. When the first group of students finishes the violin section, group 2 starts at the beginning of the song. When group 2 finishes the violin section, group 3 starts at the beginning of the song. When a group finishes the song, they should keep singing the final lines of the song until group 3 arrives at the final line.

Your community may choose to handle this study in different ways, depending on the makeup of the group. Larger communities may opt to complete orchestra activities within individual classes during the Fine Arts component. Smaller communities may opt to do these activities as one big group, directly after morning assembly.

WEEK TWENTY-FOUR
Review and Celebration

EXPRESSING

Play *Mary Had a Little Lamb* with the whole community. Sing the *Orchestra Song* with the whole community.

Resources

Classical Music for Dummies (Pogue and Speck)

Trivium Tables®: Music

Instrument pictures if desired (see pages 112–116)

Foundations Audio CD (any cycle) for the *Orchestra Song*

Orchestra Song

Violins:
The violins ringing like lovely singing.
The violins ringing like lovely song.

Clarinets:
The clarinet, the clarinet, goes doodle doodle doodle doodle dat.
The clarinet, the clarinet, goes doodle doodle doodle dat.

Trumpets:
The trumpet is braying,
Ta-ta-ta-ta TA ta-ta-ta-ta ta ta TAH.
The trumpet is braying,
Ta-ta-ta-ta TA ta-ta-ta-ta ta ta TAH.

Horns:
The horn, the horn, awakes me at morn.
The horn, the horn, awakes me at morn.

Drums:
The drum's playing two tones.
They're always the same tones.
5-1, 1-5, 5-5-5-5-1.

 To which instrument family (strings, woodwinds, brass, percussion) does the violin belong? the clarinet? the trumpet? the horn? the drums?

WEEK	PROJECT
1	#2 Shaded*
	#17 Same Place*
2	#24 Mirage*
	#26 Distortion*
3	#9 See Through*
4	#11 On the Move*
	#12 Speedy*
5	#13 Expanding*
	#16 In and Out*
6	#3 Cover Up*
	#4 Thick*
7	Sun Prints
8	Proportional Solar System
9	Rockets
10	Facility Clean-Up
11	Solar Model
12	Constellations
13	#161 Spoon Bell*
	#162 Humming Glass*
14	#165 Cold Foot*
	#171 Pepper Run*
15	#164 Bottle Organ*
16	#189 Shape Up*
	#190 Breakthrough*
17	#174 Energy Change*
	#177 Snap!*
18	#184 Lifter*
	#185 Ramp*
19	Paper Airplanes
20	Straw Bridge
21	Tower Construction
22	Popsicle Stick Catapult
23	Egg Protector
24	Outdoor Contest

* *201 Awesome, Magical, Bizarre &
Incredible Experiments*

Hands-on Science

In Weeks 1 through 24, students practice scientific discussions using *201 Awesome, Magical, Bizarre & Incredible Experiments* and create awesome projects. For the full text on these weeks' study, please refer to Cycle 1 (page 117).

For Weeks 1–6 and 13–18, see Scientific Method Discussion (page 129).

WEEK SEVEN
Sun Prints

A photogram of algae made by Anna Atkins as part of her 1843 book *Photographs of British Algae: Cyanotype Impressions.*

ATTENDING

Follow the instructions in the Sun Print Kit. (Sun print kits can be found through an Internet search or from a science supply store, school supply store, or craft store.)

NAMING

Today we are going to make pictures using the sun's rays. Do you remember the parts of the sun? [*Week 9 memory work*] What are some different ways to make pictures? [*drawing, painting, camera, etc.*]

EXPRESSING

What did we use? What did we do? What did we see?

Materials

A sunny day!
Sun Print Kits (one per student)
one dishpan of water per class
simple objects like leaves, small toys,
    small action figures (for the class)

In addition to using the sun print paper, older students can also make sun prints using colored construction paper and clear plastic wrap (or Plexiglas). Compare the two sun prints and processes.

WEEK EIGHT
Proportional Solar System (outside)

ATTENDING

1. Take students to a large open area like a parking lot or a large play area.

2. Start by placing the "sun" (beach ball) at the farthest point of the parking lot or large play area.

3. Use the chart on these pages to measure and place variously-sized balls at their approximate distances from the sun.

4. Place variously-sized marbles between Mars and Jupiter to represent the asteroid belt.

Materials

one beach ball
one dime-sized bead
200 marbles of various sizes (for moons and asteroid belt)
2 golf balls
2 tennis balls
2 soccer balls
20 ft. tape measure
flexible wire (for rings around planets)

NAMING

What planets do the different pieces (bead, marbles, balls) represent?

EXPRESSING

Allow older students to lead by using the chart to measure and place variously-sized balls at their approximate distances from the sun.

What did we use? What did we do? What did we see?

Planet	Diameter (km)	Shape	1 Rotation	Year	Sun Distance (km)	Inches	Moons
Mercury	4,900	bead	59 days	88 days	57.9 mill	5.8	0
Venus	12,100	golf ball	243 days	224.7 days	108.2 mill	10.8	0
Earth	12,756	golf ball	24 hours	365.3 days	149.6 mill	14.9	1
Mars	6,800	marble	24.5 hours	687 days	227.8 mill	22.8	2
Jupiter	142,800	soccer ball	9.8 hours	12 Earth years	778 mill	77.8	66
Saturn	120,660	soccer ball	10.7 hours	29.5 Earth years	1,427 mill	142.7	62
Uranus	52,400	tennis ball	17 hours	84 Earth years	2,870 mill	287	27
Neptune	49,500	tennis ball	16 hours	165 Earth years	4,500 mill	450	14

How to Build a Proportional Solar System Outside

Asteroid belt between the orbits of Mars and Jupiter— use various marbles to illustrate

WEEK NINE
Rockets

 ## ATTENDING

Blow up a balloon, then let out the air all at once. What happens?

Activity:

Take classes out in groups or all at once. You can do one or multiple rockets for each class, or multiple rockets all together.

Option: Award students who know the memory work with the honor of launching a rocket!

 ## NAMING

Discuss how rockets work. *[Combustion propels a rocket upward.]*

 ## EXPRESSING

What did we use? What did we do? What did we see?

Materials

Rocket Kits (assembly needed;
    consult kit for other supplies)
Outside area without many tall trees
Stomp rockets if a large, clear outside
    area is not available

 Older students could lead the rocket launch with adult supervision. Encourage the students to read the rocket directions themselves and then launch the rockets.

WEEK TEN
Facility Clean-up or Community Service

ATTENDING

Look around. Do you see a place where you can help? Ask facility administrators what they would like help with. Some suggestions might be giving baked goods for breakfast or cleaning the foyer or bathrooms.

Materials

Your community

Community Service

- washing windows

- planting flowers or plants

- making care kits for the homeless

- putting together chemo care packages

- writing postcards to senior citizens, or members of the armed forces, law enforcement, or fire department

NAMING

What does it mean to have a nurturing community? What kinds of things can we do to be more nurturing as a community?

EXPRESSING

What did we use? What did we do? What did we see?

 Encourage students to come up with their own ideas of how they can serve their community.

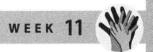
WEEK ELEVEN
Solar System Model (inside)

ATTENDING

1. First, place the "sun" (2" yellow strip) at the (shorter, if rectangular) edge of the black paper.

2. Use the chart on these pages to measure and glue the different objects at their approximate distances from the sun.

3. Direct students to add the names of the planets to the background as they proceed.

4. Put glitter glue between Mars and Jupiter to represent the asteroid belt.

TIPS

• Write the planet names on the bags of jewels.

• Rough up the back of the jewels to help them adhere better.

• Use glow-in-the-dark glitter glue pens.

Materials

Option 1 (older students)
large black construction paper (18"–22" long)
yellow construction paper (sun)
rulers
glue
small, dome-shaped half jewels
medium half jewels
glitter or glitter glue pens (for asteroid belt)
large half beads, or large half marbles
large half marbles

Option 2 (younger students)
pre-measured black paper
yellow construction paper (sun)
small planet stickers

NAMING

Discuss the planets' names, sizes, and distances from the sun.

EXPRESSING

What did we use? What did we do? What did we see?

 Encourage students to draw all the elements of the proportional solar system on paper and color them.

HOW TO BUILD A PROPORTIONAL SOLAR SYSTEM (INSIDE)		
Body	**Distance from the edge of the sun**	**Represented by**
Sun	sticks out 2 inches	large strip of yellow construction paper
Mercury	.20 (1/5) inch	smallest half-jewel
Venus	.33 (1/3) inch	medium half-jewel
Earth	.5 (1/2) inch	medium half-jewel
Mars	.8 (4/5) inch	smallest half-jewel
Asteroid belt	(between the orbits of Mars and Jupiter)	star glitter in an arch; use glitter glue pens for less mess
Jupiter	2.5 inches	largest bead
Saturn	4 inches	largest bead
Uranus	9.5 inches	large half-marble
Neptune	15 inches	large half-marble

© 2018 Classical Conversations® MultiMedia, Inc.

WEEK TWELVE
Constellations

 ATTENDING

Direct students to draw several constellations on paper (one per sheet). Younger students can use star stickers to represent the major stars.

Another option is to use glow-in-the-dark craft paint to draw the major stars.

Materials

Black construction paper

Glow-in-the-dark craft paint

Optional: small Christmas lights, glow-in-the-dark stickers, star stickers

 NAMING

Discuss and show pictures of some constellations. Many diagrams of constellations can be found online.

 EXPRESSING

What did we use? What did we do? What did we see?

 Older students can take poster board and use a pencil to punch out holes where the major stars in their constellations would be. Christmas lights can be inserted into the holes.

WEEK NINETEEN
Paper Airplanes

ATTENDING

Fly some of the pre-made paper airplanes.

Activity:

Direct pairs, teams or individual students to use the materials to make paper airplanes. More adult instruction may be needed for younger students, and some adult instruction may be needed for older students. The goal is not for every student to design and build the same paper airplane, but for every student to have an opportunity to think through the process of making a paper airplane and to work as a team. On Week 24, the airplanes will be tested to see which one can fly the farthest.

NAMING

Have pre-made designs to show to the students. What are some of the designs called?

TIP

You may want to save completed projects from weeks 19–23 for the outdoor contest on week 24.

EXPRESSING

What did we use? What did we do? What did we see?

Materials

Construction paper

Paper airplane books (cut designs out ahead of time)

Consult Classical Conversations online subscription services through ClassicalConversations.com or the Internet for many airplane designs

Older students can make different or more advanced airplane designs and hold a flying competition.

WEEK TWENTY
Straw Bridge Construction

 ATTENDING

Direct pairs or teams of students to use the supplies to design and build a straw bridge. More adult instruction may be needed for younger students, and some adult instruction may be needed for older students. The goal is not for every student to design and build the same bridge, but for every student to have an opportunity to think through the process of building a bridge and to work as a team. On Week 24, the bridges will be tested to see which one can hold the most weight. Some examples to test the bridge's sturdiness might be books, cups of pennies, or other weights.

Materials

Option 1 (for older students)
50 drinking straws
200 rubber bands
Play-Doh® or tape (be careful of allergies)

Option 2 (for younger students)
toothpicks
mini marshmallows

 NAMING

What are some types of bridges? What is the purpose of a bridge?

 EXPRESSING

What did we use? What did we do? What did we see?

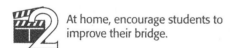 At home, encourage students to improve their bridge.

WEEK TWENTY-ONE
Tower Construction

ATTENDING

Direct pairs or teams of students to use the materials to design and construct a tower. More adult instruction may be needed for younger students, and some adult instruction may be needed for older students. The goal is not for every student to design and build the same tower, but for every student to have an opportunity to think through the process of building a tower and to work as a team. On Week 24, the towers will be tested to see which one is the tallest.

TIP

Students will have better success if they start with a strong base.

Materials

Drinking straws
Sturdy tape
Measuring stick (to measure
    completed projects)
Consult the Internet for images

NAMING

What are some different types of towers? What is the purpose of a tower?

EXPRESSING

What did we use? What did we do? What did we see?

Discuss math used in designing large structures like the tower and the bridge.

WEEK TWENTY-TWO
Popsicle Stick Catapult

Materials

craft sticks (7 per student)

rubber bands

glue or glue stick

soft items to serve as projectiles
(like mini marshmallows, small
pompoms, popcorn)

small bottle cap (optional)

Consult the Internet for images

 ATTENDING

Direct pairs, teams, or individual students to use the materials to make a popsicle stick catapult. More adult instruction may be needed for younger students, and some adult instruction may be needed for older students. The goal is not for every student to design and build the same catapult, but for every student to have an opportunity to think through the process of building a catapult and to work as a team. On Week 24, the catapults will be tested to see which catapult can throw the farthest.

1. Lay five craft sticks one on top of the other (all going the same direction) and rubber band the sticks together at each end.

2. Take the two remaining craft sticks and place them together in the same manner, but only rubber band one end together.

3. Take a rubber band and wrap it around both bundles, making an "X."

4. Optional: Take a small bottle cap and glue it to the open end of the two-banded craft sticks to hold a projectile.

5. Slide the five-stick bundle into the open end of the two-stick bundle and push it as far to the end as it can go. This will form a "T" or cross shape with both bundles.

6. Place a soft projectile on the top of the open end or in the small bottle cap, press down at the very top and release.

 NAMING

What are some types of catapults? What is the purpose of a catapult?

 EXPRESSING

What did we use? What did we do? What did we see?

 More advanced designs for older students can be found online. Students may experiment with different numbers of sticks in the larger bundle, or different strength rubber bands.

WEEK TWENTY-THREE
Egg Protector

ATTENDING

Direct pairs, teams, or individual students to use the materials to make an egg protector. More adult instruction may be needed for younger students, and some adult instruction may be needed for older students. The goal is not for every student to design and build the same egg protector, but for every student to have an opportunity to think through the process of building an egg protector and to work as a team. On Week 24, the egg protectors will be tested with real eggs to see which one protected the egg the best. When building the egg protector, students should think about building the protector so that the egg can be inserted later for testing in week 24.

TIP

Use the craft sticks to build a box secured by the rubber bands. Use the napkins to cushion the egg.

Materials

50 craft sticks
rubber bands
12 napkins
plastic egg for practice

NAMING

What are some types of eggs? What other materials could have been used to protect the egg?

EXPRESSING

What did we use? What did we do? What did we see?

 If time allows, let the older students give the experiment a second try now that they have observed and discussed mistakes from the first round.

WEEK TWENTY-FOUR
Outdoor Contest

Materials
Completed projects from weeks
　19–23

 ATTENDING

Time to test the students' creations! This can be a competition either between individuals or between classes. Explain the contest rules. Encourage good sportsmanship!

Which airplane can fly the farthest?

Test straw bridges with books, cups of pennies, or other weights.

Who has the tallest tower?

Which catapult can throw the farthest?

Test egg protectors using real eggs.

Be sure to clean up after the competition; teams play AND teams clean up.

 NAMING

Celebrate accomplishments!

 EXPRESSING

What did we use? What did we do? What did we see?

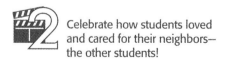 Celebrate how students loved and cared for their neighbors—the other students!

200

SAMPLE JOURNAL ENTRY

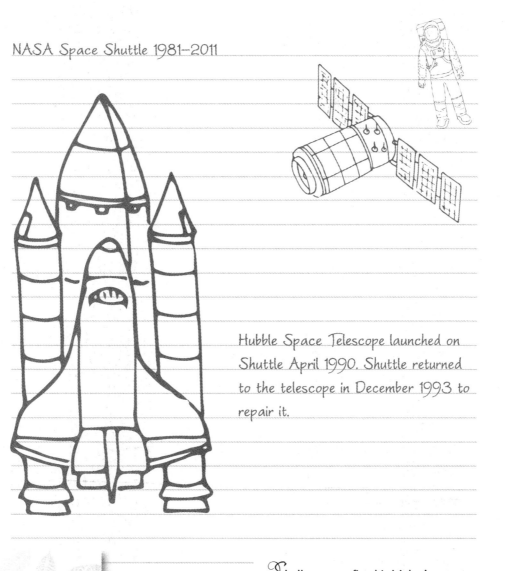

NASA Space Shuttle 1981–2011

Hubble Space Telescope launched on
Shuttle April 1990. Shuttle returned
to the telescope in December 1993 to
repair it.

Nature Sketch Journal

Drawing and Writing Pages and
References for Budding Scientists

Shall man confine his Maker's sway
    To Gothic domes of mouldering stone?
Thy temple is the face of day;
    Earth, ocean, heaven thy boundless
throne.
    —Lord Byron, "The Prayer of Nature" (excerpt)

Go further at home:

Explore (and sketch) the orbits of the bodies in our solar system.

Available from
CLASSICALCONVERSATIONSBOOKS.COM

RISING TO THE CHALLENGE
TEACHER CERTIFICATE

Congratulations

FOR SUCCESSFULLY
COMPLETING

CYCLE

2

IN YOUR HOME
SCHOOL

It is the glory of God to conceal a thing: but the honour of kings is to search out a matter.

Proverbs 25:2

_____

Parents' Names

Classical Conversations® honors your commitment to learn alongside your children and values your service to family and community.

Classical Conversations recognizes your achievements as parents who completed Foundations Cycle 2. You have taught your children and continued your own education by leading others through the grammar of math, Latin, science, English, history, geography, art, and music. This Cycle 2 knowledge, enhanced by weekly community training in the classical model, has equipped you to homeschool with confidence during the exciting high school years ahead. You are prepared to consider future roles tutoring the Foundations, Essentials, and Challenge programs.

_____
Licensed Classical Conversations™ Community Name

_____
Director Signature

_____
Date

Through wisdom is an house builded; and by understanding it is established:
And by knowledge shall the chambers be filled with all precious and pleasant riches.

—PROVERBS 24:3–4

A CYCLE 3 MEMORY MASTER KNOWS...

U.S. HISTORY

161 EVENTS AND PEOPLE

in a chronological timeline

24 HISTORY SENTENCES

including the Preamble to the U.S. Constitution and the Bill of Rights, which add depth to the timeline

120 GEOGRAPHIC FEATURES

and locations in North America

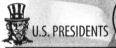

45 U.S. PRESIDENTS

24 SCIENCE FACTS

including the first 12 elements of the periodic table and the parts of 8 body systems

8 VERSES OF JOHN 1 IN LATIN

with English translation

15s MULTIPLICATION TABLES

as well as common squares and cubes, basic geometry formulas, and unit conversions

11 IRREGULAR VERB CONJUGATIONS

along with other grammar facts

not to mention drawing techniques, music theory, and tin whistle, **6** great artists and related projects, introduction to orchestra and **3** classical composers, **12** science experiments, **12** science projects, and **24** oral presentations!

For practice on the go, download our mobile app!

THAT'S OVER **400** pieces of information **in one year!**

WEEK	MATH	LATIN	SCIENCE	ENGLISH	TIMELINE	HISTORY	GEOGRAPHY	PROJECTS	FINE ARTS
1	1s and 2s	prepositions	4 types of tissue	an infinitive	1–7	Columbus	states and capitals	68 Blinking	basic shapes
2	3s and 4s	conjunctions and adverbs	bones of axial skeleton	a present participle	8–14	Pilgrims	states and capitals	70 Water Drop Lens	mirror images
3	5s and 6s	pronouns	3 kinds of muscle	a past participle	15–21	Boston Tea Party	states and capitals	74 Fingerprints	upside-down
4	7s and 8s	verbs	3 parts of nervous system	verbs: principal parts	22–28	Declaration of Independence	states and capitals	76 Lung Capacity	abstract
5	9s and 10s	verbs	5 main senses	to be	29–35	George Washington	states and capitals	72 Sound/Direct. 77 Rubbed Off	perspective
6	11s and 12s	nouns	digestive system	to do	36–42	Louisiana Purchase	states and capitals	78 How Do You…? 79 Spinning 80 Pattern	final project
7	13s	nouns	excretory system	to rise	43–49	Monroe Doctrine	states and capitals	brain, heart, kidney, bladder	tin whistle
8	14s	nouns	circulatory system	to raise	50–56	Missouri Compromise	states and capitals	cells, spleen, pancreas, gallbladder	dynamics
9	15s	verb rules	lymph system	to lay	57–63	Secession of Southern States	states and capitals	skeleton, muscles, stomach	note values and staff
10	squares	article rules	respiratory system	to lie	64–70	Manifest Destiny	states and capitals	intestines, liver, lungs, skin	rhythm
11	cubes	nouns/ pronouns rules	endocrine system	to set	71–77	Civil War	N. Appalachian Mountains	eyes, nose, ears, tongue, face	note names and scales
12	tsp. and tbsp.	John 1:1	purposes of blood	to sit	78–84	General Robert E. Lee	S. Appalachian Mountains	life-sized poster	review and celebration
13	liquid equivalents	John 1:1	atomic number	to beat	85–91	Fourteenth Amendment	Western Mountains	86 Where Did It Go?	Grandma Moses
14	linear equivalents	John 1:2	element	to break	92–98	Tycoons	Northwest Mountains	83 Not Same Time 84 Dry Paper	Picasso
15	metric measurements	John 1:3	parts of atom	to write	99–105	Immigrants	Great Lakes	91 Magic Solution	O'Keeffe
16	area rectangle	John 1:3	first 4 elements	to go	106–112	U.S. and WW I	bays	93 Bubbler	Rockwell
17	area square	John 1:4	second 4 elements	subject	113–119	Nineteenth Amendment	rivers (east)	99 Testing for Starch	Wyeth
18	area triangle	John 1:5	third 4 elements	predicate	120–126	Pearl Harbor	rivers (west)	102 Hard Water	Lichtenstein
19	area circle	John 1:5	acid and base	clause	127–133	NATO	trails	Coin Toss	Romantic & Modern
20	circumference	John 1:6	heavens declare	independent clause	134–140	Brown v. Board of Education	canals	Candy Probability	Tchaikovsky
21	Associative Law	John 1:6	theory of evolution	subordinate clause	141–147	U.S. astronauts	Native Amer. regions	Pizza Combinations	Debussy
22	Commutative Law	John 1:7	intelligent design	phrase	148–154	September 11, 2001	deserts	Bluberry Pancakes	Stravinsky
23	Distributive Law	John 1:7	preserve Earth's history	4 sentence structures	155–161	Preamble	prominent features	What are the Odds?	orchestra
24	Identity Law	John 1:7	natural selection	7 sentence patterns	U. S. Presidents	Bill of Rights	more prominent features	What Does All That Data Mean?	review

MATH

MULTIPLICATION TABLES
1s and 2s

1 × 1 = 1	2 × 1 = 2
1 × 2 = 2	2 × 2 = 4
1 × 3 = 3	2 × 3 = 6
1 × 4 = 4	2 × 4 = 8
1 × 5 = 5	2 × 5 = 10
1 × 6 = 6	2 × 6 = 12
1 × 7 = 7	2 × 7 = 14
1 × 8 = 8	2 × 8 = 16
1 × 9 = 9	2 × 9 = 18
1 × 10 = 10	2 × 10 = 20
1 × 11 = 11	2 × 11 = 22
1 × 12 = 12	2 × 12 = 24
1 × 13 = 13	2 × 13 = 26
1 × 14 = 14	2 × 14 = 28
1 × 15 = 15	2 × 15 = 30

 ENGLISH

AN INFINITIVE
An **infinitive** is "to" plus a verb, used as a noun, adjective, or adverb.

 LATIN

PREPOSITIONS

in	in
apud	with
per	by
sine	without
a	from
de	of

TIMELINE

Classical Acts & Facts® History Cards

1	**AGE OF ANCIENT EMPIRES**
2	Creation and the Fall
3	The Flood and the Tower of Babel
4	Mesopotamia and Sumer
5	Egyptians
6	Indus River Valley Civilization
7	Minoans and Mycenaeans

 SCIENCE 1

Classical Acts & Facts® Science Cycle 3

What are four types of tissue?
connective
epithelial
muscle
nerve

PRESENTATION NOTES

 Recite math memory work in speed rounds.

 HISTORY 92

Tell me about Columbus.
In 1492, Columbus made the first of four trips to the Caribbean on three Spanish ships named the *Niña*, the *Pinta*, and the *Santa María*.

 GEOGRAPHY

STATES AND CAPITALS
Augusta, ME
Concord, NH
Boston, MA
Providence, RI
Hartford, CT

 HANDS-ON

FINE ARTS
Drawing Introduction (see page 80)
Five Elements of Shape (see page 81)

SCIENCE
Blinking (#68)

MATH

MULTIPLICATION TABLES
3s and 4s

3 × 1 = 3	4 × 1 = 4
3 × 2 = 6	4 × 2 = 8
3 × 3 = 9	4 × 3 = 12
3 × 4 = 12	4 × 4 = 16
3 × 5 = 15	4 × 5 = 20
3 × 6 = 18	4 × 6 = 24
3 × 7 = 21	4 × 7 = 28
3 × 8 = 24	4 × 8 = 32
3 × 9 = 27	4 × 9 = 36
3 × 10 = 30	4 × 10 = 40
3 × 11 = 33	4 × 11 = 44
3 × 12 = 36	4 × 12 = 48
3 × 13 = 39	4 × 13 = 52
3 × 14 = 42	4 × 14 = 56
3 × 15 = 45	4 × 15 = 60

 ENGLISH

A PRESENT PARTICIPLE
A **present participle** is a verb plus "-ing," used as an adjective or a verb.

 HISTORY 100

Tell me about the Pilgrims.
In 1620, the Pilgrims sailed from Plymouth, England and signed the Mayflower Compact before founding Plymouth Colony in North America.

 LATIN

CONJUNCTIONS and ADVERBS

et	and
ut	that
non	not

 TIMELINE

Classical Acts & Facts® History Cards

8 Seven Wonders of the Ancient World
9 Patriarchs of Israel
10 Hittites and Canaanites
11 Kush
12 Assyrians
13 Babylonians
14 China's Shang Dynasty

 **GEOGRAPHY**

STATES AND CAPITALS
Montpelier, VT
Albany, NY
Trenton, NJ
Harrisburg, PA
Dover, DE

 **SCIENCE** CYCLE 3 2

Classical Acts & Facts® Science Cycle 3

Which bones make up the axial skeleton?
skull
vertebrae
ribs
sternum

PRESENTATION NOTES

 Set a goal of drawing a map a day.

 HANDS-ON

FINE ARTS
Mirror Images (see page 82)

SCIENCE
Water Drop Lens (#70)

What are some outside activities you enjoy at night?

MATH

MULTIPLICATION TABLES
5s and 6s

5 × 1 = 5	6 × 1 = 6
5 × 2 = 10	6 × 2 = 12
5 × 3 = 15	6 × 3 = 18
5 × 4 = 20	6 × 4 = 24
5 × 5 = 25	6 × 5 = 30
5 × 6 = 30	6 × 6 = 36
5 × 7 = 35	6 × 7 = 42
5 × 8 = 40	6 × 8 = 48
5 × 9 = 45	6 × 9 = 54
5 × 10 = 50	6 × 10 = 60
5 × 11 = 55	6 × 11 = 66
5 × 12 = 60	6 × 12 = 72
5 × 13 = 65	6 × 13 = 78
5 × 14 = 70	6 × 14 = 84
5 × 15 = 75	6 × 15 = 90

 ENGLISH

A PAST PARTICIPLE
A **past participle** is a verb plus "-ed," used as an adjective or a verb.

 HISTORY 108

Tell me about the Boston Tea Party.

In 1773, colonists disguised as Mohawks dumped tea from the British East India Company into the Boston Harbor.

 LATIN

PRONOUNS

hic	this
hoc	same
ipso, ipsum	him
cui	whose
quod	that
eam	it
illum	him

 **TIMELINE**

Classical Acts & Facts® History Cards

15	Hinduism in India
16	Phoenicians and the Alphabet
17	Olmecs of Mesoamerica
18	Israelite Exodus and Desert Wandering
19	Israelite Conquest and Judges
20	Greek Dark Ages
21	Israel's United Kingdom

 GEOGRAPHY

STATES AND CAPITALS
Annapolis, MD
Richmond, VA
Charleston, WV
Raleigh, NC
Columbia, SC
Washington, DC

 SCIENCE

Classical Acts & Facts® Science Cycle 3

What are three kinds of muscle?
skeletal
smooth
cardiac

PRESENTATION NOTES

 Review Cycle 1 history.

 HANDS-ON

FINE ARTS
Upside-down image (see page 83)

SCIENCE
Fingerprints (#74)

Memoria

MATH

MULTIPLICATION TABLES
7s and 8s

$7 \times 1 = 7$	$8 \times 1 = 8$
$7 \times 2 = 14$	$8 \times 2 = 16$
$7 \times 3 = 21$	$8 \times 3 = 24$
$7 \times 4 = 28$	$8 \times 4 = 32$
$7 \times 5 = 35$	$8 \times 5 = 40$
$7 \times 6 = 42$	$8 \times 6 = 48$
$7 \times 7 = 49$	$8 \times 7 = 56$
$7 \times 8 = 56$	$8 \times 8 = 64$
$7 \times 9 = 63$	$8 \times 9 = 72$
$7 \times 10 = 70$	$8 \times 10 = 80$
$7 \times 11 = 77$	$8 \times 11 = 88$
$7 \times 12 = 84$	$8 \times 12 = 96$
$7 \times 13 = 91$	$8 \times 13 = 104$
$7 \times 14 = 98$	$8 \times 14 = 112$
$7 \times 15 = 105$	$8 \times 15 = 120$

 ENGLISH

VERB: PRINCIPAL PARTS
infinitive
present
past
present participle
past participle

 LATIN

VERBS

erat	was
venit	came
perhiberet	bear
crederent	believe

 **TIMELINE**

Classical Acts & Facts® History Cards

22	Early Native Americans
23	Israel Divides into Two Kingdoms
24	Homer and Hesiod
25	Rome Founded by Romulus and Remus
26	Israel Falls to Assyria
27	Assyria Falls to Babylon
28	Lao-Tzu, Confucius, Buddha

SCIENCE CYCLE 3 4

Classical Acts & Facts® Science Cycle 3

What are three parts of the nervous system?
brain
spinal cord
nerves

PRESENTATION NOTES

 Review Cycle 1 English.

 HISTORY 108

Tell me about the Declaration of Independence.
In 1776, the Continental Congress published the Declaration of Independence in Philadelphia, announcing the colonists' intent to separate from England.

 GEOGRAPHY

STATES AND CAPITALS
Atlanta, GA
Tallahassee, FL
Montgomery, AL
Jackson, MS
Baton Rouge, LA

HANDS-ON

FINE ARTS
Abstract Art (see page 84)

SCIENCE
Lung Capacity (#76)

Memoria
What are you praying for?

 MATH

MULTIPLICATION TABLES
9s and 10s

9 × 1 = 9	10 × 1 = 10
9 × 2 = 18	10 × 2 = 20
9 × 3 = 27	10 × 3 = 30
9 × 4 = 36	10 × 4 = 40
9 × 5 = 45	10 × 5 = 50
9 × 6 = 54	10 × 6 = 60
9 × 7 = 63	10 × 7 = 70
9 × 8 = 72	10 × 8 = 80
9 × 9 = 81	10 × 9 = 90
9 × 10 = 90	10 × 10 = 100
9 × 11 = 99	10 × 11 = 110
9 × 12 = 108	10 × 12 = 120
9 × 13 = 117	10 × 13 = 130
9 × 14 = 126	10 × 14 = 140
9 × 15 = 135	10 × 15 = 150

 ENGLISH

TO BE

infinitive	to be
present	am, are, is
past	was, were
present participle	being
past participle	been

 LATIN

VERBS

facta sunt	were made
factum est	was made
missus	sent
conprehenderunt	comprehended
lucet	shineth
fuit	there was

TIMELINE

Classical Acts & Facts® History Cards

29   Judah falls to Babylon, Temple Destroyed
30   Babylon Falls to Persia
31   Jews Return and Rebuild the Temple
32   Roman Republic
33   Golden Age of Greece
34   Peloponnesian Wars
35   Persia Falls to Alexander the Great

 SCIENCE

Classical Acts & Facts® Science Cycle 3

What are the five main senses?
sight
hearing
taste
smell
touch

PRESENTATION NOTES

 Recite Cycle 3 Latin vocabulary in speed rounds.

 HISTORY 108

Tell me about George Washington.
In 1789, in New York, George Washington was granted the full powers and responsibilities of the presidency by the U.S. Constitution.

 **GEOGRAPHY**

STATES AND CAPITALS
Lansing, MI
Columbus, OH
Indianapolis, IN
Frankfort, KY
Nashville, TN

 **HANDS-ON**

FINE ARTS
Perspective (see page 85)

SCIENCE
Sound and Direction (#72)
Rubbed Off (#77)

MATH

MULTIPLICATION TABLES
11s and 12s

11 × 1 = 11	12 × 1 = 12
11 × 2 = 22	12 × 2 = 24
11 × 3 = 33	12 × 3 = 36
11 × 4 = 44	12 × 4 = 48
11 × 5 = 55	12 × 5 = 60
11 × 6 = 66	12 × 6 = 72
11 × 7 = 77	12 × 7 = 84
11 × 8 = 88	12 × 8 = 96
11 × 9 = 99	12 × 9 = 108
11 × 10 = 110	12 × 10 = 120
11 × 11 = 121	12 × 11 = 132
11 × 12 = 132	12 × 12 = 144
11 × 13 = 143	12 × 13 = 156
11 × 14 = 154	12 × 14 = 168
11 × 15 = 165	12 × 15 = 180

ENGLISH

TO DO

infinitive	to do
present	do, does
past	did
present participle	doing
past participle	done

LATIN

NOUNS

verbum	word
Deus, Deum, Deo	God
principio	beginning
omnia, omnes	all
nihil	nothing

TIMELINE

Classical Acts & Facts® History Cards

36 India's Mauryan Empire
37 Mayans of Mesoamerica
38 Punic Wars
39 Rome Conquers Greece
40 Roman Dictator Julius Caesar
41 Caesar Augustus and the *Pax Romana*
42 John the Baptist

SCIENCE

Cycle 3 • 7

Classical Acts & Facts® Science Cycle 3

What are some parts of the digestive system?
mouth
esophagus
stomach
liver
small intestine
large intestine

PRESENTATION NOTES

HISTORY
  112

Tell me about the Louisiana Purchase.
In 1803, the purchase of Louisiana from France prompted westward exploration by pioneers such as Lewis and Clark and Congressman Davy Crockett.

GEOGRAPHY

STATES AND CAPITALS
Madison, WI
Springfield, IL
Des Moines, IA
Jefferson City, MO
Little Rock, AR

HANDS-ON

FINE ARTS
Drawing Review and Final Project (see page 86)

SCIENCE
How Do You Feel? (#78)
Spinning (#79)
Change of Pattern (#80)

What do you want to do differently next week?

MATH

MULTIPLICATION TABLES

13s

$13 \times 1 = 13$
$13 \times 2 = 26$
$13 \times 3 = 39$
$13 \times 4 = 52$
$13 \times 5 = 65$
$13 \times 6 = 78$
$13 \times 7 = 91$
$13 \times 8 = 104$
$13 \times 9 = 117$
$13 \times 10 = 130$
$13 \times 11 = 143$
$13 \times 12 = 156$
$13 \times 13 = 169$
$13 \times 14 = 182$
$13 \times 15 = 195$

ENGLISH

TO RISE

infinitive	to rise
present	rise, rises
past	rose
present participle	rising
past participle	risen

HISTORY 115

Tell me about the Monroe Doctrine. 118

After victory in the War of 1812, the United States wrote the Monroe Doctrine, which warned Europeans not to attempt to colonize the Americas.

LATIN

NOUNS

vita	life
lux	light
homo, hominum	man
nomen	name

TIMELINE

Classical Acts & Facts® History Cards

43   Jesus the Messiah
44   Pentecost and the Early Church
45   Persecution Spreads the Gospel
46   Herod's Temple Destroyed by Titus
47   Diocletian Divides the Roman Empire
48   Constantine Legalizes Christianity
49   India's Gupta Dynasty

GEOGRAPHY

STATES AND CAPITALS

St. Paul, MN
Bismarck, ND
Pierre, SD
Cheyenne, WY
Lincoln, NE

SCIENCE

Classical Acts & Facts® Science Cycle 3

What are four parts of the excretory system?

urinary tract
lungs
skin
intestines

PRESENTATION NOTES

 Choose a *Classical Acts & Facts® History Card* at random and recite cards that come after it.

HANDS-ON

FINE ARTS

Music Theory and Practice Introduction (see page 87)
Parts of the Tin Whistle (see pages 88, 90–91)

SCIENCE

Anatomy: brain, heart, kidney, bladder (see pages 261–262)

CYCLE 3 | 9

 MATH

MULTIPLICATION TABLES
14s
$14 \times 1 = 14$
$14 \times 2 = 28$
$14 \times 3 = 42$
$14 \times 4 = 56$
$14 \times 5 = 70$
$14 \times 6 = 84$
$14 \times 7 = 98$
$14 \times 8 = 112$
$14 \times 9 = 126$
$14 \times 10 = 140$
$14 \times 11 = 154$
$14 \times 12 = 168$
$14 \times 13 = 182$
$14 \times 14 = 196$
$14 \times 15 = 210$

 ENGLISH

TO RAISE

infinitive	to raise
present	raise, raises
past	raised
present participle	raising
past participle	raised

NOTE: Weeks 5 through 16 are irregular verb tenses. Week 8, *to raise*, is a regular verb but is shown for comparison to *to rise*.

 HISTORY 116

Tell me about the Missouri Compromise.

In 1820, Henry Clay worked out the Missouri Compromise, allowing Missouri to enter the Union as a slave state and Maine as a free state.

 LATIN

NOUNS

testimonium	witness, testimony
lumine	light
Iohannes	John
tenebris, tenebrae	darkness

TIMELINE

Classical Acts & Facts® History Cards

50 Council of Nicea
51 Augustine of Hippo
52 Jerome Completes the Vulgate
53 Visigoths Sack Rome
54 THE MIDDLE AGES
55 Council of Chalcedon
56 Western Roman Empire Falls to Barbarians

 SCIENCE

Classical Acts & Facts® Science Cycle 3

What are six parts of the circulatory system?

heart
arteries
veins
capillaries
red and white blood cells
platelets

PRESENTATION NOTES

 Refer to *Trivium Tables®: Rhetoric* for ways to enhance your presentation this week.

GEOGRAPHY

STATES AND CAPITALS
Topeka, KS
Oklahoma City, OK
Austin, TX
Denver, CO
Santa Fe, NM

HANDS-ON

FINE ARTS
Dynamics (see pages 92–93)

SCIENCE
Anatomy: cells, spleen, pancreas, gallbladder (see pages 261–262)

Memoria

What new discovery about God's world brought you joy?

MATH

MULTIPLICATION TABLES
15s
15 × 1 = 15
15 × 2 = 30
15 × 3 = 45
15 × 4 = 60
15 × 5 = 75
15 × 6 = 90
15 × 7 = 105
15 × 8 = 120
15 × 9 = 135
15 × 10 = 150
15 × 11 = 165
15 × 12 = 180
15 × 13 = 195
15 × 14 = 210
15 × 15 = 225

ENGLISH

TO LAY

infinitive	to lay
present	lay, lays
past	laid
present participle	laying
past participle	laid

HISTORY

Tell me about the secession of the Southern states.

The Compromise of 1850, the Fugitive Slave Act, and the *Dred Scott* decision preceded the secession of the Southern states.

LATIN

VERB RULES
Latin verbs have different endings called **conjugations**.

TIMELINE

Classical Acts & Facts® History Cards

57 Byzantine Emperor Justinian
58 Benedict and Monasticism
59 Muhammad Founds Islam
60 Zanj and Early Ghana in Africa
61 Franks Defeat Muslims at the Battle of Tours
62 Golden Age of Islam
63 Vikings Raid and Trade

GEOGRAPHY

STATES AND CAPITALS
Salt Lake City, UT
Phoenix, AZ
Carson City, NV
Sacramento, CA
Honolulu, HI

SCIENCE

Classical Acts & Facts® Science Cycle 3

What are four parts of the lymph system?
lymph vessels
lymph nodes
spleen
thymus

PRESENTATION NOTES

 Review Cycle 1 science.

HANDS-ON

FINE ARTS
Note Values and Staff (see pages 94–95)

SCIENCE
Anatomy: skeleton, muscles, stomach (see pages 261–262)

MATH

SQUARES
$1 \times 1 = 1$
$2 \times 2 = 4$
$3 \times 3 = 9$
$4 \times 4 = 16$
$5 \times 5 = 25$
$6 \times 6 = 36$
$7 \times 7 = 49$
$8 \times 8 = 64$
$9 \times 9 = 81$
$10 \times 10 = 100$
$11 \times 11 = 121$
$12 \times 12 = 144$
$13 \times 13 = 169$
$14 \times 14 = 196$
$15 \times 15 = 225$

ENGLISH

TO LIE
infinitive	to lie
present	lie, lies
past	lay
present participle	lying
past participle	lain

HISTORY 121

Tell me about Manifest Destiny.
President Polk believed that the Mexican War and the Gadsden Purchase in the mid-1800s affirmed America's manifest destiny to spread across the continent.

LATIN

ARTICLE RULES
Latin has no translation for articles *a, an, the*. (These rules are observable in the passage you translated.)

 **TIMELINE**

Classical Acts & Facts® History Cards

64 Japan's Heian Period
65 Charlemagne Crowned Emperor of Europe
66 Alfred the Great of England
67 Erik the Red and Leif Eriksson, Norse Explorers
68 Vladimir I of Kiev
69 Byzantine Emperor Basil II
70 East-West Schism of the Church

 **GEOGRAPHY**

STATES AND CAPITALS
Helena, MT
Boise, ID
Olympia, WA
Salem, OR
Juneau, AK

SCIENCE

Classical Acts & Facts® Science Cycle 3

What are some parts of the respiratory system?
nose
pharynx
larynx
trachea
bronchi
bronchioles
alveoli
lungs

PRESENTATION NOTES

Review Cycle 1 geography.

HANDS-ON

FINE ARTS
Rhythm (see pages 96–97)

SCIENCE
Anatomy: intestines, liver, lungs, skin (see pages 261–262)

Memoria
Share some details from a field trip.

MATH

CUBES
$1 \times 1 \times 1 = 1$
$2 \times 2 \times 2 = 8$
$3 \times 3 \times 3 = 27$
$4 \times 4 \times 4 = 64$
$5 \times 5 \times 5 = 125$
$6 \times 6 \times 6 = 216$
$7 \times 7 \times 7 = 343$
$8 \times 8 \times 8 = 512$
$9 \times 9 \times 9 = 729$
$10 \times 10 \times 10 = 1{,}000$
$11 \times 11 \times 11 = 1{,}331$
$12 \times 12 \times 12 = 1{,}728$
$13 \times 13 \times 13 = 2{,}197$
$14 \times 14 \times 14 = 2{,}744$
$15 \times 15 \times 15 = 3{,}375$

ENGLISH

TO SET
infinitive	to set
present	set, sets
past	set
present participle	setting
past participle	set

LATIN

NOUNS/PRONOUNS RULES
Latin nouns and pronouns have different endings called **declensions**.

TIMELINE

Classical Acts & Facts® History Cards

71 Norman Conquest and Feudalism in Europe
72 The Crusades
73 Zimbabwe and Early Mali in Africa
74 Aztecs of Mesoamerica
75 Francis of Assisi and Thomas Aquinas
76 Japan's Shoguns
77 Incas of South America

SCIENCE

Classical Acts & Facts® Science Cycle 3

What is the endocrine system?
The endocrine system consists of glands and organs that use hormones to send messages through the bloodstream to the rest of the body.

PRESENTATION NOTES

Recite timeline forwards and backwards.

HISTORY 127

Tell me about the Civil War.
In 1861, the Civil War began when President Abraham Lincoln went to war with the Southern states that had seceded from the Union.

GEOGRAPHY

NORTHERN APPALACHIAN MOUNTAINS
White Mountains
Green Mountains
Adirondack Mountains
Allegheny Mountains

HANDS-ON

FINE ARTS
Note Names and Scales (see pages 98–101)

SCIENCE
Anatomy: eyes, nose, ears, tongue, face (see pages 261–262)

Memoria

MATH

TEASPOONS AND TABLESPOONS
3 teaspoons (tsp.) =
1 tablespoon (tbsp.)

2 tablespoons (tbsp.) =
1 fluid ounce (fl. oz.)

 LATIN

JOHN 1:1
in principio erat Verbum

in the beginning was the Word

 SCIENCE

Classical Acts & Facts® Science Cycle 3

What are the major purposes of blood?
transportation
protection
communication
regulation

 ENGLISH

TO SIT

infinitive	to sit
present	sit, sits
past	sat
present participle	sitting
past participle	sat

TIMELINE

Classical Acts & Facts® History Cards

78 Genghis Khan Rules the Mongols
79 England's Magna Carta
80 Ottoman Empire
81 Marco Polo's Journey to China
82 The Hundred Years' War and Black Death
83 The Renaissance
84 China's Ming Dynasty

PRESENTATION NOTES

 Choose a series of history sentences and create a history story.

 HISTORY 127

Tell me about General Robert E. Lee.

In 1865, General Robert E. Lee surrendered to General Ulysses S. Grant at Appomattox Court House in Virginia.

GEOGRAPHY

SOUTHERN APPALACHIAN MOUNTAINS
The Great Valley
Blue Ridge Mountains
Great Smoky Mountains
Cumberland Mountains
Mt. Mitchell

HANDS-ON

FINE ARTS
Review and Celebration (see pages 102–103)

SCIENCE
Anatomy: create life-sized poster (see pages 261–262)

Memoria
Who are some mentors you value?

CYCLE 3 **WEEK 13**

MEMORY WORK

 MATH

LIQUID EQUIVALENTS

8 fluid ounces (fl. oz.) = 1 cup (c.)

2 cups (c.) = 1 pint (pt.)

2 pints (pt.) = 1 quart (qt.)

4 quarts (qt.) = 1 gallon (gal.)

 LATIN

JOHN 1:1

et Verbum erat apud Deum

and the Word was with God

et Deus erat Verbum

and the Word was God

 SCIENCE 17

Classical Acts & Facts® Science Cycle 3

What is the atomic number?

The atomic number is the number of protons in the nucleus of an atom, which is also the number of electrons in a neutral atom.

 ENGLISH

TO BEAT

infinitive	to beat
present	beat, beats
past	beat
present participle	beating
past participle	beaten

TIMELINE

Classical Acts & Facts® History Cards

85 **AGE OF EXPLORATION**
86 Prince Henry Founds School of Navigation
87 Slave Trade in Africa
88 Gutenberg's Printing Press
89 Songhai in Africa
90 Czar Ivan the Great of Russia
91 The Spanish Inquisition

PRESENTATION NOTES

 Recite irregular Latin verbs in a speed round.

 HISTORY 128

Tell me about the Fourteenth Amendment. 150

In 1868, the Fourteenth Amendment made all former slaves U.S. citizens and paved the way for the Civil Rights Movement.

 GEOGRAPHY

WESTERN MOUNTAINS
Rocky Mountains
Pikes Peak
Mt. Elbert
Sierra Nevadas
Mt. Whitney

HANDS-ON 35

FINE ARTS

Introduction to Great Artists (see pages 104–105, 254)
Grandma Moses (see page 255)

SCIENCE

Where Did It Go? (#86)

Memoria

218

MEMORY WORK WEEK **14**

 M A T H

LINEAR EQUIVALENTS
2.54 centimeters (cm) = 1 inch (in.)

12 inches (in.) = 1 foot (ft.)

5,280 feet (ft.) = 1 mile (mi.)

1 kilometer (km) = ⅝ mile (mi.)

 L A T I N

JOHN 1:2
hoc erat in principio apud Deum

the same was in the beginning with God

 S C I E N C E 18

Classical Acts & Facts® Science Cycle 3

What is an element?
An element is a basic chemical substance defined by its atomic number and atomic mass.

 E N G L I S H

TO BREAK
infinitive	to break
present	break, breaks
past	broke
present participle	breaking
past participle	broken

 **T I M E L I N E**

Classical Acts & Facts® History Cards

92 Columbus Sails to the Caribbean

93 AGE OF ABSOLUTE MONARCHS

94 Protestant Reformation

95 Spanish Conquistadors in the Americas

96 Calvin's *Institutes of the Christian Religion*

97 Council of Trent

98 Baroque Period of the Arts

P R E S E N T A T I O N   N O T E S

 Review Cycle 1 Latin.

 H I S T O R Y 106

Tell me about tycoons.
During the late 1800s, tycoons like Vanderbilt, Rockefeller, Carnegie, and Swift fueled the nation's Industrial Age by developing American resources.

 G E O G R A P H Y

NORTHWEST MOUNTAINS
Cascade Mountains
Mt. Rainier
Mt. St. Helens
Denali

 H A N D S - O N 38

FINE ARTS
Pablo Picasso (see page 255)

SCIENCE
Not at the Same Time (#83)
Dry Paper (#84)

Memoria
Describe God's goodness to your family.

MATH

 LATIN

 SCIENCE 19

METRIC MEASUREMENTS

10 millimeters (mm) =
1 centimeter (cm)

100 centimeters (cm) = 1 meter (m)

1,000 meters (m) = 1 kilometer (km)

JOHN 1:3
omnia per ipsum facta sunt

all things were made by him

Classical Acts & Facts® Science Cycle 3

What are some parts of an atom?
nucleus
protons
electrons
quarks
leptons
neutrons

 ENGLISH

TIMELINE

PRESENTATION NOTES

TO WRITE

infinitive	to write
present	write, writes
past	wrote
present participle	writing
past participle	written

Classical Acts & Facts® History Cards

99	Japan's Isolation
100	Jamestown and Plymouth Colony Founded
101	**AGE OF ENLIGHTENMENT**
102	Hudson's Bay Company
103	First Great Awakening
104	Classical Period of the Arts
105	The Seven Years' War

 Review Cycle 2 history.

 HISTORY 117

 GEOGRAPHY

 HANDS-ON 40

Tell me about immigrants coming to America.
From 1820 to 1930, more than 37 million immigrants came to America, seeking freedom and the opportunity to increase their personal wealth.

GREAT LAKES

H uron
O ntario
M ichigan
E rie
S uperior

FINE ARTS

Georgia O'Keeffe (see page 255)

SCIENCE

Magic Solution (#91)

Memoria

MATH

 LATIN

 SCIENCE

AREA OF A RECTANGLE

The area of a rectangle equals length times width.

JOHN 1:3

et sine ipso factum est nihil

and without him was made nothing

quod factum est

that was made

Classical Acts & Facts® Science Cycle 3

What are the first four elements in the periodic table by number, element, symbol, and mass?

1	Hydrogen	H	1
2	Helium	He	4
3	Lithium	Li	7
4	Beryllium	Be	9

 ENGLISH

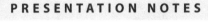 **TIMELINE**

PRESENTATION NOTES

TO GO

infinitive	to go
present	go, goes
past	went
present participle	going
past participle	gone

Classical Acts & Facts® History Cards

106 AGE OF INDUSTRY
107 James Cook Sails to Australia and Antarctica
108 American Revolution and Gen. George Washington
109 Madison's Constitution and the Bill of Rights
110 French Revolution
111 Second Great Awakening
112 Louisiana Purchase and Lewis and Clark Expedition

 Categorize timeline cards by continent.

 HISTORY

 **GEOGRAPHY**

HANDS-ON

Tell me about the United States and World War I.

In 1917, President Wilson asked Congress to enter World War I against the Central Powers two years after German U-boats sank the *Lusitania*, killing American citizens.

BAYS

Chesapeake Bay
Hudson Bay
San Francisco Bay
Puget Sound
Pamlico Sound

FINE ARTS

Norman Rockwell (see page 256)

SCIENCE

Bubbler (#93)

Memoria
What are you learning about yourself?

MATH

AREA OF A SQUARE
The area of a square equals length of its side squared.

LATIN

JOHN 1:4
in ipso vita erat

in him was life

et vita erat lux hominum

and the life was the light of men

SCIENCE

Classical Acts & Facts® Science Cycle 3

What are the second four elements in the periodic table by number, element, symbol, and mass?

5	Boron	B	11
6	Carbon	C	12
7	Nitrogen	N	14
8	Oxygen	O	16

ENGLISH

SENTENCE PARTS: SUBJECT
The **subject** is that part of a sentence about which something is being said.

TIMELINE

Classical Acts & Facts® History Cards

113	Napoleon Crowned Emperor of France
114	Liberation of South America
115	The War of 1812
116	The Missouri Compromise
117	Immigrants Flock to America
118	The Monroe Doctrine
119	Romantic Period of the Arts

PRESENTATION NOTES

 In ten minutes, draw as much of the world as you can remember, with locations and features.

HISTORY

Tell me about the Nineteenth Amendment.
Elizabeth Cady Stanton and Susan B. Anthony led the women's suffrage movement in the United States, resulting in the Nineteenth Amendment in 1920 that granted women the right to vote.

GEOGRAPHY

RIVERS (East)
St. Lawrence River
Ohio River
Mississippi River
Missouri River
Arkansas River

HANDS-ON 43

FINE ARTS

Andrew Wyeth (see page 256)

SCIENCE

Testing for Starch (#99)

Memoria

MEMORY WORK WEEK **18**

 M A T H

AREA OF A TRIANGLE
The area of a triangle equals one-half base times height.

L A T I N

JOHN 1:5
et lux in tenebris lucet

and the light shineth in the darkness

 S C I E N C E 25

Classical Acts & Facts® Science Cycle 3

What are the third four elements in the periodic table by number, element, symbol, and mass?

9	Fluorine	F	19
10	Neon	Ne	20
11	Sodium	Na	23
12	Magnesium	Mg	24

 E N G L I S H

SENTENCE PARTS: PREDICATE
The **predicate** is that part of a sentence that says something about the subject.

T I M E L I N E

Classical Acts & Facts® History Cards

120 Cherokee Trail of Tears
121 U.S. Westward Expansion
122 Marx Publishes *The Communist Manifesto*
123 The Compromise of 1850 and the *Dred Scott* Decision
124 U.S. Restores Trade with Japan
125 British Queen Victoria's Rule Over India
126 Darwin Publishes *The Origin of Species*

P R E S E N T A T I O N   N O T E S

 Recite Cycle 3 Latin rules in speed rounds.

H I S T O R Y 141

Tell me about Pearl Harbor.
On December 7, 1941, the Japanese bombed Pearl Harbor, Hawaii, causing the United States to join the Allies in World War II.

G E O G R A P H Y

RIVERS (West)
Colorado River
Red River
Rio Grande River
Columbia River
Great Salt Lake

 H A N D S - O N 44

FINE ARTS
Roy Lichtenstein (see page 256)

SCIENCE
Hard Water (#102)

Memoria
How did your parents contribute to your success?

MATH

AREA OF A CIRCLE
The area of a circle equals pi (3.14) times the radius squared.

 LATIN

JOHN 1:5
et tenebrae eam non conpre-henderunt

and the darkness did not comprehend it

 SCIENCE 29

Classical Acts & Facts® Science Cycle 3

What is the difference between an acid and a base?
An acid donates a hydrogen ion and a base accepts a hydrogen ion.

 ENGLISH

SENTENCE PARTS: CLAUSE
A **clause** is a group of words that contains both a subject and a verb.

TIMELINE

Classical Acts & Facts® History Cards

127 Lincoln's War Between the States
128 Reconstruction of the Southern States
129 Dominion of Canada
130 Otto von Bismarck Unifies Germany
131 Boer Wars in Africa
132 The Spanish-American War
133 The Progressive Era

PRESENTATION NOTES

  Review Cycle 2 science.

 HISTORY 148

Tell me about NATO.
In 1949, the United States and its allies formed NATO to resist the spread of Soviet communism.

 GEOGRAPHY

TRAILS
Cumberland Road
Santa Fe Trail
Mormon Trail
Gila Trail
Old Spanish Trail
California Trail
Oregon Trail

HANDS-ON 139

FINE ARTS
Composers and Orchestra Introduction (see pages 108–109, 257)
Romantic and Modern Periods (see page 258)

SCIENCE
Probability (see page 263)
Coin Toss (see pages 264–265)

Memoria

MEMORY WORK   **WEEK 20**

 MATH

CIRCUMFERENCE OF A CIRCLE
The circumference of a circle equals two times pi (3.14) times the radius.

LATIN

JOHN 1:6
fuit homo missus a Deo

there was a man sent from God

 SCIENCE 31

Classical Acts & Facts® Science Cycle 3

What do the heavens declare?
The heavens declare the glory of God: the skies proclaim the work of his hands. (Psalm 19:1, NIV)

ENGLISH

INDEPENDENT CLAUSE
An **independent clause** expresses a complete thought like a sentence.

TIMELINE

Classical Acts & Facts® History Cards

134 Australia Becomes a Commonwealth
135 Mexican Revolution
136 World War I and President Wilson
137 Lenin and the Bolshevik Revolution in Russia
138 U.S. Evangelist Billy Graham
139 Modern Period of the Arts
140 The Great Depression and the New Deal

PRESENTATION NOTES

Review Cycle 2 English.

 HISTORY 150

Tell me about *Brown v. Board of Education*.
In 1954, in *Brown v. Board of Education*, the U.S. Supreme Court ruled that the segregation of public schools by race is unconstitutional.

GEOGRAPHY

CANALS
Erie Canal
Pennsylvania Canal
Chesapeake and Ohio Canal
Ohio and Erie Canal
Miami and Erie Canal

HANDS-ON 31

FINE ARTS
Tchaikovsky *Symphony no. 6* (see page 258)

SCIENCE
Candy Probability (see pages 266–267)

Memoria
What did you struggle with this week?

MATH

The Associative Law
for addition states:
$(a + b) + c = a + (b + c)$

The Associative Law
for multiplication states:
$(a \times b) \times c = a \times (b \times c)$

LATIN

JOHN 1:6
cui nomen erat Iohannes

whose name was John

SCIENCE 32

Classical Acts & Facts® Science Cycle 3

What does the theory of evolution rely on?
The theory of evolution relies on the belief that life began as a chance combination of non-living things.

ENGLISH

SUBORDINATE CLAUSE
A **subordinate clause**, also known as a dependent clause, does not express a complete thought and cannot stand alone.

TIMELINE

Classical Acts & Facts® History Cards

141 World War II and President Franklin D. Roosevelt
142 Stalin of the USSR and the Katyn Massacre
143 The United Nations Formed
144 The Cold War
145 Gandhi and India's Independence
146 Jewish State Established
147 Mao and Communist Victory in China

PRESENTATION NOTES

Review Cycle 2 geography.

HISTORY 154

Tell me about U.S. astronauts.
In 1969, U.S. astronauts Neil Armstrong and Edwin Aldrin were the first men to walk on the moon.

GEOGRAPHY

NATIVE AMERICAN REGIONS
Eastern Woodlands
Plains
Plateau
Northwest Coast
California
Great Basin
Southwest

HANDS-ON 36

FINE ARTS

Debussy "La Mer" (see page 258)

SCIENCE

Pizza Combinations (see page 268)

Memoria

18-21, 26-28, 31-48

MATH

The Commutative Law for addition states:
$$a + b = b + a$$

The Commutative Law for multiplication states:
$$a \times b = b \times a$$

LATIN

JOHN 1:7
hic venit in testimonium

this man came for a witness

SCIENCE

CYCLE 3   33

Classical Acts & Facts® Science Cycle 3

What does the theory of intelligent design rely on?
The theory of intelligent design relies on the belief that life began as a result of intention and purpose.

ENGLISH

SENTENCE PARTS: PHRASE

A **phrase** is a group of words that does not contain both a subject and a verb and may be used as a single part of speech.

TIMELINE

Classical Acts & Facts® History Cards

148   North Atlantic Treaty Organization
149   The Korean War
150   Martin Luther King, Jr. and the Civil Rights Movement
151   Jim and Elisabeth Elliot, Missionaries to Ecuador
152   The Antarctic Treaty
153   The Vietnam War
154   U.S. Astronauts Walk on the Moon

PRESENTATION NOTES

Substitute different numbers in the equation and calculate to prove commutative laws.

HISTORY

160

Tell me about September 11, 2001.
On September 11, 2001, terrorists hijacked four airplanes. They flew two into the World Trade Center in New York City and one into the Pentagon in Washington, DC. The fourth plane crashed into a Pennsylvania field.

GEOGRAPHY

DESERTS
Mojave Desert
Sonoran Desert
Colorado Desert
Painted Desert
Great Salt Lake Desert

HANDS-ON

 39

FINE ARTS

Stravinsky *The Rite of Spring* (see page 258)

SCIENCE

Blueberry Pancakes (see page 269)

Memoria
How did your family grow this year?

MATH

The Distributive Law states:
$$a(b + c) = ab + ac$$

 LATIN

JOHN 1:7
ut testimonium perhiberet de lumine

to give testimony of the light

 SCIENCE

Classical Acts & Facts® Science Cycle 3

What are some ways earth's history is preserved?
rocks
fossils
ice
tar
amber

 ENGLISH

FOUR SENTENCE STRUCTURES
simple
compound
complex
compound-complex

TIMELINE

Classical Acts & Facts® History Cards

155 AGE OF INFORMATION AND GLOBALIZATION
156 Watergate, President Nixon Resigns
157 Fall of Communism in Eastern Europe
158 European Union Formed
159 Apartheid Abolished in South Africa
160 September 11, 2001
161 Rising Tide of Freedom

PRESENTATION NOTES

 Review Cycle 2 Latin.

 HISTORY 109

Tell me the Preamble to the U.S. Constitution.
We the People of the United States, in order to form a more perfect Union, establish Justice, insure domestic Tranquility, provide for the common defense, promote the general Welfare, and secure the Blessings of Liberty to ourselves and our Posterity, do ordain and establish this Constitution for the United States of America.

 GEOGRAPHY

PROMINENT FEATURES
Grand Canyon
Black Hills
Ozark Highlands
Okefenokee Swamp
Olympic rainforests
Niagara Falls

 HANDS-ON

FINE ARTS
Orchestra Overview (see page 259)

SCIENCE

What are the Odds? (see pages 270–271)

MATH

The Identity Law
for addition states:
$$a + 0 = a$$

The Identity Law
for multiplication states:
$$a \times 1 = a$$

 LATIN

JOHN 1:7
ut omnes crederent per illum

that all men might believe through him

 SCIENCE 35

Classical Acts & Facts® Science Cycle 3

What is natural selection?
Natural selection is the idea that the fittest survive and pass along their traits to their offspring.

 ENGLISH

SEVEN SENTENCE PATTERNS
Subject–Verb
Subject–Verb–Direct Object
Subject–Verb–Predicate Nominative
Subject–Verb–Predicate Adjective
Subject–Verb–Indirect Object–Direct Object
Subject–Verb–Direct Object–Object Complement Noun
Subject–Verb–Direct Object–Object Complement Adjective

 TIMELINE

Classical Acts & Facts® History Cards

U.S. Presidents:
Washington, Adams, Jefferson, Madison, Monroe, Adams, Jackson, Van Buren, Harrison, Tyler, Polk, Taylor, Fillmore, Pierce, Buchanan, Lincoln, Johnson, Grant, Hayes, Garfield, Arthur, Cleveland, Harrison, Cleveland, McKinley, Roosevelt, Taft, Wilson, Harding, Coolidge, Hoover, Roosevelt, Truman, Eisenhower, Kennedy, Johnson, Nixon, Ford, Carter, Reagan, Bush, Clinton, Bush, Obama, Trump

PRESENTATION NOTES

Recite the first *and* last name of each president. List each president's political party. List the state in which each president was born.

 HISTORY 109

Tell me the Bill of Rights.
1. Freedoms
2. Own guns
3. Quartering soldiers
4. Warrants
5. Cannot testify against self
6. Right to speedy trial
7. Right to a jury
8. Cruel, unusual punishment
9. People's rights
10. States' rights

 **GEOGRAPHY**

MORE PROMINENT FEATURES
Mississippi River Delta
Mammoth Cave
San Andreas Fault
Gulf of Mexico
Death Valley

HANDS-ON

FINE ARTS
Orchestra Review and Celebration (see page 259)

SCIENCE

What Does All That Data Mean? (see pages 272–273)

Celebrate!

1 1s and 2s

- [ ] 1 × 1 = 1
- [ ] 1 × 2 = 2
- [ ] 1 × 3 = 3
- [ ] 1 × 4 = 4
- [ ] 1 × 5 = 5
- [ ] 1 × 6 = 6
- [ ] 1 × 7 = 7
- [ ] 1 × 8 = 8
- [ ] 1 × 9 = 9
- [ ] 1 × 10 = 10
- [ ] 1 × 11 = 11
- [ ] 1 × 12 = 12
- [ ] 1 × 13 = 13
- [ ] 1 × 14 = 14
- [ ] 1 × 15 = 15
- [ ] 2 × 1 = 2
- [ ] 2 × 2 = 4
- [ ] 2 × 3 = 6
- [ ] 2 × 4 = 8
- [ ] 2 × 5 = 10
- [ ] 2 × 6 = 12
- [ ] 2 × 7 = 14
- [ ] 2 × 8 = 16
- [ ] 2 × 9 = 18
- [ ] 2 × 10 = 20
- [ ] 2 × 11 = 22
- [ ] 2 × 12 = 24
- [ ] 2 × 13 = 26
- [ ] 2 × 14 = 28
- [ ] 2 × 15 = 30

2 3s and 4s

- [ ] 3 × 1 = 3
- [ ] 3 × 2 = 6
- [ ] 3 × 3 = 9
- [ ] 3 × 4 = 12
- [ ] 3 × 5 = 15
- [ ] 3 × 6 = 18
- [ ] 3 × 7 = 21
- [ ] 3 × 8 = 24
- [ ] 3 × 9 = 27
- [ ] 3 × 10 = 30
- [ ] 3 × 11 = 33
- [ ] 3 × 12 = 36
- [ ] 3 × 13 = 39
- [ ] 3 × 14 = 42
- [ ] 3 × 15 = 45
- [ ] 4 × 1 = 4
- [ ] 4 × 2 = 8
- [ ] 4 × 3 = 12
- [ ] 4 × 4 = 16
- [ ] 4 × 5 = 20
- [ ] 4 × 6 = 24
- [ ] 4 × 7 = 28
- [ ] 4 × 8 = 32
- [ ] 4 × 9 = 36
- [ ] 4 × 10 = 40
- [ ] 4 × 11 = 44
- [ ] 4 × 12 = 48
- [ ] 4 × 13 = 52
- [ ] 4 × 14 = 56
- [ ] 4 × 15 = 60

3 5s and 6s

- [ ] 5 × 1 = 5
- [ ] 5 × 2 = 10
- [ ] 5 × 3 = 15
- [ ] 5 × 4 = 20
- [ ] 5 × 5 = 25
- [ ] 5 × 6 = 30
- [ ] 5 × 7 = 35
- [ ] 5 × 8 = 40
- [ ] 5 × 9 = 45
- [ ] 5 × 10 = 50
- [ ] 5 × 11 = 55
- [ ] 5 × 12 = 60
- [ ] 5 × 13 = 65
- [ ] 5 × 14 = 70
- [ ] 5 × 15 = 75
- [ ] 6 × 1 = 6
- [ ] 6 × 2 = 12
- [ ] 6 × 3 = 18
- [ ] 6 × 4 = 24
- [ ] 6 × 5 = 30
- [ ] 6 × 6 = 36
- [ ] 6 × 7 = 42
- [ ] 6 × 8 = 48
- [ ] 6 × 9 = 54
- [ ] 6 × 10 = 60
- [ ] 6 × 11 = 66
- [ ] 6 × 12 = 72
- [ ] 6 × 13 = 78
- [ ] 6 × 14 = 84
- [ ] 6 × 15 = 90

4 7s and 8s

- [ ] 7 × 1 = 7
- [ ] 7 × 2 = 14
- [ ] 7 × 3 = 21
- [ ] 7 × 4 = 28
- [ ] 7 × 5 = 35
- [ ] 7 × 6 = 42
- [ ] 7 × 7 = 49
- [ ] 7 × 8 = 56
- [ ] 7 × 9 = 63
- [ ] 7 × 10 = 70
- [ ] 7 × 11 = 77
- [ ] 7 × 12 = 84
- [ ] 7 × 13 = 91
- [ ] 7 × 14 = 98
- [ ] 7 × 15 = 105
- [ ] 8 × 1 = 8
- [ ] 8 × 2 = 16
- [ ] 8 × 3 = 24
- [ ] 8 × 4 = 32
- [ ] 8 × 5 = 40
- [ ] 8 × 6 = 48
- [ ] 8 × 7 = 56
- [ ] 8 × 8 = 64
- [ ] 8 × 9 = 72
- [ ] 8 × 10 = 80
- [ ] 8 × 11 = 88
- [ ] 8 × 12 = 96
- [ ] 8 × 13 = 104
- [ ] 8 × 14 = 112
- [ ] 8 × 15 = 120

5 9s and 10s

- [ ] 9 × 1 = 9
- [ ] 9 × 2 = 18
- [ ] 9 × 3 = 27
- [ ] 9 × 4 = 36
- [ ] 9 × 5 = 45
- [ ] 9 × 6 = 54
- [ ] 9 × 7 = 63
- [ ] 9 × 8 = 72
- [ ] 9 × 9 = 81
- [ ] 9 × 10 = 90
- [ ] 9 × 11 = 99
- [ ] 9 × 12 = 108
- [ ] 9 × 13 = 117
- [ ] 9 × 14 = 126
- [ ] 9 × 15 = 135
- [ ] 10 × 1 = 10
- [ ] 10 × 2 = 20
- [ ] 10 × 3 = 30
- [ ] 10 × 4 = 40
- [ ] 10 × 5 = 50
- [ ] 10 × 6 = 60
- [ ] 10 × 7 = 70
- [ ] 10 × 8 = 80
- [ ] 10 × 9 = 90
- [ ] 10 × 10 = 100
- [ ] 10 × 11 = 110
- [ ] 10 × 12 = 120
- [ ] 10 × 13 = 130
- [ ] 10 × 14 = 140
- [ ] 10 × 15 = 150

6 11s and 12s

- [ ] 11 × 1 = 11
- [ ] 11 × 2 = 22
- [ ] 11 × 3 = 33
- [ ] 11 × 4 = 44
- [ ] 11 × 5 = 55
- [ ] 11 × 6 = 66
- [ ] 11 × 7 = 77
- [ ] 11 × 8 = 88
- [ ] 11 × 9 = 99
- [ ] 11 × 10 = 110
- [ ] 11 × 11 = 121
- [ ] 11 × 12 = 132
- [ ] 11 × 13 = 143
- [ ] 11 × 14 = 154
- [ ] 11 × 15 = 165
- [ ] 12 × 1 = 12
- [ ] 12 × 2 = 24
- [ ] 12 × 3 = 36
- [ ] 12 × 4 = 48
- [ ] 12 × 5 = 60
- [ ] 12 × 6 = 72
- [ ] 12 × 7 = 84
- [ ] 12 × 8 = 96
- [ ] 12 × 9 = 108
- [ ] 12 × 10 = 120
- [ ] 12 × 11 = 132
- [ ] 12 × 12 = 144
- [ ] 12 × 13 = 156
- [ ] 12 × 14 = 168
- [ ] 12 × 15 = 180

7 | 13s

- [ ] $13 \times 1 = 13$
- [ ] $13 \times 2 = 26$
- [ ] $13 \times 3 = 39$
- [ ] $13 \times 4 = 52$
- [ ] $13 \times 5 = 65$
- [ ] $13 \times 6 = 78$
- [ ] $13 \times 7 = 91$
- [ ] $13 \times 8 = 104$
- [ ] $13 \times 9 = 117$
- [ ] $13 \times 10 = 130$
- [ ] $13 \times 11 = 143$
- [ ] $13 \times 12 = 156$
- [ ] $13 \times 13 = 169$
- [ ] $13 \times 14 = 182$
- [ ] $13 \times 15 = 195$

8 | 14s

- [ ] $14 \times 1 = 14$
- [ ] $14 \times 2 = 28$
- [ ] $14 \times 3 = 42$
- [ ] $14 \times 4 = 56$
- [ ] $14 \times 5 = 70$
- [ ] $14 \times 6 = 84$
- [ ] $14 \times 7 = 98$
- [ ] $14 \times 8 = 112$
- [ ] $14 \times 9 = 126$
- [ ] $14 \times 10 = 140$
- [ ] $14 \times 11 = 154$
- [ ] $14 \times 12 = 168$
- [ ] $14 \times 13 = 182$
- [ ] $14 \times 14 = 196$
- [ ] $14 \times 15 = 210$

9 | 15s

- [ ] $15 \times 1 = 15$
- [ ] $15 \times 2 = 30$
- [ ] $15 \times 3 = 45$
- [ ] $15 \times 4 = 60$
- [ ] $15 \times 5 = 75$
- [ ] $15 \times 6 = 90$
- [ ] $15 \times 7 = 105$
- [ ] $15 \times 8 = 120$
- [ ] $15 \times 9 = 135$
- [ ] $15 \times 10 = 150$
- [ ] $15 \times 11 = 165$
- [ ] $15 \times 12 = 180$
- [ ] $15 \times 13 = 195$
- [ ] $15 \times 14 = 210$
- [ ] $15 \times 15 = 225$

10 | SQUARES

- [ ] $1 \times 1 = 1$
- [ ] $2 \times 2 = 4$
- [ ] $3 \times 3 = 9$
- [ ] $4 \times 4 = 16$
- [ ] $5 \times 5 = 25$
- [ ] $6 \times 6 = 36$
- [ ] $7 \times 7 = 49$
- [ ] $8 \times 8 = 64$
- [ ] $9 \times 9 = 81$
- [ ] $10 \times 10 = 100$
- [ ] $11 \times 11 = 121$
- [ ] $12 \times 12 = 144$
- [ ] $13 \times 13 = 169$
- [ ] $14 \times 14 = 196$
- [ ] $15 \times 15 = 225$

11 | CUBES

- [ ] $1 \times 1 \times 1 = 1$
- [ ] $2 \times 2 \times 2 = 8$
- [ ] $3 \times 3 \times 3 = 27$
- [ ] $4 \times 4 \times 4 = 64$
- [ ] $5 \times 5 \times 5 = 125$
- [ ] $6 \times 6 \times 6 = 216$
- [ ] $7 \times 7 \times 7 = 343$
- [ ] $8 \times 8 \times 8 = 512$
- [ ] $9 \times 9 \times 9 = 729$
- [ ] $10 \times 10 \times 10 = 1,000$
- [ ] $11 \times 11 \times 11 = 1,331$
- [ ] $12 \times 12 \times 12 = 1,728$
- [ ] $13 \times 13 \times 13 = 2,197$
- [ ] $14 \times 14 \times 14 = 2,744$
- [ ] $15 \times 15 \times 15 = 3,375$

12 | TEASPOONS AND TABLESPOONS

- [ ] 3 teaspoons equals 1 tablespoon
- [ ] 2 tablespoons equals 1 fluid ounce

13 | LIQUID EQUIVALENTS

- [ ] 8 fluid ounces equals 1 cup
- [ ] 2 cups equals 1 pint
- [ ] 2 pints equals 1 quart
- [ ] 4 quarts equals 1 gallon

14 | LINEAR EQUIVALENTS

- [ ] 2.54 centimeters equals 1 inch
- [ ] 12 inches equals 1 foot
- [ ] 5,280 feet equals 1 mile
- [ ] 1 kilometer equals ⅝ mile

15 | METRIC MEASUREMENTS

- [ ] 10 millimeters equals 1 centimeter
- [ ] 100 centimeters equals 1 meter
- [ ] 1000 meters equals 1 kilometer

16 | AREA OF A RECTANGLE

- [ ] The area of a rectangle equals length times width.

17 | AREA OF A SQUARE

- [ ] The area of a square equals the length of its side squared.

18 | AREA OF A TRIANGLE

- [ ] The area of a triangle equals one-half base times height.

19 | AREA OF A CIRCLE

- [ ] The area of a circle equals pi (3.14) times the radius squared.

20 | CIRCUMFERENCE OF A CIRCLE

- [ ] The circumference of a circle equals 2 times pi (3.14) times the radius.

21 | ASSOCIATIVE LAW

- [ ] The Associative Law for addition states: $(a + b) + c = a + (b + c)$
- [ ] The Associative Law for multiplication states: $(a \times b) \times c = a \times (b \times c)$

22 | COMMUTATIVE LAW

- [ ] The Commutative Law for addition states: $a + b = b + a$
- [ ] The Commutative Law for multiplication states: $a \times b = b \times a$

23 | DISTRIBUTIVE LAW

- [ ] The Distributive Law states: $a(b + c) = ab + ac$

24 | IDENTITY LAW

- [ ] The Identity Law for addition states: $a + 0 = a$
- [ ] The Identity Law for multiplication states: $a \times 1 = a$

1	PREPOSITIONS	
☐	in	in
☐	apud	with
☐	per	by
☐	sine	without
☐	a	from
☐	de	of
2	CONJUNCTIONS and ADVERBS	
☐	et	and
☐	ut	that
☐	non	not
3	PRONOUNS	
☐	hic	this
☐	hoc	same
☐	ipso, ipsum	him
☐	cui	whose
☐	quod	that
☐	eam	it
☐	illum	him
4	VERBS	
☐	erat	was
☐	venit	came
☐	perhiberet	bear
☐	crederent	believe
5	VERBS	
☐	facta sunt	were made
☐	factum est	was made
☐	missus	sent
☐	conpre-henderunt	comprehended
☐	lucet	shineth
☐	fuit	there was

6	NOUNS	
☐	verbum	word
☐	Deus, Deum, Deo	God
☐	principio	beginning
☐	omnia, omnes	all
☐	nihil	nothing
7	NOUNS	
☐	vita	life
☐	lux	light
☐	homo, hominum	man
☐	nomen	name
8	NOUNS	
☐	testimonium	witness, testimony
☐	lumine	light
☐	Iohannes	John
☐	tenebris, tenebrae	darkness
9	VERB RULES	
☐	Latin verbs have different endings called **conjugations**.	
10	ARTICLE RULES	
☐	Latin has no translation for articles *a*, *an*, *the*. (These rules are observable in the passage you translated.)	
11	NOUNS/PRONOUNS RULES	
☐	Latin nouns and pronouns have different endings called **declensions**.	
12	JOHN 1:1	
☐	in principio erat Verbum	
	in the beginning was the Word	

13	JOHN 1:1
☐	et Verbum erat apud Deum
	and the Word was with God
	et Deus erat Verbum
	and the Word was God

14	JOHN 1:2
☐	hoc erat in principio apud Deum
	the same was in the beginning with God

15	JOHN 1:3
☐	omnia per ipsum facta sunt
	all things were made by him

16	JOHN 1:3
☐	et sine ipso factum est nihil
	and without him was made nothing
	quod factum est
	that was made

17	JOHN 1:4
☐	in ipso vita erat
	in him was life
	et vita erat lux hominum
	and the life was the light of men

18	JOHN 1:5
☐	et lux in tenebris lucet
	and the light shineth in the darkness

19	JOHN 1:5
☐	et tenebrae eam non conprehenderunt
	and the darkness did not comprehend it

20	JOHN 1:6
☐	fuit homo missus a Deo
	there was a man sent from God

21	JOHN 1:6
☐	cui nomen erat Iohannes
	whose name was John

22	JOHN 1:7
☐	hic venit in testimonium
	this man came for a witness

23	JOHN 1:7
☐	ut testimonium perhiberet de lumine
	to give testimony of the light

24	JOHN 1:7
☐	ut omnes crederent per illum
	that all men might believe through him

1 **What are four types of tissue?**

- [ ] connective
- [ ] epithelial
- [ ] muscle
- [ ] nerve

2 **Which bones make up the axial skeleton?**

- [ ] skull
- [ ] vertebrae
- [ ] ribs
- [ ] sternum

3 **What are three kinds of muscle?**

- [ ] skeletal
- [ ] smooth
- [ ] cardiac

4 **What are three parts of the nervous system?**

- [ ] brain
- [ ] spinal cord
- [ ] nerves

5 **What are the five main senses?**

- [ ] sight
- [ ] hearing
- [ ] taste
- [ ] smell
- [ ] touch

6 **What are some parts of the digestive system?**

- [ ] mouth
- [ ] esophagus
- [ ] stomach
- [ ] liver
- [ ] small intestine
- [ ] large intestine

7 **What are four parts of the excretory system?**

- [ ] urinary tract
- [ ] lungs
- [ ] skin
- [ ] intestines

8 **What are six parts of the circulatory system?**

- [ ] heart
- [ ] arteries
- [ ] veins
- [ ] capillaries
- [ ] red and white blood cells
- [ ] platelets

9 **What are four parts of the lymph system?**

- [ ] lymph vessels
- [ ] lymph nodes
- [ ] spleen
- [ ] thymus

10 **What are some parts of the respiratory system?**

- [ ] nose
- [ ] pharynx
- [ ] larynx
- [ ] trachea
- [ ] bronchi
- [ ] bronchioles
- [ ] alveoli
- [ ] lungs

11 **What is the endocrine system?**

- [ ] The endocrine system consists of glands and organs that use hormones to send messages through the bloodstream to the rest of the body.

12 **What are the major purposes of blood?**

- [ ] transportation
- [ ] protection
- [ ] communication
- [ ] regulation

13 What is the atomic number?

☐ The atomic number is the number of protons in the nucleus of an atom, which is also the number of electrons in a neutral atom.

14 What is an element?

☐ An element is a basic chemical substance defined by its atomic number and atomic mass.

15 What are some parts of an atom?

☐ nucleus
☐ protons
☐ electrons
☐ quarks
☐ leptons
☐ neutrons

16 What are the first four elements in the periodic table by number, element, symbol, and mass?

☐ 1 Hydrogen   H   1
☐ 2 Helium   He 4
☐ 3 Lithium   Li 7
☐ 4 Beryllium Be 9

17 What are the second four elements in the periodic table by number, element, symbol, and mass?

☐ 5 Boron   B   11
☐ 6 Carbon   C   12
☐ 7 Nitrogen N   14
☐ 8 Oxygen   O   16

18 What are the third four elements in the periodic table by number, element, symbol, and mass?

☐ 9 Fluorine   F   19
☐ 10 Neon   Ne 20
☐ 11 Sodium   Na 23
☐ 12 Magnesium Mg 24

19 What is the difference between an acid and a base?

☐ An acid donates a hydrogen ion and a base accepts a hydrogen ion.

20 What do the heavens declare?

☐ The heavens declare the glory of God: the skies proclaim the work of his hands. (Psalm 19:1)

21 What does the theory of evolution rely on?

☐ The theory of evolution relies on the belief that life began as a chance combination of non-living things.

22 What does the theory of intelligent design rely on?

☐ The theory of intelligent design relies on the belief that life began as a result of intention and purpose.

23 What are some ways earth's history is preserved?

☐ rocks
☐ fossils
☐ ice
☐ tar
☐ amber

24 What is natural selection?

☐ Natural selection is the idea that the fittest survive and pass along their traits to their off-spring.

1   AN INFINITIVE

☐ An **infinitive** is "to" plus a verb, used as a noun, adjective, or adverb.

2   A PRESENT PARTICIPLE

☐ A **present participle** is a verb plus "-ing," used as an adjective or a verb.

3   A PAST PARTICIPLE

☐ A **past participle** is a verb plus "-ed," used as an adjective or a verb.

4   VERB: PRINCIPAL PARTS

☐ infinitive

☐ present

☐ past

☐ present participle

☐ past participle

5   TO BE

☐ infinitive — to be

☐ present — am, are, is

☐ past — was, were

☐ present participle — being

☐ past participle — been

6   TO DO

☐ infinitive — to do

☐ present — do, does

☐ past — did

☐ present participle — doing

☐ past participle — did

7   TO RISE

☐ infinitive — to rise

☐ present — rise, rises

☐ past — rose

☐ present participle — rising

☐ past participle — risen

8   TO RAISE

☐ infinitive — to raise

☐ present — raise, raises

☐ past — raised

☐ present participle — raising

☐ past participle — raised

9   TO LAY

☐ infinitive — to lay

☐ present — lay, lays

☐ past — laid

☐ present participle — laying

☐ past participle — laid

10   TO LIE

☐ infinitive — to lie

☐ present — lie, lies

☐ past — lay

☐ present participle — lying

☐ past participle — lain

11   TO SET

☐ infinitive — to set

☐ present — set, sets

☐ past — set

☐ present participle — setting

☐ past participle — set

12   TO SIT

☐ infinitive — to sit

☐ present — sit, sits

☐ past — sat

☐ present participle — sitting

☐ past participle — sat

13 TO BEAT

- [ ] infinitive — to beat
- [ ] present — beat, beats
- [ ] past — beat
- [ ] present participle — beating
- [ ] past participle — beaten

14 TO BREAK

- [ ] infinitive — to break
- [ ] present — break, breaks
- [ ] past — broke
- [ ] present participle — breaking
- [ ] past participle — broken

15 TO WRITE

- [ ] infinitive — to write
- [ ] present — write, writes
- [ ] past — wrote
- [ ] present participle — writing
- [ ] past participle — written

16 TO GO

- [ ] infinitive — to go
- [ ] present — go, goes
- [ ] past — went
- [ ] present participle — going
- [ ] past participle — gone

17 SENTENCE PARTS: SUBJECT

- [ ] The **subject** is that part of a sentence about which something is being said.

18 SENTENCE PARTS: PREDICATE

- [ ] The **predicate** is that part of a sentence that says something about the subject.

19 SENTENCE PARTS: CLAUSE

- [ ] A **clause** is a group of words that contains both a subject and a verb.

20 INDEPENDENT CLAUSE

- [ ] An **independent clause** expresses a complete thought like a sentence.

21 SUBORDINATE CLAUSE

- [ ] A **subordinate clause**, also known as a dependent clause, does not express a complete thought and cannot stand alone.

22 SENTENCE PARTS: PHRASE

- [ ] A **phrase** is a group of words that does not contain both a subject and a verb and may be used as a single part of speech.

23 FOUR SENTENCE STRUCTURES

- [ ] simple
- [ ] compound
- [ ] complex
- [ ] compound-complex

24 SEVEN SENTENCE PATTERNS

- [ ] subject–verb
- [ ] subject–verb–direct object
- [ ] subject–verb–predicate nominative
- [ ] subject–verb–predicate adjective
- [ ] subject–verb–indirect object–direct object
- [ ] subject–verb–direct object–object complement noun
- [ ] subject–verb–direct object–object complement adjective

WEEK 1	1	**AGE OF ANCIENT EMPIRES**
	2	Creation and the Fall
	3	The Flood and the Tower of Babel
	4	Mesopotamia and Sumer
	5	Egyptians
	6	Indus River Valley Civilization
	7	Minoans and Mycenaeans
WEEK 2	8	Seven Wonders of the Ancient World
	9	Patriarchs of Israel
	10	Hittites and Canaanites
	11	Kush
	12	Assyrians
	13	Babylonians
	14	China's Shang Dynasty
WEEK 3	15	Hinduism in India
	16	Phoenicians and the Alphabet
	17	Olmecs of Mesoamerica
	18	Israelite Exodus and Desert Wandering
	19	Israelite Conquest and Judges
	20	Greek Dark Ages
	21	Israel's United Kingdom
WEEK 4	22	Early Native Americans
	23	Israel Divides into Two Kingdoms
	24	Homer and Hesiod
	25	Rome Founded by Romulus and Remus
	26	Israel Falls to Assyria
	27	Assyria Falls to Babylon
	28	Lao-Tzu, Confucius, Buddha

WEEK 5	29	Judah falls to Babylon, Temple Destroyed
	30	Babylon Falls to Persia
	31	Jews Return and Rebuild the Temple
	32	Roman Republic
	33	Golden Age of Greece
	34	Peloponnesian Wars
	35	Persia Falls to Alexander the Great
WEEK 6	36	India's Mauryan Empire
	37	Mayans of Mesoamerica
	38	Punic Wars
	39	Rome Conquers Greece
	40	Roman Dictator Julius Caesar
	41	Caesar Augustus and the Pax Romana
	42	John the Baptist
WEEK 7	43	Jesus the Messiah
	44	Pentecost and the Early Church
	45	Persecution Spreads the Gospel
	46	Herod's Temple Destroyed by Titus
	47	Diocletian Divides the Roman Empire
	48	Constantine Legalizes Christianity
	49	India's Gupta Dynasty
WEEK 8	50	Council of Nicea
	51	Augustine of Hippo
	52	Jerome Completes the Vulgate
	53	Visigoths Sack Rome
	54	**THE MIDDLE AGES**
	55	Council of Chalcedon
	56	Western Roman Empire Falls to Barbarians

WEEK 9	57	Byzantine Emperor Justinian
	58	Benedict and Monasticism
	59	Muhammad Founds Islam
	60	Zanj and Early Ghana in Africa
	61	Franks Defeat Muslims at the Battle of Tours
	62	Golden Age of Islam
	63	Vikings Raid and Trade
WEEK 10	64	Japan's Heian Period
	65	Charlemagne Crowned Emperor of Europe
	66	Alfred the Great of England
	67	Erik the Red and Leif Eriksson, Norse Explorers
	68	Vladimir I of Kiev
	69	Byzantine Emperor Basil II
	70	East-West Schism of the Church
WEEK 11	71	Norman Conquest and Feudalism in Europe
	72	The Crusades
	73	Zimbabwe and Early Mali in Africa
	74	Aztecs of Mesoamerica
	75	Francis of Assisi and Thomas Aquinas
	76	Japan's Shoguns
	77	Incas of South America
WEEK 12	78	Genghis Khan Rules the Mongols
	79	England's Magna Carta
	80	The Ottoman Empire
	81	Marco Polo's Journey to China
	82	The Hundred Years' War and Black Death
	83	The Renaissance
	84	China's Ming Dynasty

WEEK 24 U. S. PRESIDENTS

162		163		164		165		166		167	
	Washington		Monroe		Harrison		Fillmore		Johnson		Arthur
	Adams		Adams		Tyler		Pierce		Grant		Cleveland
	Jefferson		Jackson		Polk		Buchanan		Hayes		Harrison
	Madison		Van Buren		Taylor		Lincoln		Garfield		Cleveland

WEEK 13
- 85 **AGE OF EXPLORATION**
- 86 Prince Henry Founds School of Navigation
- 87 Slave Trade in Africa
- 88 Gutenberg's Printing Press
- 89 Songhai in Africa
- 90 Czar Ivan the Great of Russia
- 91 The Spanish Inquisition

WEEK 14
- 92 Columbus Sails to the Caribbean
- 93 **AGE OF ABSOLUTE MONARCHS**
- 94 Protestant Reformation
- 95 Spanish Conquistadors in the Americas
- 96 Calvin's *Institutes of the Christian Religion*
- 97 Council of Trent
- 98 Baroque Period of the Arts

WEEK 15
- 99 Japan's Isolation
- 100 Jamestown and Plymouth Colony Founded
- 101 **AGE OF ENLIGHTENMENT**
- 102 Hudson's Bay Company
- 103 First Great Awakening
- 104 Classical Period of the Arts
- 105 The Seven Years' War

WEEK 16
- 106 **AGE OF INDUSTRY**
- 107 James Cook Sails to Australia and Antarctica
- 108 American Revolution and General George Washington
- 109 Madison's Constitution and the Bill of Rights
- 110 French Revolution
- 111 Second Great Awakening
- 112 Louisiana Purchase and Lewis and Clark Expedition

WEEK 17
- 113 Napoleon Crowned Emperor of France
- 114 Liberation of South America
- 115 The War of 1812
- 116 The Missouri Compromise
- 117 Immigrants Flock to America
- 118 The Monroe Doctrine
- 119 Romantic Period of the Arts

WEEK 18
- 120 Cherokee Trail of Tears
- 121 U.S. Westward Expansion
- 122 Marx Publishes *The Communist Manifesto*
- 123 The Compromise of 1850 and the *Dred Scott* Decision
- 124 U.S. Restores Trade with Japan
- 125 British Queen Victoria's Rule Over India
- 126 Darwin Publishes *The Origin of Species*

WEEK 19
- 127 Lincoln's War Between the States
- 128 Reconstruction of the Southern States
- 129 Dominion of Canada
- 130 Otto von Bismarck Unifies Germany
- 131 Boer Wars in Africa
- 132 The Spanish-American War
- 133 The Progressive Era

WEEK 20
- 134 Australia Becomes a Commonwealth
- 135 Mexican Revolution
- 136 World War I and President Wilson
- 137 Lenin and the Bolshevik Revolution in Russia
- 138 U.S. Evangelist Billy Graham
- 139 Modern Period of the Arts
- 140 The Great Depression and the New Deal

WEEK 21
- 141 World War II and President Franklin D. Roosevelt
- 142 Stalin of the USSR and the Katyn Massacre
- 143 The United Nations Formed
- 144 The Cold War
- 145 Gandhi and India's Independence
- 146 Jewish State Established
- 147 Mao and Communist Victory in China

WEEK 22
- 148 North Atlantic Treaty Organization
- 149 The Korean War
- 150 Martin Luther King, Jr. and the Civil Rights Movement
- 151 Jim and Elisabeth Elliot, Missionaries to Equador
- 152 The Antarctic Treaty
- 153 The Vietnam War
- 154 U.S. Astronauts Walk on the Moon

WEEK 23
- 155 **AGE OF INFORMATION AND GLOBALIZATION**
- 156 Watergate, President Nixon Resigns
- 157 Fall of Communism in Eastern Europe
- 158 European Union Formed
- 159 Apartheid Abolished in South Africa
- 160 September 11, 2001
- 161 Rising Tide of Freedom

168	McKinley Roosevelt Taft Wilson	169	Harding Coolidge Hoover Roosevelt	170	Truman Eisenhower Kennedy Johnson	171	Nixon Ford Carter Reagan	172	Bush Clinton Bush Obama	173	Trump

1   **Tell me about Columbus.**

☐ In 1492, Columbus made the first of four trips to the Caribbean on three Spanish ships named the *Niña*, the *Pinta*, and the *Santa María*.

2   **Tell me about the Pilgrims.**

☐ In 1620, the Pilgrims sailed from Plymouth, England and signed the Mayflower Compact before founding Plymouth Colony in North America.

3   **Tell me about the Boston Tea Party.**

☐ In 1773, colonists disguised as Mohawks dumped tea from the British East India Company into the Boston Harbor.

4   **Tell me about the Declaration of Independence.**

☐ In 1776, the Continental Congress published the Declaration of Independence in Philadelphia, announcing the colonists' intent to separate from England.

5   **Tell me about George Washington.**

☐ In 1789, in New York, George Washington was granted the full powers and responsibilities of the presidency by the U.S. Constitution.

6   **Tell me about the Louisiana Purchase.**

☐ In 1803, the purchase of Louisiana from France prompted westward exploration by pioneers such as Lewis and Clark and Congressman Davy Crockett.

7   **Tell me about the Monroe Doctrine.**

☐ After victory in the War of 1812, the United States wrote the Monroe Doctrine, which warned Europeans not to attempt to colonize the Americas.

8   **Tell me about the Missouri Compromise.**

☐ In 1820, Henry Clay worked out the Missouri Compromise, allowing Missouri to enter the Union as a slave state and Maine as a free state.

9   **Tell me about the secession of the Southern states.**

☐ The Compromise of 1850, the Fugitive Slave Act, and the *Dred Scott* decision preceded the secession of the Southern states.

10   **Tell me about Manifest Destiny.**

☐ President Polk believed that the Mexican War and the Gadsden Purchase in the mid-1800s affirmed America's manifest destiny to spread across the continent.

11   **Tell me about the Civil War.**

☐ In 1861, the Civil War began when President Abraham Lincoln went to war with the Southern states that had seceded from the Union.

12   **Tell me about General Robert E. Lee.**

☐ In 1865, General Robert E. Lee surrendered to General Ulysses S. Grant at Appomattox Court House in Virginia.

13 Tell me about the Fourteenth Amendment.

☐ In 1868, the Fourteenth Amendment made all former slaves U.S. citizens and paved the way for the Civil Rights Movement.

14 Tell me about tycoons.

☐ During the late 1800s, tycoons like Vanderbilt, Rockefeller, Carnegie, and Swift fueled the nation's Industrial Age by developing American resources.

15 Tell me about immigrants coming to America.

☐ From 1820 to 1930, more than 37 million immigrants came to America, seeking freedom and the opportunity to increase their personal wealth.

16 Tell me about the United States and World War I.

☐ In 1917, President Wilson asked Congress to enter World War I against the Central Powers two years after German U-boats sank the *Lusitania*, killing American citizens.

17 Tell me about the Nineteenth Amendment.

☐ Elizabeth Cady Stanton and Susan B. Anthony led the women's suffrage movement in the United States, resulting in the Nineteenth Amendment in 1920 that granted women the right to vote.

18 Tell me about Pearl Harbor.

☐ On December 7, 1941, the Japanese bombed Pearl Harbor, Hawaii, causing the United States to join the Allies in World War II.

19 Tell me about NATO.

☐ In 1949, the United States and its allies formed NATO to resist the spread of Soviet communism.

20 Tell me about *Brown v. Board of Education*.

☐ In 1954, in *Brown v. Board of Education,* the U.S. Supreme Court ruled that the segregation of public schools by race is unconstitutional.

21 Tell me about U.S. astronauts.

☐ In 1969, U.S. astronauts Neil Armstrong and Edwin Aldrin were the first men to walk on the moon.

22 Tell me about September 11, 2001.

☐ On September 11, 2001, terrorists hijacked four airplanes. They flew two into the World Trade Center in New York City and one into the Pentagon in Washington, DC. The fourth plane crashed into a Pennsylvania field.

23 Tell me the Preamble to the U.S. Constitution.

☐ We the People of the United States, in order to form a more perfect Union, establish Justice, insure domestic Tranquility, provide for the common defense, promote the general Welfare, and secure the Blessings of Liberty to ourselves and our Posterity, do ordain and establish this Constitution for the United States of America.

24 Tell me the Bill of Rights.

☐
1. Freedoms
2. Own guns
3. Quartering soldiers
4. Warrants
5. Cannot testify against self
6. Right to speedy trial
7. Right to a jury
8. Cruel, unusual punishment
9. People's rights
10. States' rights

1 STATES AND CAPITALS
- [ ] Augusta, ME
- [ ] Concord, NH
- [ ] Boston, MA
- [ ] Providence, RI
- [ ] Hartford, CT

2 STATES AND CAPITALS
- [ ] Montpelier, VT
- [ ] Albany, NY
- [ ] Trenton, NJ
- [ ] Harrisburg, PA
- [ ] Dover, DE

3 STATES AND CAPITALS
- [ ] Annapolis, MD
- [ ] Richmond, VA
- [ ] Charleston, WV
- [ ] Raleigh, NC
- [ ] Columbia, SC
- [ ] **Washington, DC**

4 STATES AND CAPITALS
- [ ] Atlanta, GA
- [ ] Tallahassee, FL
- [ ] Montgomery, AL
- [ ] Jackson, MS
- [ ] Baton Rouge, LA

5 STATES AND CAPITALS
- [ ] Lansing, MI
- [ ] Columbus, OH
- [ ] Indianapolis, IN
- [ ] Frankfort, KY
- [ ] Nashville, TN

6 STATES AND CAPITALS
- [ ] Madison, WI
- [ ] Springfield, IL
- [ ] Des Moines, IA
- [ ] Jefferson City, MO
- [ ] Little Rock, AR

7 STATES AND CAPITALS
- [ ] St. Paul, MN
- [ ] Bismarck, ND
- [ ] Pierre, SD
- [ ] Cheyenne, WY
- [ ] Lincoln, NE

8 STATES AND CAPITALS
- [ ] Topeka, KS
- [ ] Oklahoma City, OK
- [ ] Austin, TX
- [ ] Denver, CO
- [ ] Sante Fe, NM

9 STATES AND CAPITALS
- [ ] Salt Lake City, UT
- [ ] Phoenix, AZ
- [ ] Carson City, NV
- [ ] Sacramento, CA
- [ ] Honolulu, HI

10 STATES AND CAPITALS
- [ ] Helena, MT
- [ ] Boise, ID
- [ ] Olympia, WA
- [ ] Salem, OR
- [ ] Juneau, AK

11 NORTHERN APPALACHIAN MOUNTAINS
- [ ] White Mountains
- [ ] Green Mountains
- [ ] Adirondack Mountains
- [ ] Allegheny Mountains

12 SOUTHERN APPALACHIAN MOUNTAINS
- [ ] The Great Valley
- [ ] Blue Ridge Mountains
- [ ] Great Smoky Mountains
- [ ] Cumberland Mountains
- [ ] Mt. Mitchell

13 WESTERN MOUNTAINS
- [ ] Rocky Mountains
- [ ] Pikes Peak
- [ ] Mt. Elbert
- [ ] Sierra Nevadas
- [ ] Mt. Whitney

14 NORTHWEST MOUNTAINS
- [ ] Cascade Mountains
- [ ] Mt. Rainier
- [ ] Mt. St. Helens
- [ ] Denali

15 GREAT LAKES
- [ ] **H** uron
- [ ] **O** ntario
- [ ] **M** ichigan
- [ ] **E** rie
- [ ] **S** uperior

16 BAYS
- [ ] Chesapeake Bay
- [ ] Hudson Bay
- [ ] San Francisco Bay
- [ ] Puget Sound
- [ ] Pamlico Sound

17 RIVERS (EAST)
- [ ] St. Lawrence River
- [ ] Ohio River
- [ ] Mississippi River
- [ ] Missouri River
- [ ] Arkansas River

18 RIVERS (WEST)
- [ ] Colorado River
- [ ] Red River
- [ ] Rio Grande River
- [ ] Columbia River
- [ ] Great Salt Lake

19 TRAILS
- [ ] Cumberland Road
- [ ] Santa Fe Trail
- [ ] Mormon Trail
- [ ] Gila Trail
- [ ] Old Spanish Trail
- [ ] California Trail
- [ ] Oregon Trail

20 CANALS
- [ ] Erie Canal
- [ ] Pennsylvania Canal
- [ ] Chesapeake and Ohio Canal
- [ ] Ohio and Erie Canal
- [ ] Miami and Erie Canal

21 NATIVE AMERICAN REGIONS
- [ ] Eastern Woodlands
- [ ] Plains
- [ ] Plateau
- [ ] Northwest Coast
- [ ] California
- [ ] Great Basin
- [ ] Southwest

22 DESERTS
- [ ] Mojave Desert
- [ ] Sonoran Desert
- [ ] Colorado Desert
- [ ] Painted Desert
- [ ] Great Salt Lake Desert

23 PROMINENT FEATURES
- [ ] Grand Canyon
- [ ] Black Hills
- [ ] Ozark Highlands
- [ ] Okefenokee Swamp
- [ ] Olympic rainforests
- [ ] Niagara Falls

24 MORE PROMINENT FEATURES
- [ ] Mississippi River Delta
- [ ] Mammoth Cave
- [ ] San Andreas Fault
- [ ] Gulf of Mexico
- [ ] Death Valley

UNITED STATES: STATES AND CAPITALS

Black Line Master

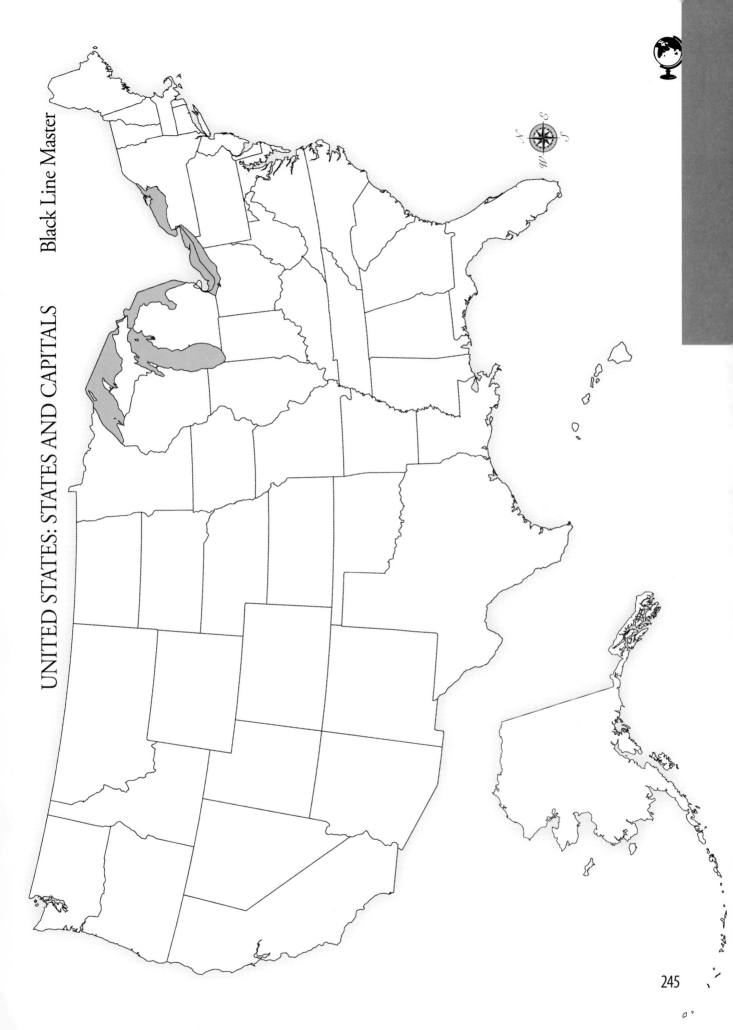

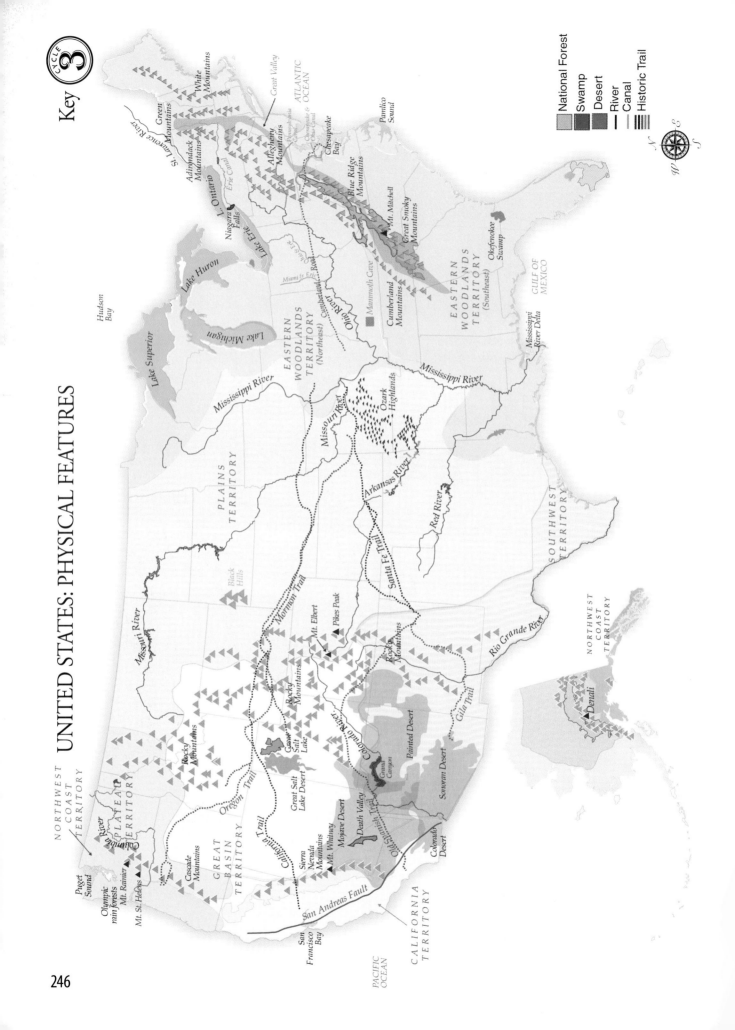

UNITED STATES: PHYSICAL FEATURES

National Forest
Swamp
Desert
River
Canal
Historic Trail

N
W   E
S

246

UNITED STATES: PHYSICAL FEATURES

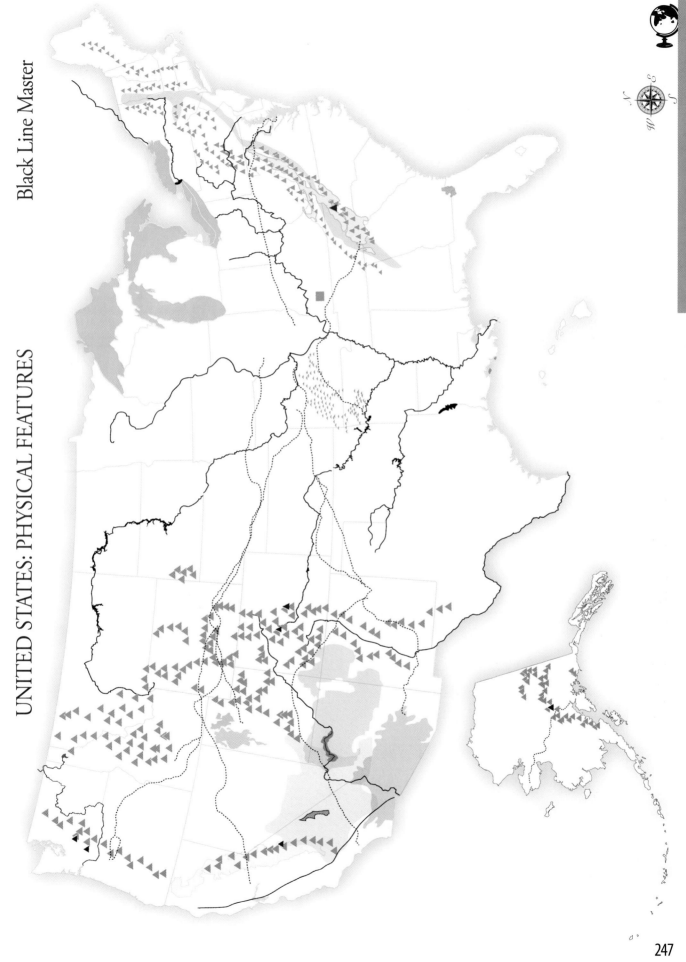

United States States and Capitals

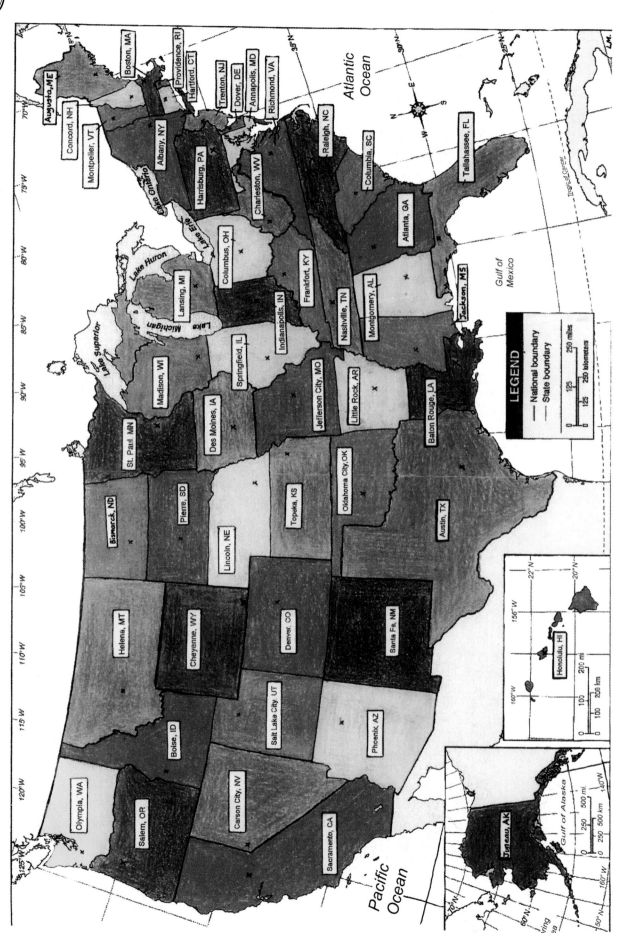

United States Physical Features

Student Sample

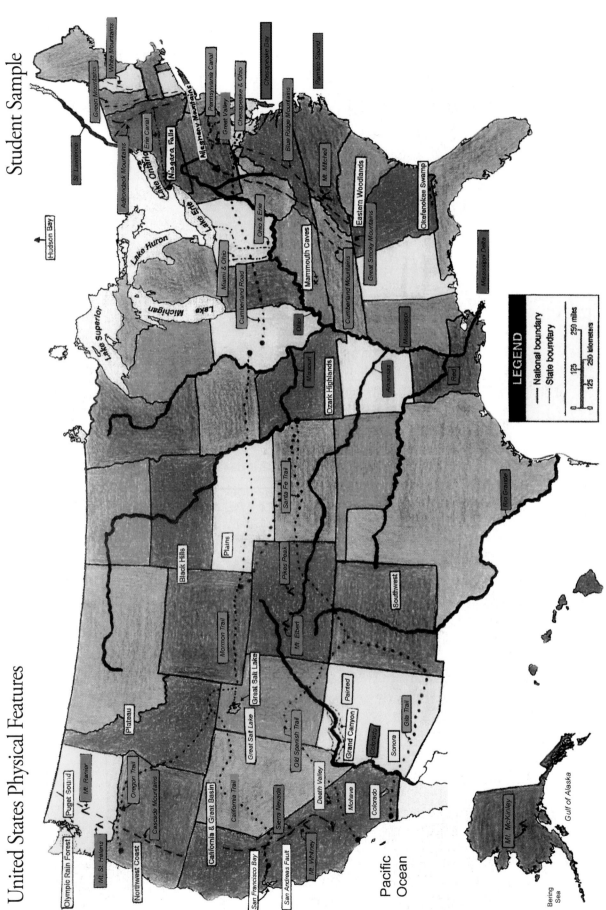

LEGEND
- - - National boundary
—— State boundary

125   250 miles
125   250 kilometers

Olympic Rain Forest
Mt. St. Helens
Northwest Coast
Puget Sound
Mt. Rainier
Oregon Trail
Cascade Mountains
California & Great Basin
California Trail
Sierra Nevada
San Francisco Bay
San Andreas Fault
Mt. Whitney
Death Valley
Old Spanish Trail
Great Salt Lake
Mormon Trail
Mohave
Colorado
Grand Canyon
Colorado
Sonora
Gila Trail
Painted
Plateau
Black Hills
Plains
Pikes Peak
Mt. Elbert
Santa Fe Trail
Southwest
Rio Grande
Ozark Highlands
Missouri
Arkansas
Red
Mississippi
Mississippi Delta
Okefenokee Swamp
Great Smoky Mountains
Eastern Woodlands
Cumberland Mountains
Mt. Mitchell
Blue Ridge Mountains
Mammouth Caves
Cumberland Road
Miami & Ohio
Ohio
Ohio & Erie
Lake Michigan
Lake Superior
Lake Huron
Lake Erie
Lake Ontario
Hudson Bay
St. Lawrence
Green Mountains
White Mountains
Adirondack Mountains
Niagara Falls
Erie Canal
Allegheny Mountains
Great Valley
Pennsylvania Canal
Chesapeake & Ohio
Chesapeake Bay
Pamlico Sound
Pacific Ocean
Bering Sea
Mt. McKinley
Gulf of Alaska

INSTRUCTIONS FOR RIGHTEOUS LIVING
JOHN 1:1–7 (VULGATE)

NOTES ABOUT THIS SECTION:

The King James Version was selected for some Foundations Scripture passages because of the beauty of the language style; however, the spelling of words such as *honour/honor* and *shewing/showing* was intentionally changed to American-English spelling to minimize confusion in our young readers.

We do not wish to usurp your church or family Scripture memory work. Rather, we have chosen a few designated verses per cycle to augment the **Foundations** memory work. We are using a translation of the Latin Vulgate for this passage, but please feel free to use the translation of your choice.

[1]In the beginning was the Word, and the Word was with God, and the Word was God.

[2]The same was in the beginning with God.

[3]All things were made by him; and without him was made nothing that was made.

[4]In him was life; and the life was the light of men.

[5]And the light shineth in darkness; and the darkness did not comprehend it.

[6]There was a man sent from God, whose name was John.

[7]This man came for a witness, to give testimony of the light, that all men might believe through him.

PRESENTATIONS

Let's make public speaking a pleasant part of our culture for our children. Feel free to suggest to your older child that he or she could read the IEW paper from Essentials or explain more thoroughly a *Classical Acts & Facts® Science Card*. However, if your child just wants to tell the class about their grandparent or model car, say, "Good idea! Think about what you'll say while I get a glass of iced tea." Then listen as he or she gives their story a whirl.

Remind your child to:

1. Take a clearing breath while he sees if everyone is ready to listen.
2. Introduce himself and his presentation.
3. Speak clearly and audibly and take care to look each audience member in the eye as he speaks.
4. Let the audience know he is finished by ending with, "Are there any questions?"

Just smile at your child when they present in public. And remember, ideas need time to digest and settle. Next week while listening with a glass of iced tea in your hand, ask if there's anything he wants to improve on from the previous week. Time allows ears to hear comments without taking them as criticism.

A good audience listens and participates by asking questions of other presenters. Occasionally have the students hold up eyeballs drawn on index cards and then put the card down when the presenter has caught their eye.

In community, each student presents twenty-four times a year, which provides over one hundred formal public speaking opportunities in kindergarten thru sixth grade. Success comes from consistency over many years.

More Resources to Help

Classical Conversations students exercise the skills of rhetorical presentation through all program levels, from these short presentations in Foundations to science fair, mock trial, and formal debate in Challenge. You might consider attending one of these Challenge events—this will be your child in just a few years! Additionally, we've developed some resources to serve families all the way through the high school years.

Trivium Tables®: Rhetoric

This laminated, double-sided resource has four panels on each side that describe different aspects of rhetoric—presenting—for your student to learn, review, and practice. Please see the bookstore for more information.

See our online subscription service through ClassicalConversations. com, word search: *presentation* for more ideas.

For families who subscribe, there are dozens of resources in the file-sharing area of our membership site.

Let your speech be always with grace, seasoned with salt, that ye may know how ye ought to answer every man.
—COLOSSIANS 4:6 (KJV)

Students love to dress up in character for presentations.

"Presentations are not about the material presented, they are about building the child's confidence and poise."

—LEIGH A. BORTINS
THE CORE (p. 175)

FINE ARTS
Drawing

Resources

Drawing with Children, Mona Brookes (for visual game ideas, scaling of drawing projects)

Classical Conversations online subscription services through ClassicalConversations.com

WEEK	PROJECT
1	five elements of shape *Drawing with Children* (Mona Brookes)
2	mirror images *Drawing with Children* (Mona Brookes)
3	upside-down image *Drawing with Children* (Mona Brookes)
4	abstract art *Drawing with Children* (Mona Brookes)
5	perspective *Drawing with Children* (Mona Brookes)
6	review and final project

In Weeks 1 through 6, students practice various drawing techniques using the OiLS technique from *Drawing with Children.* For the full text on these weeks' study, please refer to Cycle 1 (pages 80–86).

Required Resources

Tin whistle in the key of D
Reproducible handouts included in this curriculum (see pages 88, 100, 101, 103, 253)

Recommended Resources

Classical Music for Dummies (Pogue and Speck)
Sheet music (to practice)
Recorded music (to enjoy at home)

Music

In Weeks 7 through 12, we introduce very basic music theory while students learn a tune on the tin whistle. For the full text on these weeks' study, please refer to Cycle 1 (pages 87–103).

Yankee Doodle

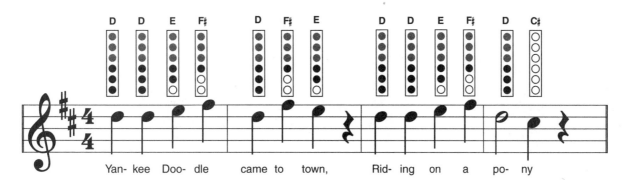

Yan- kee Doo- dle came to town, Rid- ing on a po- ny

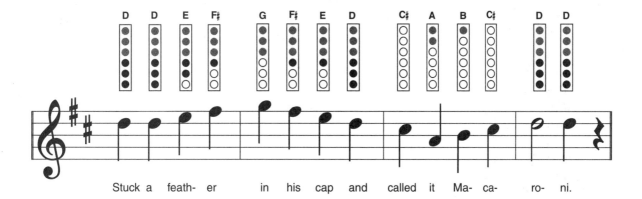

Stuck a feath- er in his cap and called it Ma- ca- ro- ni.

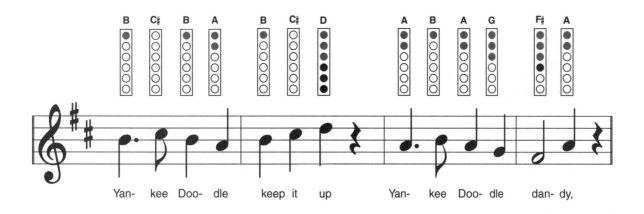

Yan- kee Doo- dle keep it up Yan- kee Doo- dle dan- dy,

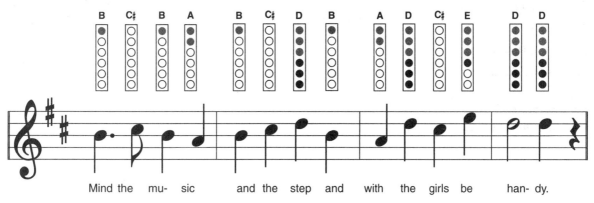

Mind the mu- sic and the step and with the girls be han- dy.

Resources

Discovering Great Artists (Kohl and Solga)

Classical Acts and Facts® History Cards: Artists and Composers, Set 3

Marvelous to Behold (Classical Conversations® MultiMedia)

Great Artists

In Weeks 13 through 18, we learn about six artists from the Baroque, Romantic, and Modern periods. For the full introductory text on these weeks' study, please refer to Cycle 1 (pages 104–105).

WEEK	CYCLE 1		CYCLE 2		CYCLE 3	
	ARTIST	TECHNIQUE	ARTIST	TECHNIQUE	ARTIST	TECHNIQUE
13	Giotto (c. 1266–1337)	Paint (Gothic)	Rembrandt 1606–1669	Drawing (Baroque)	Grandma Moses 1860–1961	Painting Folk Art
14	Ghiberti 1378–1455	Sculpt/Relief (Renaissance)	Gainsborough 1727–1788	Drawing/Painting (Romantic)	Picasso 1881–1973	Painting Abstract
15	Angelico c. 1395–1455	Drawing (Renaissance)	Degas 1834–1917	Painting (Impressionist)	O'Keeffe 1887–1986	Watercolors Romantic
16	Dürer 1471–1528	Print (Renaissance)	Monet 1840–1926	Painting (Impressionist)	Rockwell 1895–1978	Illustration/ Painting Realism
17	Michelangelo 1475–1564	Paint (Renaissance)	Morisot 1841–1895	Painting (Impressionist)	Wyeth 1917–2009	Tempera Realism
18	El Greco 1541–1614	Drawing (Baroque)	van Gogh 1853–1890	Modern Impressionist	Lichtenstein 1923–1997	Illustration Modern Pop

WEEK THIRTEEN
Grandma Moses ("Busy Folk Art Scene")

ATTENDING

At home, observe the *Classical Acts & Facts® History Cards: Artists and Composers* #35, and other artists and composers cards from Cycle 3, Cycle 1, and Cycle 2.

Use the sample conversation starters from the list below.

Sample conversation starters:

What do you see in this work of art?

How is this work of art similar to others from the same time period? Other time periods?

How is this work of art different from others from the same time period? Other time periods?

How similar or different are these comparisons?

What was happening during the time this artwork was created?

At the same time this work of art was created, where was the artist? Who else was there? What was happening?

What do others say about the artwork? What do you think the artist wanted to express?

Resources
Discovering Great Artists (Kohl and Solga)

Classical Acts & Facts® History Cards #139

Classical Acts & Facts® History Cards: Artists and Composers #35 (Grandma Moses); #38 (Picasso); #40 (O'Keeffe); and #45.

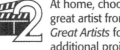 At home, choose another great artist from *Discovering Great Artists* for an additional project.

EXPRESSING

Do the assigned project from *Discovering Great Artists*.

WEEK FOURTEEN
Pablo Picasso ("One Color Painting" or "Fractured Friend")

WEEK FIFTEEN
Georgia O'Keeffe ("Close-Up Flower Painting")

WEEK SIXTEEN
Norman Rockwell ("Tell-A-Story Illustration")

Resources

Discovering Great Artists (Kohl and Solga)

Classical Acts & Facts® History Cards: Artists and Composers #41 (Rockwell); #43 (Wyeth); #44 (Lichtenstein); and #45.

 At home, watch a documentary on a modern artist.

WEEK SEVENTEEN
Andrew Wyeth ("First Snow")

 Evaluate and update the art in your home.

TIP

You can use cotton swabs or toothpicks instead of toothbrushes to dot the rubber cement.

WEEK EIGHTEEN
Roy Lichtenstein ("Comic Dots")

 Create an art project from items in your garage.

TIP

If there is not enough room for a 4' by 8' piece of paper, then use 11" x 14" paper, and cotton swabs instead of sponges. Another option is to use regular-sized paper or cardstock and bingo markers to make the dots.

Composers and Orchestra

In weeks 19 through 24, students practice listening skills using music and listening guides from *Classical Music for Dummies*. For the full text on these weeks' study, please refer to Cycle 1 (pages 108–109).

Resources

Classical Music for Dummies (Pogue and Speck)
Classical Acts & Facts® *History Cards*
Classical Acts & Facts® *History Cards: Artists and Composers*
Instrument pictures (if desired; see pages 112–116)
Foundations Audio CD (any cycle) for the *Orchestra Song*

		LESSONS		
		CYCLE 1	CYCLE 2	CYCLE 3
WEEK		PROJECT	PROJECT	PROJECT
19		Baroque and Classical Periods *Classical Music for Dummies* (Pogue and Speck)	Classical and Romantic Periods *Classical Music for Dummies* (Pogue and Speck)	Romantic and Modern Periods *Classical Music for Dummies* (Pogue and Speck)
20		Handel: *Water Music Suite* *Classical Music for Dummies* (Pogue and Speck)	Beethoven: *Symphony no. 5* *Classical Music for Dummies* (Pogue and Speck)	Tchaikovsky: *Symphony no. 6*, Fourth Movement *(Symphony Pathétique)* *Classical Music for Dummies* (Pogue and Speck)
21		Bach: *The Well-Tempered Clavier* Prelude and Fugue in C Major *Classical Music for Dummies* (Pogue and Speck)	Brahms: *Symphony no. 4* *Classical Music for Dummies* (Pogue and Speck)	Debussy: *La Mer* *Classical Music for Dummies* (Pogue and Speck)
22		Mozart: *Piano Concerto no. 22 in E-flat*, Third Movement *Classical Music for Dummies* (Pogue and Speck)	Dvořák: *Serenade for Strings* *Classical Music for Dummies* (Pogue and Speck)	Stravinsky: *The Rite of Spring* *Classical Music for Dummies* (Pogue and Speck)
23		orchestra overview *Classical Music for Dummies* (Pogue and Speck)	orchestra overview *Classical Music for Dummies* (Pogue and Speck)	orchestra overview *Classical Music for Dummies* (Pogue and Speck)
24		review and celebration	review and celebration	review and celebration

WEEK NINETEEN
Romantic and Modern Periods

Resources

Classical Music for Dummies (Pogue and Speck)

Classical Acts & Facts® History Cards #139

Classical Acts & Facts® History Cards: Artists and Composers #31 (Tchaikovsky); #36 (Debussy); and #39 (Stravinsky)

 ATTENDING

Without naming the composers, listen to pieces by Tchaikovsky, Debussy, and Stravinsky. Over the next three weeks, we will spend more time with each piece as families get to know those pieces more intimately. Each subsequent week, listen to the individual composer's piece while a parent-tutor reads the listening outline aloud. Practice cultivating restful listening in community.

Here are some suggestions:

1. Turn out the lights and have students get into a restful position. Have them close their eyes and listen.

2. Turn on the lights. Have students listen again. What do they notice?

3. Listen again. Have students stand up each time the piece gets loud and sit back down when the piece gets quiet.

 EXPRESSING

Focus on active listening, not busy hands. Learn to have ears that hear. Pause music and ask questions that accompany the listening outline.

WEEK TWENTY
Tchaikovsky *(Symphony no. 6)*

WEEK TWENTY-ONE
Debussy ("La Mer")

WEEK TWENTY-TWO
Stravinsky ("The Rite of Spring")

WEEK TWENTY-THREE
Orchestra Overview

ATTENDING

Teach the children the *Orchestra Song*.

EXPRESSING

1. Practice the orchestra seating chart (see *Trivium Tables®: Music*) by assigning students to be in the different instrument families (strings, woodwinds, brass, percussion). Hand out instrument pictures if desired.

2. Practice singing the orchestra song as a group while students are in the orchestra seating arrangement.

3. If students are getting to know the piece well, you can consider singing it as a round. When the first group of students finishes the violin section, group 2 starts at the beginning of the song. When group 2 finishes the violin section, group 3 starts at the beginning of the song. When a group finishes the song, they should keep singing the final lines of the song until group 3 arrives at the final line.

Your community may choose to handle this study in different ways, depending on the makeup of the group. Larger communities may opt to complete orchestra activities within individual classes during the Fine Arts component. Smaller communities may opt to do these activities as one big group, directly after morning assembly.

WEEK TWENTY-FOUR
Review and Celebration

EXPRESSING

Play *Yankee Doodle* with the whole community. Sing the *Orchestra Song* with the whole community.

Resources
Classical Music for Dummies (Pogue and Speck)
Trivium Tables®: Music
Instrument pictures if desired (see pages 112–116)
Foundations Audio CD (any cycle) for the *Orchestra Song*

Orchestra Song

Violins:
The violins ringing like lovely singing.
    The violins ringing like lovely song.

Clarinets:
The clarinet, the clarinet, goes doodle doodle doodle doodle dat.
The clarinet, the clarinet, goes doodle doodle dat.

Trumpets:
The trumpet is braying,
Ta-ta-ta-ta TA ta-ta-ta-ta ta ta TAH.
The trumpet is braying,
Ta-ta-ta-ta TA ta-ta-ta-ta ta ta TAH.

Horns:
The horn, the horn, awakes me at morn.
The horn, the horn, awakes me at morn.

Drums:
The drum's playing two tones.
They're always the same tones.
5-1, 1-5, 5-5-5-5-1.

 To which instrument family (strings, woodwinds, brass, percussion) does the violin belong? the clarinet? the trumpet? the horn? the drums?

WEEK	PROJECT
1	#68 Blinking*
2	#70 Water Drop Lens*
3	#74 Fingerprints*
4	#76 Lung Capacity*
5	#72 Sound and Direction*
	#77 Rubbed Off
6	#78 How Do You Feel*
	#79 Spinning*
	#80 Change of Pattern*
7	**Anatomy** (brain, heart, kidney, bladder)
8	**Anatomy** (cells, spleen, pancreas, gallbladder)
9	**Anatomy** (skeleton, muscles, stomach)
10	**Anatomy** (intestines, liver, lungs, skin)
11	**Anatomy** (eyes, nose, ears, tongue, face)
12	**Anatomy** Create life-sized poster
13	#86 Where Did It Go?*
14	#83 Not at the Same Time*
	#84 Dry Paper
15	#91 Magic Solution*
16	#93 Bubbler*
17	#99 Testing for Starch*
18	#102 Hard Water*
19	**Coin Toss**
20	**Candy Probability**
21	**Pizza Combinations**
22	**Blueberry Pancakes**
23	**What are the Odds?**
24	**What Does All That Data Mean?**

* *201 Awesome, Magical, Bizarre & Incredible Experiments*

We perish from want of wonder, not from want of wonders.

–G. K. CHESTERTON

Hands-on Science

In Weeks 1 through 24, students practice scientific discussions using *201 Awesome, Magical, Bizarre & Incredible Experiments* and create awesome projects. For the full text on these weeks' study, please refer to Cycle 1 (page 117).

For Weeks 1–6 and 13–18, see Scientific Method Discussion (page 129).

WEEKS SEVEN THROUGH ELEVEN
Student Body

ATTENDING

Direct students to color and cut out the body parts for each week. Collect completed parts and store in folders, envelopes, or zip-top bags for Week 12.

NAMING

Present the current week's body parts. Review various anatomy memory work. See weeks 7–11 below and *My Body*.

Materials

My Body (Patricia Carratello)
Crayons and colored pencils
Scissors
Copies of that week's body parts
Large pieces of white paper (e.g., butcher paper, newspaper end-roll, a white paper table cover, or roll of craft paper)

TIP

Write the student's name on the back of each completed body part.

NOTE

The organs of the smaller students tend to be crowded in the life-sized poster, while the older students' organs tend to be more spread out.

LESSONS				
WEEK 7	**WEEK 8**	**WEEK 9**	**WEEK 10**	**WEEK 11**
brain, heart, kidney, bladder	cells, spleen, pancreas, gallbladder	skeleton, muscles, stomach	intestines, liver, lungs, skin	eyes, nose, ears, tongue, face

Continued on next page

WEEK TWELVE
Student Body

Continued from previous page

LESSON
WEEK 12
1. Place the **brain** onto the head of the body outline. Tape the top and bottom. (Refer to *My Body* page 4.)
2. Place the **heart** in the middle of the chest, centered between the armpits. Tape the top and bottom. (Refer to *My Body* page 4.)
3. Place the **face** over the outline of the head. Tape the face on the left and right sides ONLY, leaving flaps for viewing the brain (top) and for fitting in the trachea later (bottom). See *My Body* page 6.
4. Place the **bones** onto the left leg, matching the image in *My Body* (page 6). Tape the top and bottom. The kneecaps will overlap the leg bones. Tape the foot bones onto the outline of the foot.
5. Tape the **muscles** on the right, matching the image in *My Body* page 6. Large muscles go on the upper leg, small muscles on the lower leg.
6. Place the **kidneys** just above belly button level. The left kidney should be a little higher than the right. Tape the top and bottom. Refer to *My Body* page 4.
7. Place the **pancreas** lengthwise across the kidneys. Center a piece of tape along the top and bottom, leaving flaps on either side to view the kidneys. Refer to *My Body* page 4.
8. Place the **gallbladder** on top of the right kidney. Tape ONLY the top of it so that you can lift it up to see the kidney. See *My Body* page 4.
9. Place the **spleen** at the top of the left kidney. Tape ONLY the top so that you can lift it up to see the kidney. Refer to *My Body* page 4.
10. Center the **bladder** just above where the legs meet. Tape ONLY on one side. Refer to *My Body* page 4.
11. Align the **large intestine** over the **small intestine** along the lines that read "Attach to the large (small) intestine." Tape them together. You should be able to fold up the edge of the large intestine to see the end of the small intestine tube, where there is a note that reads "attach to stomach."   Place the large and small intestines (they should be taped together) so that the rectum is right where the legs meet.   Slide the rectum under the bladder. (Refer to Body Pattern #2 in *My Body* page 6.)   Hold the intestines in place and fasten them with a brad, pushing it through the circle marked "brad" in the center of the small intestines.
12. Place the **stomach** as shown on page 26 of *My Body*. The stomach connects to the small intestine at a bit of an angle. Attach the stomach to the outline with a brad through the marked hole.
13. Place the **lungs** on the chest, with the trachea just under the chin. The lungs will partially cover the heart. Tape the trachea securely, but ONLY tape to the very top of the lungs. This will allow you to lift the lungs to see the other organs.
14. Place the **liver** under the bottom of the lungs. The bottom of the liver will overlap the right kidney. Hold the liver in place and attach it with a brad at the marked hole.

 Instead of cutting out body parts from the book, encourage older students to draw their own using *My Body* as a reference.

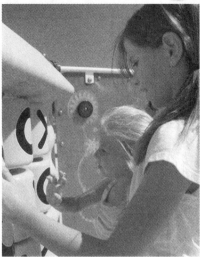

Probability

God is 100 percent certain and faithful. Everything else has a degree of chance. **Probability** is the mathematical study of chance.

Probability is a subject that we have a good intuitive sense about but that we often get wrong when we start working with more than simple examples. Much of our lives are governed by principles of probability from insurance and mortgage rates to whether your doctor prescribes a certain medicine. Every conclusion that follows the scientific method (see page 129) answers the question: Could we have gotten this result by chance? As your students grow in their scientific and mathematical understanding, they will see how a well-crafted experiment will aid them in answering this question.

They will also come to see that not all questions can be answered by an experiment. The science of Origins cannot be studied using conventional scientific methods, yet understanding and calculating probabilities is an essential part of understanding what could, or couldn't have simply happened.

Foundations students will use the following projects to practice collecting good data and calculating probability.

WEEK NINETEEN
COIN TOSS

Materials

One coin per student

Paper to record tallies

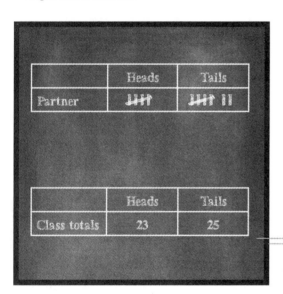

	Heads	Tails
Partner	卌	卌 II

	Heads	Tails
Class totals	23	25

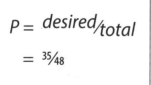

$$P = \frac{desired}{total}$$
$$= \frac{35}{48}$$

ATTENDING

Display a coin like a quarter. Explain that every coin has two sides, heads and tails. Tell the students you want to play a game, but you are not sure who should go first. Often at the beginning of an athletic game, the referee hosts a coin toss between the two teams to choose who goes first. Is it fair to toss a coin? Why?[*Because it's an even chance of heads or tails.*]

Activity: Have the students find a partner and then take turns tossing a coin. One person will toss the coin six times and the other person will toss the coin an additional six times. The total number of coin tosses will be twelve.

1. Have the students tally on a piece of paper how many times they get heads and how many times they get tails.

2. Work together to sum up class results.

NAMING

If your coin landed on heads, did you always get a tails on the next flip? No, we all understand that every flip of the coin is **independent,** and that is why we are usually happy to use a coin to get a chance outcome. The mathematical study of this chance is called **probability**. Each time we flipped the coin our result was the **outcome**.

In the study of probability, we generally refer to *desired* outcomes (the outcome that we want or are interested in) and *total* outcomes (everything that happened). We may also refer to **events** which means an outcome or group of outcomes.

Sometimes we use words to describe the chance of something happening: *impossible, unlikely, possible, an even chance, likely,* or *certain*. Mathematically, probability is the measure of how likely an outcome is and is expressed as a number between 0 and 1. To find the probability of an event, we use this fraction: desired outcomes/ total outcomes.

Let's discuss how to calculate some probabilities for our coin flip:

   i. the probability that a coin flip is both heads and tails =
      $^0\!/_2 = 0$ = never

  ii. the probability of heads = 1 head/2 sides = ½

 iii. the probability of tails = 1 tail/2 sides = ½

 iv. the probability that a coin flip is heads or tails =
      2/2 = 1 = always

How does this compare with your results? [*They are probably different.*] This is important to know. Probability is about chance and the likelihood of a specific event happening over many outcomes. Our actual results for fewer repetitions often will NOT match our calculated probability.

 Use dice or cards to compare calculated probabilities to actual results, e.g., with a die: rolling a 1, rolling a number greater than 3, rolling an even or with cards: drawing a red even card, drawing an ace.

STORYTELLING

Often when we are hearing or telling a story, we talk about probability as a percentage. A percentage is just another way of writing a special fraction where our total outcomes is 100. If there is an 80 percent chance of rain, it means that if the viewing area were broken into 100 parts, then 80 of those parts should see rain. If a survey is reported that the crime rate is 2.5 percent, then that means that 2.5 days out of 100 there is a crime reported.

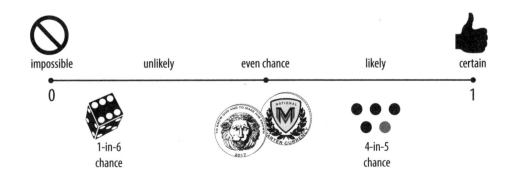

impossible   unlikely   even chance   likely   certain

0   1

1-in-6 chance   4-in-5 chance

WEEK TWENTY
CANDY PROBABILITY

Materials

One brown paper lunch bag

100 poker chips or colored candies

 ATTENDING

What is your favorite color of candy?

I have a roll of candy in my hand that has 3 white candies and 1 red. If red is your favorite color, what is the chance you will get your favorite color? [*Probability (P) = 1 red candy/4 total candies = ¼*]

If I wanted to make sure you had an even chance of getting your favorite color, what should I do? [*Have an equal number of each color in my hand. P = 2/4 = ½ for each one.*]

What if I had a big bag of candy and you wanted to know how many of your favorite color candies there were? Could I use what I know about probability to find out?

Activity: Use an opaque bag with a known number of poker chips (or candy). Begin with a bag full of at least 100 chips of 3 or 4 colors. Ensure that you know the distribution and that they are not evenly distributed, e.g., 60 white, 40 red, 20 blue.

1. Create a chart on the board to keep track of the draws (see sample on graphic, next page).

2. Allow the students to take turns drawing out a chip or candy, and record the result in your chart as a fraction of how many of that color divided by the total draws so far. DO NOT replace the chip or candy in the bag.

3. Pass the bag and continue having the student draw until a pattern emerges in the fractions on the chart. You can convert to percentages to help them see this.

4. Tell the students the total number of items in the bag and ask them how many draws are needed to make a close guess of how many of each color item are in the bag. (Math help: Multiply the last fraction for that color in your chart times the total number that you tell the students.)

5. Reveal the actual numbers of each color and see how close the students come to the calculated numbers. How many draws did it take? Did they have to draw every chip out of the bag?

Draw	White— Fraction	Red— Fraction	Blue— Fraction
1. White	1/1	0/1	0/1
2. Blue	1/2	0/2	1/2
3. White	2/3	0/3	1/3

NAMING

In this activity, we used a technique called **sampling** to figure out something about the whole group based on a part of the group.

Sometimes we know the probability and use that to estimate what our actual results will be, but sometimes we use our actual results to estimate our probabilities.

In this activity, suppose we drew out 17 white chips in 25 tries. Our actual result = 17/25. If we estimate that the probability is 17/25 and multiply that by 100, then we would estimate that we had 68 white chips, which is close to the 60 we actually had.

This method of sampling is useful for estimates about large groups and is used in many different kinds of studies, including science, polling and surveys, and production planning in manufacturing. A sample can give accurate information about a larger group because of the principles of probability.

WEEK TWENTY-ONE
PIZZA COMBINATIONS

Materials
Whiteboard
Poker chips (optional)

 ATTENDING

Imagine that you walked into a pizza shop and were handed a box. What do you think your chances are of getting the kind you ordered? Is it as easy to figure out as the chance of rolling an even number? What do you need to know? *How many different kinds of pizza are there?*

If your local pizza shop has lots of options, this is a harder problem. Let's start with something simple.

Activity: To build a pizza at the Classical Pizza Parlor, you can choose between cheese, pepperoni, and sausage toppings. One of the most important things to remember when listing the possibilities is to be organized!

One topping	Two toppings	Three toppings
1-Cheese	4-Cheese and pepperoni	7-Cheese, pepperoni,
2-Pepperoni	5-Cheese and sausage	and sausage
3-Sausage	6-Pepperoni and sausage	

There are 7 different possibilities, so the probability of getting the one you ordered is 1/7.

Have the students choose different toppings that they like and see how many combinations you can make. Keep a list or make a menu of the options as a class.

Younger students could have fewer topping choices and can use poker chips to represent the toppings so that they can "make" the different pizzas. Older students could have more options for their pizzas and use a whiteboard to work out the menu.

As time allows, have students repeat the activity individually.

 How does the problem change if order *does* matter? Research **permutations**.

 NAMING

A **combination** is an arrangement of objects in which the order does not matter.

WEEK TWENTY-TWO
BLUEBERRY PANCAKES

ATTENDING

So far we have talked about fairly simple probabilities such as the chance of something happening on one try. Often though we have more complicated questions that are harder to solve mathematically. Let's examine the Blueberry Pancakes problem to see a great example.

Activity

Together: Our pancake batter recipe makes 6 pancakes and has 15 blueberries. We will use 6 circles to represent the pancakes and we will use a die to represent the blueberries. Each roll will be a different blueberry— if you roll a 1, the blueberry goes on pancake 1 and so on. Allow the students to roll the die 15 times to simulate the 15 blueberries and collect the class results.

How many pancakes got at least 4 blueberries? Less than 4? More than 4? Exactly 4?

Based on this, what do you think the chances are of getting 4 blueberries on one pancake?

The calculated probabilities are pretty complicated, but you made a model of the problem to estimate the answers. This is a great way to approach math problems that you aren't sure about!

Individually or in pairs: Use the same method to model this problem of the same mix but with 30 blueberries.

What is the likelihood of getting 6 blueberries? Less than 2 blueberries? Ask the likelihood for different quantities of blueberries.

Compare the students' results. Are they similar? Are there any outliers? What results are most common?

Materials
Six-sided die

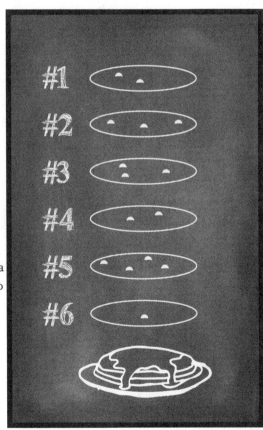

NAMING

An **outlier** is a result that doesn't seem to fit the pattern.

The **distribution** is the pattern of your results or your probabilities.

WEEK TWENTY-THREE
WHAT ARE THE ODDS?

Materials
One coin
Six-sided die

COIN TOSS RESULTS

	Heads	Tails
Partner	卌 II	卌

	Heads	Tails
Class totals	26	22

$$P(A) = \tfrac{1}{2}$$
$$P(B) = \tfrac{1}{2}$$
$$\text{Odds}(A) = \tfrac{1}{2} : \tfrac{1}{2} = 1 : 1$$

 STORYTELLING

In our storytelling, we talk more often about odds than we do probability. An underdog may have the odds stacked against them while the hero often has the odds in their favor. If students are well behaved, they might know that the odds are good that their parents will be pleased, while poor behavior quickly changes those to poor odds! Discuss how you use odds in the stories you might tell about your day.

 ATTENDING

Activity: Split your class in half and tell them that you will decide who gets a treat based on a coin toss. Ask if that is fair. Why or why not?

Assign the students a partner. Then have each pair flip a coin 12 times and keep track of how many heads and how many tails. Remind the students that probability means desired outcomes divided by total outcomes (d/t). Our expected probability is ½. Are your students' totals close to this? If you add all the flips together are you closer?

If the probability of heads is ½ and the probability of tails is ½, is it a fair coin? Do your students agree that these are even odds?

Now change the problem. Instead of a coin flip, roll a die. If it's a 1 or 2, group A gets the treat. If it's 3, 4, 5, or 6, then group B gets the treat.

Do your students think this is fair?

Have each pair model this question with 12 rolls of the die.

Now calculate the probability (*P*) of each outcome:

- P(A getting treat) = 2/6 = 1/3

- P(B getting treat) = 4/6 = 2/3

Is that close to the students' results?

In this example, the odds favor group B.

NAMING

Odds are a ratio of probabilities. In other words, it is the ratio of desired outcomes to not desired outcomes.

Typically we use a fraction bar (/) for probabilities and a colon (:) for odds.

So with our game of rolling the die, the odds of group A getting the treat are 2:4 (2 chances for and 4 against), which is expressed in the reduced form of 1:2 odds (1 chance for and 2 against).

Even odds are 1:1. The for and against are even. When we are playing a game, we usually consider even odds to be fair.

Why would people selling or promoting games of chance use odds instead of probabilities?

DIE ROLL RESULTS

	1, 2	3, 4, 5, 6
Partner	III	HHT IIII

	1, 2	3, 4, 5, 6
Class totals	17	31

$$P(A) = \tfrac{1}{3}$$
$$P(B) = \tfrac{2}{3}$$
$$Odds(A) = \tfrac{1}{3} : \tfrac{2}{3} = 1 : 2$$

WEEK TWENTY-FOUR
WHAT DOES ALL THAT DATA MEAN?

BIGFOOT SIGHTINGS BY STATE DATA POINTS	
Alaska	22
Alabama	98
Arizona	84
Arkansas	98
California	437
Colorado	123
Connecticut	12
Delaware	5
Florida	312
Georgia	132
Idaho	79
Illinois	286
Indiana	78
Iowa	69
Kansas	43
Kentucky	109
Louisiana	43
Maine	17
Maryland	35
Massachusetts	33
Michigan	213
Minnesota	71
Mississippi	22
Missouri	138
Montana	46
North Carolina	96
North Dakota	6
Nebraska	14
Nevada	8
New Hampshire	16
New Jersey	67
New Mexico	42
New York	104
Ohio	271
Oklahoma	94
Oregon	245
Pennsylvania	116
Rhode Island	5
South Carolina	52
South Dakota	17
Tennessee	97
Texas	228
Utah	70
Vermont	9
Virginia	77
Washington	641
West Virginia	100
Wisconsin	93
Wyoming	28

Source: http://www.bfro.net/gdb/

STORYTELLING

While probability—the study of chance—is often a part of the stories we tell, statistics is an important part of how we tell the story. Statistics allows us to take a lot of information and summarize it so that other people can understand it. If we tell the story of Jackie Robinson, we would want to know how well he played baseball. We wouldn't have time to explain what happened each time he went to bat. However, we can tell you that his batting average was .311. (This statistic means he got on base 311 times for every 1,000 times he went to bat.)

ATTENDING

Activity: You can use the data in the chart on these pages that shows the number of Bigfoot sightings by state. Hand out the data you like to your students.

Begin by asking questions about individual data points, such as which state had the most Bigfoot sightings and which one had the least. Now, ask some more general questions such as how much the sightings varied by state. Is there a trend in number of sightings according to the part of the country? These questions are best answered using a graph. Choose a bar graph or a line graph to demonstrate to students how to plot their data. (Both of these will have the categories [states] on the horizontal axis with the quantity [sightings] on the vertical axis. A bar graph will represent the sightings with a bar while the line graph will simply plot a point and then connect the points with a line.) Have them finish creating their own bar or line graph. Do these graphs help us to "see" our data more clearly? Would they help communicate our data to others?

Now we want to determine some measure of center for our data. There are three called the mean, median, and mode. Start by having the students put all of the data in order from the smallest to the largest.

Is there a value that occurs more often than all of the others? That is called the **mode**.

Which number is exactly in the middle? This is the **median**. It will have same number of data points before it and after it. In the case of an even number of values, the median is the average of the middle two values.

To find the **mean**, or average, add up all of the numbers and then divide by the number of data points.

EXAMPLE:

States that begin with "C"
12, 123, 437
Median = 123
Mean = 562/3 = 187.3

States that begin with "A"
22, 84, 98, 98
Median = (84 + 98) / 2 = 91
Mean = 302/4 = 75.5

Materials
Set of approximately 30 data points such as daily temperatures, number of siblings, etc.

NAMING

Statistics is the study of the collection, analysis, interpretation, presentation, and organization of data.

Collection is how we would measure or test to get our data.

Analysis and interpretation are where we can use math and probability to understand the results we got from our study or experiment.

Presentation and organization are done through charts and graphs in addition to summarizing measures such as mean, median, and mode.

Bar/Column Charts : Commonly used to show a summary of all the data that was collected.

Line Charts : Typically used to show trends as individual data values are plotted.

Pie Charts :Used to show percentages of each result.

Mean: Sum of the data values divided by the number of data values. [*For the Bigfoot data, mean = 104.1.*]

Median: Middle value of ordered list of data (odd number of values), mean of middle two values of an ordered list of data (even number of values). [*For the Bigfoot data, median = 77.*]

Mode: Most common data value. [*For the Bigfoot data, mode = 22.*]

BAR/COLUMN CHART
Bigfoot Sightings—New England

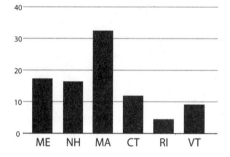

LINE CHART
Bigfoot Sightings—New England

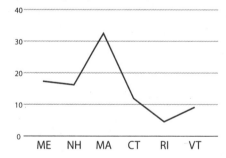

PIE CHART
Bigfoot Sightings—New England

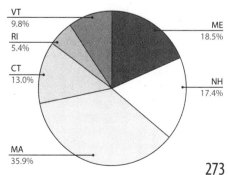

SAMPLE JOURNAL ENTRY

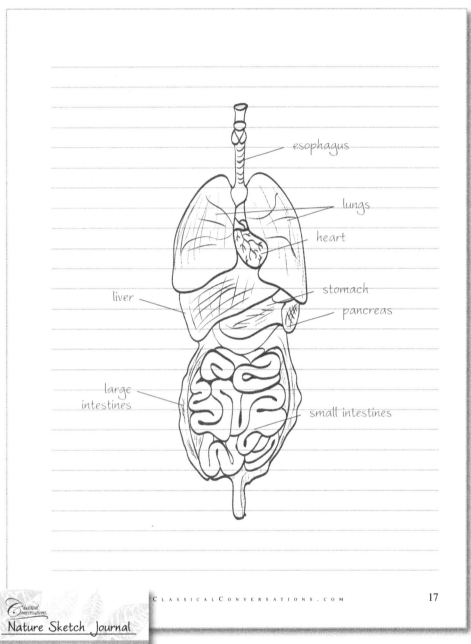

esophagus

lungs

heart

liver

stomach

pancreas

large intestines

small intestines

CLASSICALCONVERSATIONS.COM

17

At-Home Work:

Students are encouraged to properly identify and label body systems.

Classical Conversations
Nature Sketch Journal

Drawing and Writing Pages and
References for Budding Scientists

Available from

CLASSICALCONVERSATIONSBOOKS.COM

RISING TO THE CHALLENGE

CHRISTIAN

CLASSICAL COMMUNITY

Classical Conversations

It is the glory of God to conceal a thing; but the honour of kings is to search out a matter.

Proverbs 25:2

TEACHER CERTIFICATE

Congratulations

CYCLE

3

FOR SUCCESSFULLY COMPLETING

IN YOUR HOME SCHOOL

_____

Parents' Names

Classical Conversations® honors your commitment to learn alongside your children and values your service to family and community.

Classical Conversations recognizes your achievements as parents who completed Foundations Cycle 3. You have taught your children and continued your own education by leading others through the grammar of math, Latin, science, English, history, geography, art, and music. This Cycle 3 knowledge, enhanced by weekly community training in the classical model, has equipped you to homeschool with confidence during the exciting high school years ahead. You are prepared to consider future roles tutoring the Foundations, Essentials, and Challenge programs.

_____
Licensed Classical Conversations® Community Name

_____
Director Signature

_____
Date

FOUNDATIONS CURRICULUM RESOURCES

Available from
CLASSICALCONVERSATIONSBOOKS.COM

More About Classical, Christian Education

Bortins, Leigh. *The Core: Teaching Your Child the Foundations of a Classical Education.*

—. *The Question: Teaching Your Child the Essentials of a Classical Education.*

—. *The Conversation: Challenging Your Student with a Classical Education.*

—. *Echo in Celebration: A Call to Home-Centered Education.*

Classical Conversations MultiMedia. *Classical Christian Education Made Approachable.*

Sayers, Dorothy. "The Lost Tools of Learning."

More About the Art of Grammar

Bauer, Susan Wise, and Jessie Wise. *The Well-Trained Mind.*

O'Brien, Dominic. *How to Develop a Brilliant Memory Week by Week.*

Memory Work Resources

Apologia. *Exploring Creation* series.

Bauer, Susan Wise. *The Story of the World,* 4 vols.

Classical Conversations MultiMedia. *Classical Acts & Facts® History Cards,* 4 sets.

—. *Classical Acts & Facts® History Cards: Artists and Composers,* 3 sets.

—. *Classical Acts & Facts® Science Cards,* 4 sets.

—. *Exploring the World through Cartography.*

Eldon, Doug and Dorry. *Lyrical Life Science,* 3 vols.

Houghton Mifflin Harcourt. *Saxon Math™.*

Hands-on Fine Arts Resources

Brookes, Mona. *Drawing with Children.*

Classical Conversation MultiMedia. *Marvelous to Behold.*

—. *Math in Motion: First Steps in Music Theory.*

—. *Trivium Tables®: Music.*

Kohl, MaryAnn, and Kim Solga. *Discovering Great Artists.*

Pogue, David, and Scott Speck. *Classical Music for Dummies.*

Hands-on Science Resources

VanCleave, Janice. *201 Awesome, Magical, Bizarre & Incredible Experiments.*

Additional Source Documents

Encyclopædia Britannica, Inc. *Encyclopædia Britannica.* https://www.britannica.com

Kingfisher. *The Kingfisher History Encyclopedia.*

Zeman, Anne, and Kate Kelly. *Everything You Need to Know About…series.*